Participation Is Risky

Approaches to Joint Creative Processes

Liesbeth Huybrechts (ed.)

With contributions by Katrien Dreessen, Denny K.L. Ho, Liesbeth Huybrechts, Yanki Lee, Selina Schepers, Jessica Schoffelen, Cristiano Storni

Antennae
Valiz, Amsterdam

Participation Is Risky: Approaches to Joint Creative Processes

Liesbeth Huybrechts (ed.)

Preface

This book is initiated by Social Spaces and KULeuven Cultural Studies, in collaboration with BAM (Flemish Institute for Visual, Audio-visual and Media Art), Valiz Publishers, supported by the Flemish Art Fund 'Kunstendecreet' and the Dutch Mondriaan Fund, to gain more insight into the characteristics of participatory projects in art and design. Social Spaces is a research group that researches design methods, artefacts and tools that allow social exchange. The group is based at the Media, Art and Design Faculty (associated with LUCA School of Arts, University of Leuven) in the city of Genk (BE). Here, the mining industry with its large number of immigrant workers was the basis of a rich multicultural society. When, as of the 1960s, the coal-mines were forced to close down (resulting in fierce and violent social uproar), this city was confronted with a high level of unemployment. In 1964, the car factory Ford started production in Genk, offering new job opportunities. In 2012, however, the factory announced its closure in the near future, which will (again) lead to high unemployment rates. In search of an economically thriving conversion of the coal-mining heritage, the city of Genk established a creative centre (C-mine) on one of the mining sites. Social Spaces is situated at this site, once the beating heart of the region's industry. Involved in the study and practice of social design, the research group does not want to isolate its practice from that daily social context, but engages closely with it.

Over the past years, Social Spaces has been looking into how artistic, media art and design projects can be developed in participatory ways. Besides exploring the meaning of participation, the research group researches and creates approaches for designers and artists that can be used to enable participation in their projects. Working in an institutional context wherein design and art is taught, Social Spaces often finds that a participatory way of setting up projects is (often) not part of the skills of designers or artists. To support artists, designers and their participants in setting up participatory projects, the goal of this book is to describe the negotiations that designers and artists engage in when setting up participatory projects with both familiar and strange, public and private, professional or amateur and other participants. We define these negotiations as risky trade-offs, to stress that participation is a multidirectional process that is determined by the designers and artists as well as by the participants. We use the term 'risky', since it reflects the artists', designers' and participants' experience of uncertainty in participatory contexts. Working in participatory projects is often not integrated in educational and research training programmes, which results in little familiarity with participatory work. Even more experienced participatory designers and artists, who are already enjoying participatory work, need to deal with the inherent uncertainty of a participatory situation that changes repeatedly. Participatory projects thus always involve 'risky trade-offs' between — on the one hand — makers and participants taking actions with an eye on increasing participatory exchange and — on the other hand

— uncertainty about the results of this exchange. We define risk in a positive and qualitative manner (which opens possibilities to innovation), but also as something that cannot be calculated or avoided (since it is inherent to participatory projects that have uncertain and undefined outcomes). This book stimulates artists, designers and participants to engage in risky trade-offs in their participatory projects. This may occur through a conscious choice of the maker and the participants, but may also happen unintentionally. The forms which these trade-offs take (whether they occur consciously or unconsciously) depends on the artists and designers themselves, the project in question or the group of participants involved. For example, in the case study *Uncle Roy All Around You* (which is described at the end of this chapter), the art collective engaged in a specific risky trade-off when they decided to work together with different disciplines. This turned out to be a productive factor in the game they were developing, but also led to some difficult negotiations.

Based on a review of the literature and case studies of real-life participatory projects, this book will offer an overview of some of the risky trade-offs that designers, artists and participants are regularly confronted with when setting up participatory projects, art works, designs, et cetera in a hands-on way. The first chapter provides an introduction in what participatory projects are and in what sense they can be characterised by risky trade-offs between makers (designers and artists) and participants. The second chapter discusses participatory projects in design and art wherein makers and participants collaborate intensely in making new concepts, products or art works. It describes how participatory projects with a hybrid character are good facilitators of exchanges between makers and participants. The third and final chapter gives an overview of how makers set up infrastructures wherein participants can self-organise their participatory exchanges. It discusses these types of participatory projects in light of the concept of generativity. The book concludes with an overview of the risky trade-offs that are described in the previous chapters and provides some points for reflection and further research.

The book is combined with a playful participatory toolkit designed by the design collective Conditional Design, part of the Amsterdam-based design and technology studio Moniker, visualising some of the principles discussed in the book in an experimental way.[1] This toolkit can be viewed via http://conditionaldesign.org and www.socialspaces.be. Both the book and the toolkit are set up in an open way — instead of proposing 'recipes' (or determinants or prerequisites) for participatory projects — in order to allow designers and artists to interpret and use them in their own way.

1 Conditional Design is a manifesto, an experimental playground as well as a collaboration between the artists and designers Luna Maurer, Edo Paulus, Jonathan Puckey and Roel Wouters. Conditional Design focuses on designing processes rather than products. Its members design logic-based environments that use external influences to aid the development of their projects. By publishing the results of the workshops online as well as in print, the members attempt to give practice an equal footing to that of the written manifesto.

Chapter I
Participation and Risky Trade-offs

Liesbeth Huybrechts,
Selina Schepers &
Katrien Dreessen

Background, Aim and Argument

The focus of this chapter is on participatory art and design projects, such as participatory design workshops, participatory installations and participatory websites or games. These projects are all (intended to be) created together with other participants, coming from different professional domains, or communities.[1] Whether a project is defined as art or design, depends on the perspective of its maker(s). Although we provide some insight into the specific approaches to participatory design and art, we distance ourselves from the discussion whether something is art and/or design or not. After all, the focus of this book is on the issue of participation. Therefore, and to simplify things, we refer to the designers and artists as 'makers'.[2] We use the term 'participants' to identify the users, audiences or actors coming from different disciplines. Furthermore, we refer to the participatory art and design works, products, workshops and so on in which the makers and participants are involved, as 'projects' as defined by A.telier.[3] This collective describes a project as a common form in which resources, such as people and technology, are brought together in creative achievements. These achievements have objectives, timelines or deliverables. In the A.telier project, for example, the resources can include the project brief, prototypes, cultural probes and sketches, field material, project reports, engineers, architects, interaction designers, researchers, teachers, students, buildings, devices and artefacts.[4]

Literature on participation shows that the

motivations why makers and participants engage in participatory projects are quite diverse.[5] First, some makers believe that participation leads to social progress, stating that society improves when more people participate in it. They feel that people have the right to participate in a project that — potentially — concerns them.[6] In this case, social and political motivations form the basis of participatory projects. Second, makers may be interested in the technical or structural advantages of participatory projects. Ehn & Badham claim that, from a technical viewpoint, makers set up projects in participatory ways, because their participants can contribute to them and therefore perceive them as 'better'.[7] Finally, Schäfer states that, in many cases, makers set up participatory works as a cultural critique, demanding the reconfiguration of power relations.[8] In that case, participatory projects do not necessarily aim for social cohesion or technical improvements but rather take up a critical position, by questioning or disrupting the dominant structures in society.

The extensive body of literature on participation illustrates that engaging in participatory projects presents a challenge to many makers. They are used to make projects by themselves or with colleagues

1 Huybrechts, 2011.
2 Based on Sanders' distinction between 'makers' and 'users', 2001.
3 A.telier, 2011.
4 Ibid., p. 158.
5 Ehn & Badham, 2002; Schäfer, 2008; Ehn, 2002; Rheingold, 2009.
6 Ehn & Badham, 2002.
7 Ibid.
8 Schäfer, 2008.

(from the same discipline) and for a rather passive audience. Most makers are still educated in classical contexts where they are taught to create projects (like videos, photos or furniture) that are finished once they are launched onto the market. Participation stands in contrast to this 'cult of the specialist', wherein an expert is expected to provide answers to certain questions.[9] In a participatory project, not only the 'expert' but also the participants involved are central in finding these answers. Indeed, a key aspect of participatory projects is that they allow input from other participants besides the maker, by learning from and building on insights, experiences and practices of others.[10]

Since participatory projects rely on the input from both makers and participants, they are never finished. Their process and 'final' form is inherently undefined, which may lead to a feeling of uncertainty among makers and participants.[11] Uncertainty is also closely linked to creative projects in general.[12] When makers create something that is aimed at stimulating utility and efficiency, it is possible that the creation — unexpectedly — is used for unforeseen goals. For instance, unanticipated user-adaptations and user-driven developments were characteristic for the development of the Internet. The networking of computers was first intended for military goals and academic publishing, but was soon adopted for personal ways of communication.[13] Users invented their own applications, such as electronic mail and the World Wide Web.[14]

In participatory projects, makers and participants

can take several actions (for instance, organising a participatory workshop or creating an online platform) with an eye on participatory exchange, while being uncertain about the outcome. As mentioned above, since the exchanges in participatory projects are always experienced as involving uncertainty, we call these actions risky trade-offs. After all, both the participants and the maker are never sure about the results of their exchanges (brought about via negotiating). For instance, when involving local youth of 6-18 years old in the co-creation of a public space in the city, the trans-disciplinary innovation lab the Patching Zone (located in Rotterdam, NL) developed a game wherein mobile phones were used to read 'QR' codes ('Quick Response' or matrix-like barcodes). The Patching Zone explored what the local youth liked and did in their daily lives and found that they all used their mobile phones quite intensively. However, the game failed to attract significant engagement by the participants, due to the fact that the software needed for reading the QR codes did not work on all brands of mobile phones. After experimenting with other formats of games, the Patching Zone decided not to develop the phone game. They adapted an existing, popular game for a public space context: Tic-Tac-Toe (a game for two players, using a three by three grid), which they integrated as

9 Suchman, 1993; Gauntlett, 2011.
10 Norman, 2010.
11 Dreessen et al., 2011.
12 Menger, 2009.
13 Donath, 2004.
14 Abbete, 1999.

an interactive installation in the pavement, using LED lights.[15] This example shows that the interaction with the participants resulted in an outcome of the project that was unforeseen by the makers.

In this context, the goal of this first chapter is to arrive at a more specific description of the risky trade-offs between makers and participants in participatory projects and the uncertainties that are connected to these trade-offs. This requires a closer understanding of the notion of participatory projects. To make this notion more tangible, we explore the concept of 'things', which points to the specific moments in projects in which makers use objects — such as installations, prototypes and so on — to engage with diverse participants in participatory ways. We acknowledge that the term 'thing' can be criticized for reducing participation to its material or digital form. However, we use the term as described by Latour, who defines the 'thing' as an issue around which people gather, i.e. a socio-material assembly.[16] To deepen our understanding of the risky trade-offs taking place within participatory projects, an extensive literature study, in-depth interviews, observations and workshops were carried out, using the participatory mapping method and toolkit MAP-it, developed by our research group Social Spaces. By presenting two case studies at the end of the chapter, we demonstrate how risky trade-offs and uncertainties manifest themselves in two real-life participatory projects, being the game *Uncle Roy All Around You* by Blast Theory (i.e. case study 1) and the performative walk *Routes and Routines* by Constant vzw (i.e. case study 2).

To summarise, in this chapter we elaborate on the following aspects: the framing of the notion of participation in three domains (p. 18), sociologist Latour's definition of the 'thing' to describe participatory art and design projects (p. 32), the phases of a participatory project (p. 36), the definition of uncertainty and risk in participatory projects (p. 40), leading to a definition of participatory projects as risky trade-offs and two case studies in which we use the above-mentioned mapping method for analysing the risky trade-offs, 'things' and uncertainties in participatory projects (p. 57). We conclude with a discussion that leads the way to the next chapters (p. 79).

15 This case will be further explored in chapter 2. See: chapter 2, '3.1. Case study 3: Go-for-IT!'
16 Latour, 2005; Latour, 2011; Latour & Weibel, 2005.

Framing

To describe the uncertain, risky trade-offs in participatory projects, we first look into how participation is defined within several domains. We provide an overview of the literature and discuss some of the prevailing views on participation within citizen engagement, media and culture. Next, we reflect on participatory projects as 'things', corresponding to Latour's Actor-Network Theory.[17] We then describe participatory projects in relation to the phases of their creation and how they are associated with the concepts of risk and uncertainty. We conclude this section by giving our own definition of participatory projects, which we — subsequently — use throughout the rest of this book.

The Concept of Participation

How participation is defined depends largely on the domain in which the project is developed. Therefore, we describe how participation is defined within the perspective of citizen engagement (p.18) and the domains of media (p. 21) and culture (p. 25). We feel that taking a look at the definition of participation in these three domains is important and necessary for framing our own definition of participation. Of course, we acknowledge that other classifications are possible and that there is some overlap between the described definitions of participation.

Participation in Citizen Engagement

Over time, participation has mainly been referred

to as the representation of the citizen in decision-making (cfr. 'citizen power'). One of the best-known definitions of participation in this perspective must be the one by Sherry Arnstein.[18] She defines participation as:

> the redistribution of power that enables the have-not citizens, presently excluded from the political and economic processes, to be deliberately included in the future. It is the strategy by which the have-nots join in determining how information is shared, goals and policies are set, tax resources are allocated, programs are operated, and benefits like contracts and patronage are parcelled out.[19]

Arnstein describes participation as the means by which social reform can be induced, allowing the have-not citizens to share in the benefits of society. The author distinguishes between different degrees of participation. The first degree and the strongest form of participation — involving citizen control, delegated power and partnership — is called 'citizen power'. The second — 'tokenism' — involves placation, consultation and informing. Finally, she refers to therapy and manipulation as 'non-participation'.[20]

17 Latour, 2005.
18 Arnstein,1969.
19 Ibid., p. 216.
20 Ibid.

Similar to Arnstein's 'ladder of participation', Milbrath frames participation in a kind of pyramid, indicating that different types of participants have different levels of engagement in participatory projects.[21] Depending on the extent of participation in a political process, he mentions three groups of participants: 'gladiators' (who are very active in the political process), 'spectators' (who are only somewhat politically active) and 'apathetics' (who do not partake in any political process whatsoever).[22] Furthermore, Verba et al. start from a model that defines participation in relation to three criteria.[23] First, they note that participation is linked to the amount in which participants share their concerns and preferences with policy makers. Second, they emphasise that participation is related to the pressure that people can put on policy-makers in order for them to do something with these concerns and preferences. Finally, Verba et al. indicate that time, money and skills are powerful predictors for political participation and more 'measurable' than motivations.[24]

Summary

From this overview of literature, we can conclude that:

— Arnstein describes participation as the means by which social reform can be induced, allowing have-not citizens to share in the benefits of society. The limitation of her definition, for the scope of this text, is that it only focuses on the political aspects of participation.[25]

- Arnstein, Verba et al. and Milbrath all indicate that different levels of participation exist. However, they make clear that the borders between the different levels cannot always be easily distinguished.[26]
- Verba et al. illustrate why participants do not always participate in the same way and to the same extent. The three criteria that Verba et al. mention (i.e. ability to share, influence and access to time, money and skills) clearly show why different degrees of participation — in a participatory project — exist.[27]

Participation in Media

Participation is an important topic in media theory as well. Throughout history, some media were deliberately created to enhance participation between people. As early as the 17th century, Kircher created a series of boxes that allowed participants to recombine mathematical or musical elements into new compositions in order to participate in the pleasure of (the rather specialised fields of) art and science.[28] The Industrial Revolution (end 18th — beginning 19th century) brought about an optimistic view on technology. In the 19th century, inventions such as the predecessor of

21 Milbrath, 1965.
22 Devos, 2006.
23 Verba et al., 1995.
24 Ibid., 1995.
25 Arnstein, 1969.
26 Ibid.; Verba et al., 1995; Milbrath, 1965.
27 Verba et al., 1995.
28 Zielinski, 2006.

the computer by Babbage, the telegraph, Morse code, the telephone by Bell, radio and television, held a lot of promises for participation. These opportunities were explored by several art movements in the 1960s, such as Fluxus and Happening (represented by artists such as John Cage and Nam June Paik), who experimented with the participatory potential of media:

> While Cage allows the musicians and the ambient sounds to modify and co-create his pieces to a substantial extent, Paik builds an interactive installation from which sounds emerge without any compositional guidelines only when the visitors intervene. Comparably, Paik adopts the receptive analytical strategy of Cage's 1951 composition for radio sets and transfers it to television, but then takes a decisive further step from participatory reception to creative intervention by the public.[29]

Authors such as Laurel and Murray regard the advent of digital (and interactive) media in the late 20th century as a new great opportunity for participation.[30] Partly due to the increasing interactive possibilities of new media tools like websites or games, the consumer was no longer self-evidently considered as passive but rather as an active participant. Corresponding to this and in light of the rise of networked media, O'Reilly calls Web

2.0 (like the social network platform Facebook or the photo sharing site Flickr) 'an architecture of participation', a means designed for user contribution.[31] Shirky claims that networked media allow people to go beyond consuming, by producing a big mass of content with a very small individual investment.[32] Benkler observed the rise of networked media as having three important effects on people's possibilities for participation, improving people's capacity to do more for and by themselves, in loose commonality with others, without the constraints of a price system or traditional hierarchical models of social and economic organisation and in organisations that operate outside the market sphere.[33] Furthermore, authors such as Gauntlett describe how, in this context, some aspects of editorial, managerial or cultural curatorship have disappeared, causing an explosion in user-generated content.[34] Hawk et al., Ito et al., and De Waal & De Lange, discuss the possibilities of *mobile* networked media that allow people to participate regardless of time and location.[35] Furthermore, Leadbeater, Shirky and Bruns (describe popular notions such as the Do It Yourself (DIY) culture and the alleged role of social media in political change.[36]

Similar to authors discussing participation in citizen engagement, several writers in this research

29 Daniels, 2004.
30 Laurel, 1993, Murray, 1997.
31 O'Reilly, 2004.
32 Shirky, 2009.
33 Benkler, 2006.
34 Gauntlett, 20011; Jensen et al., 2008.
35 Hawk et al., 2008; Ito et al., 2007; De Waal & De Lange, 2008.
36 Leadbeater, 2008; Shirky, 2009; Bruns, 2005.

strand claim that only a minority of passionate users are truly participating in digital and networked media. They refer in this respect to 'participation inequality'.[37] In a given community, 90% of the 'users' are passive consumers and only 1% of the users is responsible for the most important contributions. Therefore, the majority of user participation in networked media is often referred to as 'pseudo-participation', since it often remains limited to clicking on pictures or liking other people's statuses.

Summary

From this overview of the literature, we may conclude that:

— different developments in media and communication technologies have allowed participation to take place on a larger scale (with more participants, over a greater distance, etc.), as well as in an easier way. Participants can do more for and by themselves, in loose commonality with others. They are no longer constrained by a price system or traditional organisational and curational models or organisations;[38]

— more participation does not necessarily imply 'better' participation. We also discussed how a lot of the literature in media (as well as in politics) refers to the fact that there is no medium that automatically allows participation, and that only a minority of people effectively participate.[39]

Participation in Culture

From a cultural perspective, in numerous published works (often closely related to the literature in the field of media) precisely these promises and pitfalls of participation are discussed. For instance, in the beginning of the 20th century, Benjamin considered the technological evolutions of his time — like photography — as opportunities for artists to rethink their autonomous practice.[40] He was convinced that the creative work is 'better, the more consumers it is able to turn into producers — that is, readers or spectators into collaborators.'[41] However, with the explosion of consumer products such as radio, television or magazines in the 20th century, Adorno & Horkheimer — exponents of the Frankfurt School — saw a lot of dangers.[42] They coined the term 'culture industry', with which they emphasised that in popular culture standardised cultural goods, such as films or radio programmes, are used to manipulate mass society by making it more docile and passive. Unlike with the telephone, they thought that mass communication media did not allow the consumer to reply or provide feedback in any way:

> The step from telephone to radio has clearly distinguished the roles. The former liberally permitted the

37 Whittaker et al.,1998; Nielsen, 2006.
38 Benkler, 2006; Gauntlett, 2011.
39 Nielsen, 2006.
40 Benjamin, 1936.
41 Ibid., p. 233.
42 Adorno & Horkheimer, 2002; Shanken, 2009.

> participant to play the role of subject. The latter democratically makes everyone equally into listeners, in order to expose them in authoritarian fashion to the same programs put out by different stations. No mechanism of reply has been developed.[43]

Framing contemporary media such as weblogs, social network sites, games or wikis, Raessens & Goldstein and Schäfer have written about participatory culture, in which the collaborative plays an important role.[44] Schäfer argues that within participatory culture people produce content, texts, software and hardware in collaboration with a large number and great diversity of participants.[45] Related to this, Jenkins et al. have called 'participatory culture' a new form of cultural production:

> 1. with relative low barriers for artistic production and civic engagement; 2. with strong support for creating and sharing one's creations with others; 3. with some type of informal mentorship whereby what is known by the most experienced is passed along to novices; 4. where members believe that their contributions matter; 5. where members feel some degree of social connection to one another

> (at the least, they care about what other people think about what they have created). Not every member must contribute, but all must believe they are free to contribute when ready and that what they contribute will be appropriately valued.[46]

Jenkins argues that platforms such as weblogs or social network sites allow new forms of debate.[47] In this what Jenkins calls 'convergence culture', classic mass media become less oriented toward a mass audience. Their digital character makes their content exchangeable between platforms and usable in a more individual and personalised manner. According to Jenkins, this allows many informal, inspiring and innovative 'collages' and collisions between different media 'types' and discourses, as well as new forms of participation.

In this context, Schäfer, however, stresses that these media are not always produced in a radically different context from the industry that Adorno & Horkheimer were talking about.[48] While they talk about the concept of 'culture industry', Schäfer introduces the concept of 'extended cultural industries' to refer to the production of cultural products that allow for participation. These extended cultural industries

43 Adorno & Horkheimer, 2002, pp. 95-96.
44 Raessens & Goldstein, 2005; Schäfer, 2008.
45 Schäfer, 2008.
46 Jenkins et al., 2006, p. 7.
47 Ibid., 2006.
48 Schäfer, 2010; Adorno & Horkheimer, 2002.

can collide with, but they can also be included in, the more traditional media practices and industries, such as the activities of the large television broadcasting industries.[49] They can, but thus do not necessarily, lead to participation.

As already became clear from the political and media discourses around participation, these participatory forms of cultural production exist in different degrees of engagement. Laermans compares the cultural audience to an onion, in which the outer peel contains incidental participants in culture.[50] The middle peel of the onion consists of an interested public that follows cultural life in specialised papers and magazines and attends cultural events more or less actively. The 'connoisseurs' can be found in the core of the onion and are perceived as part of a scene or even as a group of 'friends'. In addition to that insight into types of cultural participants, Schäfer indicates that participation can be both implicit and explicit.[51] Implicit participation processes do not, or to a lesser extent, require a conscious cultural production or choice from different methods in collaborative problem solving and communication. For example, people can contribute to the improvement of information management and services by simply 'using' platforms like Flickr. In explicit forms of participation, explicit actions contribute to communities and the conscious generation of media texts and artefacts.[52] This form of participation can be found within self-organised web communities (from fan cultures to professional development communities).

In relation to this, Schäfer distinguishes between three forms of participation by end-users in online projects on the continuum between implicit and explicit participation.[53] First, 'accumulation' refers to the rather passive and implicit activities that people engage in. These activities involve participation in popular media content and products, often developed by corporate companies. Clicking on Flickr images and bookmarking is an example of such an accumulative activity. Second, 'archiving', or organising, refers to how people store and re-organise objects and build archives and knowledge bases. This can occur on an active as well as on a more passive level. Sites like 'The Pirate Bay', for example, are spaces where people share and distribute links to movies. Finally, Schäfer defines 'construction' as the most explicit form of participation.[54] He gives the example of participants who collaborate in making so-called emulators, which, for instance, can refer to game emulators. Participants create systems to allow old computer games to be played on more recent computer systems (e.g. the old 8-bit home computer Commodore 64 on the operating system Microsoft Windows). Construction refers to:

> the emergence of new distribution and production means that are not

49 Schäfer, 2010.
50 Laermans, 2002.
51 Schäfer, 2008.
52 Schäfer, 2011.
53 Schäfer, 2008.
54 Ibid., 2008.

> institutionalized and not necessarily controlled by an owner, but rather generally at the user's disposal. It describes the production of new content and new technologies, as opposed to media that comment on or relate directly to popular media productions.[55]

Schäfer's three forms of participation are illustrated in the following diagram (see: Image 1). In this diagram, each form of participation refers to the platforms on which the specific participatory activity takes place.[56]

Summary

From this overview of the literature, we may conclude that:

- Jenkins discusses participatory culture as a new form of cultural production that evolves in a more participatory way.[57] This form of cultural production is associated with low barriers for artistic production and civic engagement, strong support for creating and sharing one's creations, attention for informal mentorship, members who believe that their contributions matter and the feeling of a degree of social connection to one another. Participatory culture — e.g. by being low-barrier and by allowing participation over different forms of media — allows the involvement of participants in the participatory process that are hard to engage otherwise;
- Jenkins points to the fact that participation goes

Framing

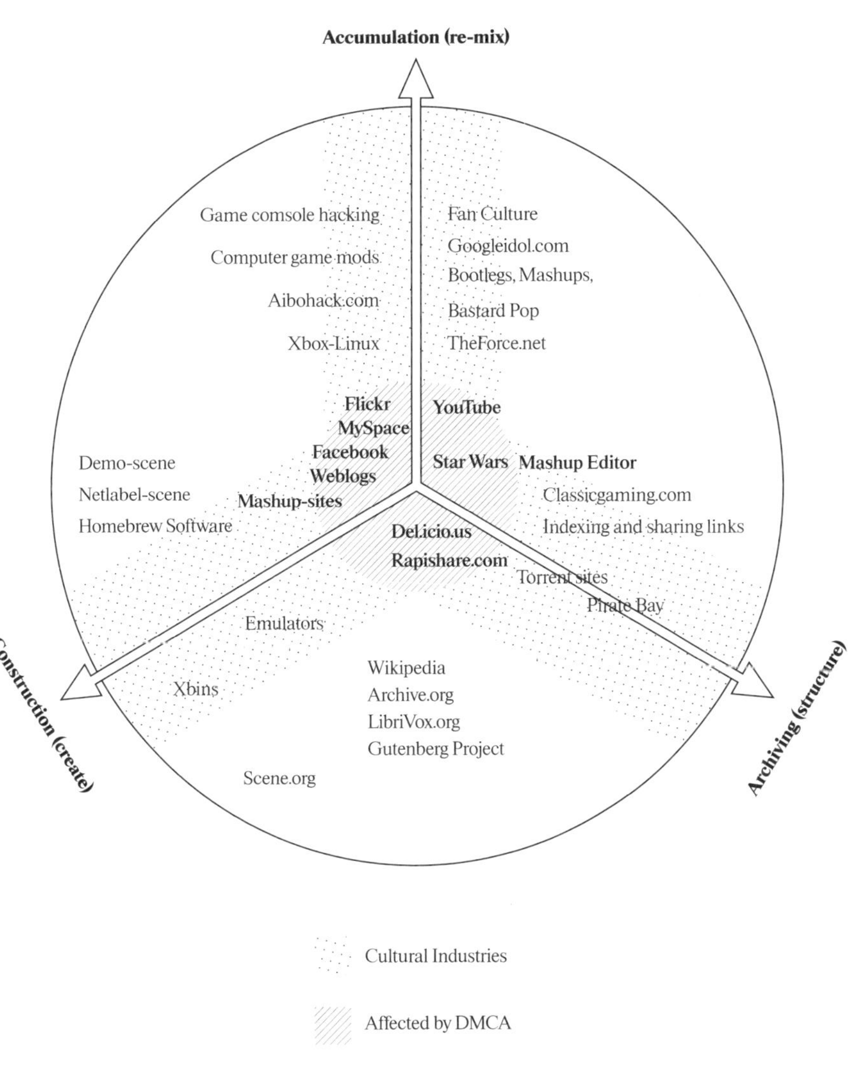

Image 1 **Mirko Tobias Schäfer**, diagram slightly adapted

55 Ibid., p. 80.
56 Ibid.
57 Jenkins, 2006.

further than merely working together with people but also includes working across the borders of media, content and disciplinary domains;[58]

— also in the domain of culture, a critical view exists on the potential of media to increase participation. Here it is also stressed that different degrees and more implicit or explicit forms of participation exist.[59]

The Concept of 'Things'

After framing the notion of participation in the above-mentioned ways, we now state that it is important in participatory art and design projects — maybe even more so than in political participatory processes — that some-*thing* is created during the project. In the cultural domain, makers of participatory projects produce various objects, games, installations, art or works in collaboration with other participants. We refer to what is produced in participatory projects as 'things', instead of traditional objects (or games, or installations, et cetera), because there are always people involved. This idea is inspired by the framework of the Actor-Network Theory, as defined by Latour.[60] In Latour & Weibel's essay *Making Things Public*, Latour states that people often present objects as 'facts' or 'matters of facts'.[61] However, he prefers to speak of 'things' or 'matters of concern' around which people gather. Latour refers to the disaster of the space shuttle Columbia (over Texas and Louisiana, U.S.A. in 2003) to explain this:

> the shuttle Columbia was not an object whose substance could be defined, but an array of conditions so unexpected that the lack of one of them (a bureaucratic routine) was enough to destroy the machine [...]. Whenever a network is deployed, a substance is transformed from an object into a thing, or to use my terms, from a matter of fact to a matter of concern.[62]

Latour thus describes a 'matter of concern' or 'thing' as much broader than a matter of 'fact' or object. To illustrate this, we refer to the A.telier collective who used this concept of thing in a participatory design context. Also inspired by Latour, they state that '... things are matters of concern insofar as they are able to offer people new possibilities of experience'.[63] The thing is, then, not only defined as an entity of matter, but also as a socio-material assembly, a collection of people and objects, dealing with a matter of concern. The example of the space shuttle disaster illustrates that a thing can refer to a device or an object (such as the shuttle Columbia itself), as well as to the assembly of people around a certain situation (such as the disaster of the space shuttle in 2003). Therefore,

58 Ibid.
59 Laermans, 2002; Schäfer, 2008.
60 Latour, 2005; Latour & Weibel, 2005.
61 Latour & Weibel, 2005.
62 Latour, 2005, p.799.
63 A.telier, 2011, p.77.

Latour states, things always include two aspects. They refer to (1) those who assemble because they are concerned, such as people who are concerned about space missions. And they refer to (2) what causes their concern and disagreement, i.e. the disaster itself. This is also illustrated by A.telier's example of a realisation of a participatory digital archive:

> the outcome of a design project is ... both a device and a thing. It can be seen as a device, the embodiment of the object of design, providing users with access to some function such as the Atelier tangible archive for storing and retrieving mixed materials. But the tangible archive as outcome of the design process is also a thing, modifying the space of interaction for the students using it, ready for unexpected use, and opening new ways of thinking and behaving.[64]

Furthermore, we consider the activity of working in participatory ways as a process of 'thinging': a continuous process of producing things. More specific, design researchers Ehn and Storni describe the participatory project as the process of producing one thing after or next to another, in relation to different groups, possibly but not necessarily leading to one or more stable objects or devices (such as a painting, a public installation or a game).[65] This term 'thinging', which is also inspired by Latour, entails that when a participatory art or design project is created or judged, not only the end-product(s) but also the various things that are created during a process have to be taken into account.[66] Defining participatory projects as processes of thinging makes clear that they always involve makers, participants and objects in subsequent and varying constellations. This means that it is not the maker, nor the participants or the objects that define the success of a project, but rather their mutual interactions. Furthermore, the 'thing' does not have the goal to close a project, but to open up new participatory engagements:

> An entire series of objectifying tendencies that push the thing to becoming an artefact is therefore counterbalanced by an entire series of thinging emergences that instead revert the tendency and bring the artefact and its associated elements to a rediscussion of their interdependencies and a reactivation of some of their virtualities and multiplicities.[67]

64 Ibid., p.158.
65 Ehn, 2008; Storni, 2012.
66 Latour, 2005.
67 Storni, 2012, p. 110.

Summary

To conclude, we can state that participatory projects can be considered as (a series of) 'things'. We claim that:

— these projects involve (several) socio-material assemblies or people assembling around a matter of concern, (such as an archive).
— this concept of thing puts our idea of participatory projects in a different perspective, considering them as an on-going, multi-directional process, in which makers, participants and objects are only a part of the whole. This implies that these projects are impossible to control by the maker alone.

The Phases of a Participatory Project

To gain more insight into what these 'things' are, it is important to describe the different phases in a participatory project, being: (1) *project-time*, referring to the creation phase and (2) *use-time*, referring to the phase during which a project is distributed and used or experienced (see: Image 2).[68]

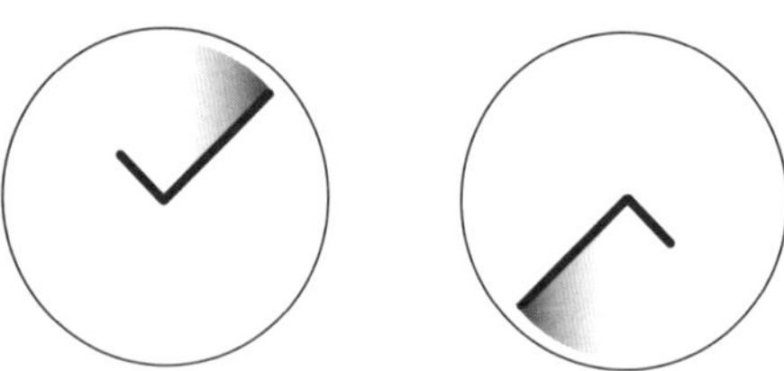

Image 2 **Visualisation project-time and use-time**

During project-time, a participatory project aims to facilitate participation in the development of a product or work that will be used afterwards. Project-time thus generally takes place before the 'public launch' of a project. The project phase involves the participation of makers and participants with different motivations, who use different working methods and have various customs.[69] The process of confronting motivations, methods and customs can be a vehicle for creativity, opening people's eyes to new types of outcomes (products, works, et cetera).[70] A large body of literature in the field of participatory design describes ways to participate in the project prior to its launch.[71] It shows that temporary forms of the project (being under development) can be used to facilitate this organised participatory confrontation. These can take on the forms of objects, like written or drawn scenarios of what the participants want to produce together or cardboard simulations of a product under development. These objects can be gradually developed further by intermixing methods and customs of the diverse participants, making the creation process tangible or readable for everybody involved and supporting them in discussing and creating collaboratively. In this phase, things are thus assemblies of various participants around 'interim' objects. For example, in the case of *Uncle Roy All Around You*, participants were engaged to evaluate and

68 A.telier, 2011.
69 Bowen, 2009.
70 Gold, 2007.
71 Simonsen & Robertson, 2012.

try out the game scenarios before the final game was completely programmed and visualised on the complex technological mobile and online platforms.

Next to project-time, there is also design in use ('at use-time').[72] During use-time, makers and participants participate in a more informal way. Ehn describes that rather than focusing on involving participants in the design process, the attention during use-time shifts towards seeing every use situation as a potential design situation. Usually, project-time precedes use-time, as these phases are often parallel trajectories, for instance, in open user innovation models. In these models, Von Hippel explains:

> economically important innovations are developed by users and other agents who divide up the tasks and costs of innovation development and then freely reveal their results. Users obtain direct use benefits from the collaborative effort. Other participants obtain diverse benefits such as enjoyment, learning, reputation, or an increased demand for complementary goods and services.[73]

The criteria of enabling participation in project-time and in use-time differ. In project-time, the project is much more controlled by the formal structure of the creative maker-team. For example, in a project that aims for the participatory creation of mobile phone interfaces, a paper simulation of a mobile phone interface design can allow a designer to talk very specifically to engineers and end-users about its functionality. However, without this professional context, this paper simulation would not have sufficient meaning in itself. In use-time, the maker is not necessarily present and therefore his or her role should be replaced by some kind of infrastructure that allows participants to continue their activities.[74] Sticking to our example of mobile phones, this infrastructure can be an online platform where participants can keep exchanging ideas about a mobile phone, such as the Android Community, exchanging around open-platform mobile devices. In use-time, a thing is thus more defined by a group of participants who self-organise their exchange around (some) objects, possibly via an infrastructure provided by the makers.

Summary

To conclude, we can state that the distinction between project and use-time helps us understand that participation can be either more maker and participant driven. We claim that:

— in project-time, participation often aids makers in developing a certain project, in dialogue with participants' desires and needs.
— in use-time, participation can be continued by the participants to develop a project further, fitting it

72 Ehn, 2008.
73 Von Hippel, 2013, p. 413.
74 Ehn, 2008; Huybrechts, 2011.

to their changing needs. This can be supported by the makers through offering participants an infrastructure via which they can exchange.

The Concepts of Uncertainties and Risk

In the literature and in previous research trajectories in which participatory projects were set up, we discovered that participatory projects always involve uncertainties and risks.[75] To explain this, we now explain the concept of uncertainty within a participatory project on the one hand and risk on the other.

Uncertainties

Although we have used the terms uncertainty and risk somewhat interchangeably throughout this chapter, they are not synonymous. We already stated that participatory projects are characterised by risky trade-offs between makers and participants, because of the many uncertainties that are involved. Participatory projects are in essence always uncertain. They rely heavily on the input from other participants.[76] This contrasts with the makers' urge to control the participatory process and its outcome.[77] We noticed that the literature roughly distinguishes four main types of uncertainty that makers deal with when they engage in participatory projects.

First, in a participatory project, the maker puts all or a selection of her or his ideas on the table where they, then, are open to adapting, changing or critiquing by the participants. By doing so, these ideas may well be transformed and personalised by the participants for new, unexpected contexts that the maker did not foresee. Makers are not used to hand over part of the control over the project to other participants in such a way.[78] Wagner et al., for example, refer to the hesitation of municipalities in engaging citizens in urban planning (instead of only experts) because they worry that citizens might even be more critical.[79] In previous research, we learned, however, that in participatory projects it is not enough to create harmony and understanding. To change a social situation, openness to critique, debate and discussion is recommended.[80]

Second, the literature shows that a specific form of uncertainty that makers deal with is that their participatory projects are spread over various domains (e.g. culture, technology or economy) and can hardly be claimed by a single domain.[81] This can make makers and participants feel uncertain about how to position these projects securely within a specific educational landscape or funding policy. We are certainly not claiming that these participatory projects are a victim of this uncertain, in-between position. Rather, we think that they deliberately embrace this uncertainty, since the viewpoints of other participants can have a radically innovative impact on the project.[82]

75 Huybrechts, 2011; Dreessen, et al., 2011.
76 Dreessen et al., 2011.
77 Huybrechts et al., 2012.
78 Ibid.
79 Wagner et al., 2009.
80 Schepers et al., 2011.
81 Twaalfhoven, 2010; Bishop, 2012.
82 Van Erven, 2010.

Third, participatory projects can provoke uncertainty, since they are complex systems developed within a network. The A.telier collective states that this complexity responds to the information society and knowledge economy in which these projects function.[83] The collective formulates three challenges that makers, consequently, are confronted with:

> 1. a complex environment in which many projects or products cross the boundaries of several organizations, stakeholder, producer and user groups;
> 2. projects or products that must meet the expectations of many organizations, stakeholders, producers, and users; and
> 3. demands at every level of production, distribution, reception and control.[84]

Fourth, Suchman describes a participatory project as a way of involving the participants and their environment into the creation process.[85] She states that there is no clear separation between makers and participants. They are all actors, with different histories, who are involved at different moments in a project. Therefore, even the role of the maker in relation to the participant can be uncertain.

Summary

By saying that makers and participants engage in risky trade-offs during a participatory project, we thus imply that:

- they can take several actions (unintentionally or intentionally) to engage in a participatory exchange, such as engaging in a network or crossing domains.
- they will, however, always be (somewhat) uncertain about many aspects of this exchange, such as the outcomes of the project, the domain in which the project will operate, the complexity of the project's context and their own roles.

Risk

We now clarify what we mean by 'risk' in participatory projects. Risk has been studied as a concept in several domains, such as sociology and philosophy, in organisational studies and in information systems.[86] The sociological literature on risk can be divided into several theoretical perspectives, each based upon different bodies of literature.[87] Each of these sociological perspectives has a different way of defining risk and its contexts. The best-known approach to risk is that of 'Risk Society', defined by Giddens and Beck and later critiqued by Lash.[88] We also discuss the philosophical approach by Stengers and the ICT (Information and Communication Technology) perspective by Hanseth & Ciborra.[89] Although we acknowledge that there are

83 A.telier, 2011.
84 Ibid., p. ix.
85 Suchman, 2006.
86 Hanseth & Ciborra, 2007.
87 Lupton, 2006; Zinn, 2004.
88 Giddens, 1999; Beck, 1992; Lash, 2000.
89 Stengers, 2002; Hanseth & Ciborra, 2007.

many other approaches to risk, we only take a closer look at these perspectives, since we feel that they are the most applicable and significant ones for explaining risk in relation to participatory projects.

Our idea of risk is inspired by Beck's and Giddens' theory of 'Risk Society'.[90] Beck claims that contemporary Western societies have shifted from an economy and way of life shaped by industrial processes 'to a late modern period in which dangers and hazards have proliferated as a result of industrialization, urbanization and globalization'.[91] Therefore, Beck states, risk has become a dominant trait of modern society and has changed, over time, in nature. While the traditional concept of risk was related to natural phenomena such as floods, new risks originate in our self-created technological and organisational environment, for instance in our ICT infrastructure.[92] All this has led to a new paradigm, which Beck calls 'Risk Society'. Then, in Beck's view, risk 'may be defined as a systematic way of dealing with hazards and insecurities induced and introduced by modernization itself.'[93] According to Beck, risk society is characterised by efforts to know and control risk.

However, a major point of critique on Beck's notion of risk society is that it might be more appropriately labelled as a 'risk-averse society' or 'angst society': 'Beck negates the possibility of a risk-seeking culture by reducing risk to risk avoidance'.[94] Beck's risk society, thus, is a society that obscures the possibility of an 'acceptable risk', which implies that some level of risk can be tolerated and is even desirable.[95] The idea of an acceptable risk corresponds to risk-taking in participatory processes, in which risk is an unavoidable and desirable factor.[96] This idea of accepting risks corresponds to Lash's definition of 'risk cultures' as alternatives to risk society.[97] Lash states that risk cultures are self-reflexive communities that are less hierarchically organised than a society, operating in a third space, being the margins or the boundary between private and public life. Risk cultures do not work with norms and are far removed from being 'security cultures' or 'consequence takers', placing themselves at the receiving ends of risk. They are risk 'cultures' because they work with values and deal with chronic uncertainty, continual questioning and with openness to innovation built into them.[98] According to Lash: 'they deal with risk, with identity-risks and ecological risks, not so much through rational calculation or normative subsumption, but through symbolic practices and especially through symbol innovation.'[99] With risk cultures Lash, in contrast to Beck, thus leaves room for 'acceptable risks': 'We need (...) to embrace, perhaps with lots of trepidation and with no small measure of fear and trembling, the risk culture.'[100]

90 Beck, 1992; Giddens, 1999.
91 Beck, 1992; Lupton, 2006, p. 12.
92 Hanseth & Ciborra, 2007; A.telier, 2011.
93 Beck, 1992, p. 21.
94 Eckberg, 2007, p. 362.
95 Scott, 2000; Eckberg, 2007.
96 Dreessen et al., 2011.
97 Lash, 2000.
98 Ibid.
99 Ibid., p. 60.
100 Beck, 1992; Lash, 2000, p. 62.

Belgian philosopher Stengers also appears to embrace this concept of acceptable risk.[101] Stengers notices that many professionals are blind to what escapes from their own paradigms. In order to produce something new, she wants to stimulate them to put their own ideas at risk. For Stengers, risk is always related to people's own experience and is closely related to trust in a certain context:

> take, for instance, the risk you might take in a new relationship with a lover or friend - you cannot foresee the outcome but you have a certain trust that can sustain its possibility. Who knows if the friendship or love will last? But we can reflect on the experience and the feelings that allow us to take risks and to experiment - the laughter and joy in the face of uncertainty. These experiments move us towards a greater possibility in life, and the potential to live, feel and experience it.[102]

Stengers mentions several risks that professionals can take, such as confrontation with groups of people that they are not familiar with.[103] She refers to an example of scientists confronting themselves with feminists or gays: 'the point is not that scientists have to accept whatever those empowered people tell them, the point is that learning from them is their chance to put their preconceived ideas at risk.'[104] Another risk a professional can take, Stengers claims, is slowing down the process of thinking. To illustrate this, she mentions the organisation of philosophical workshops in order to stimulate a collective process of thinking:

> in order to achieve this we have to produce games and rules, the aim and success of which is to slow down the qucstions/answers process in order for people not just to express what they were thinking anyway but to feel their thought becoming part of the collective adventure. When you go too fast you do not feel the possibility of new creations, new connections. The rules we invented are meant to make it impossible for anybody to be able to posit him or herself as 'I know what I think', in order for thought to emerge from a kind of collective stammering.[105]

In a recent publication, Hanseth & Ciborra place the idea of an 'acceptable risk' in the context of ICT.[106] They describe the uncertainty that results from creating complex ICT systems that involve various

101 Stengers, 2002.
102 Ibid., p. 244.
103 Ibid.
104 Ibid., pp. 264-265.
105 Ibid., p. 252.
106 Hanseth & Ciborra, 2007.

inevitable risks. Hanseth & Ciborra claim that when we are confronted with a complex ICT system, our knowledge and understanding of how its different components work and interact — and accordingly how the system as a whole works — is always incomplete. Often, the system's components act and interact in ways we cannot predict, leading to unpredictable interactions within the entire system. Furthermore, they state that the more complex a system is, the more partial our knowledge will be and the more unintended effects our interventions in the system will have. Hanseth & Ciborra indicate that to deal with this risk, a lot of tools to control risk during the creation of these systems have been developed. Examples are tools for risk management, prediction and calculation in ICT systems to control management processes. Also, ICT experts have tried to reduce the interactions between a system's components or make them easier. However, Hanseth & Ciborra consider none of these strategies as sufficient. The complexity of society grows fast and requires more and more complex systems, which will inevitably produce risk. Therefore, according to these authors, risk in ICT is a factor makers have to consciously deal with. Corresponding to Beck, they state that ICT has become a risk rather than a control technology, since it generates risk rather than controlling it.[107] The risk in ICT systems design is thus mainly related to the fact that in creating an ICT system, makers only create a small piece and seldom control the whole project. The same goes for creating a participatory project, in which makers usually create a specific part of the project. Therefore, they never know exactly how the different parts, created by different participants, eventually will interact.

Risk in participatory projects can take on many forms. For instance, building on one of the uncertainties we mentioned earlier, one form of risk-taking in participatory design processes is sharing (this will be explored further in chapter 3). This can include that a maker shares knowledge and practices surrounding a project with participants and thus risks handing over (part of the) control over the project to other participants. This type of risky trade-off is an integral and necessary part of the participatory project. Makers and participants both will constantly have to overcome their possible discomforts in these types of trade-offs and will need to look for a balance between controlling and accepting risk within their project.

However, before integrating these concepts of uncertainty and risk into our definition of participatory projects, we have to mention that when risk is defined from a maker's perspective only, it is not a useful concept for participatory projects. For instance, Storni states that risk is often defined from an expert perspective, as something that can be calculated and avoided.[108] To explain this, he quotes Callon et al. who claim that risk is a top-down concept.[109] They state that risk starts from the

107 Beck, 1986.
108 Storni, 2011.
109 Callon et al., 2009.

perspective of the expert, which 'bears the stamp of an asymmetry between experts (specialists who knows best and who are supposed to assess and manage risk) and lay people (non-specialists who instead are often at risk).'[110] In this context, Storni explains that:

> The notion of risks resonates and links to the idea of rational and informed decision, and assumes that all options have been explored and the possibility of harmful effects has been foreseen. Even though we are not able to know whether a harmful event is going to occur or not, the assumption is that we do know the statistical probability of its occurrence (thus the notion of risk). On the contrary, the notion of uncertainties underscores the fact that scientific knowledge often proves to be incapable of anticipating the effect of certain decisions, understanding all the possible options, and informing a rational decision. The idea of risks and that of uncertainties imply radically different decision-making processes in complex situations.[111]

Storni thinks that complexity is dealt with differently in participatory projects, when uncertainties instead of risks are predominant as a guideline in these projects.[112]

He claims that complexity is then approached by making risks debatable and negotiable, instead of attempting to reduce this complexity to a specific expert perspective. In this context, we believe that a definition of a participatory project needs to underline the risky trade-offs that the maker and the participants make when setting up or participating in a participatory project, instead of the risk that the expert or maker takes. This idea of risky trade-offs integrates the ideas of risk and uncertainty, by showing that risk-taking is a two-way process, involving uncertainties by all parties.

Summary

After exploring the concepts of risk and uncertainty, we can draw the following conclusion:

— makers often feel uncertain when they are involved in a participatory project.[113] These include the uncertainty of (1) sharing ideas and making them open to adapting, changing or critiquing by others, (2) their participatory project spreading over various domains, (3) acknowledging that participatory projects are complex systems developed within a network, and (4) dealing with the fact that the division of roles between makers and participants can be unclear. We also discussed how uncertainty is a necessary, integral part of the participatory project.

110 Ibid., p.1.
111 Storni, 2011, p. 169.
112 Ibid.
113 Dreessen et al., 2011.

— knowing that uncertainties are inherent to participatory projects, these projects are characterised by risky trade-offs between makers and participants. Risky trade-offs involve the conscious or unconscious negotiations between the makers, the participants in a participatory project and the objects involved in the project, with an inherently uncertain and undefined outcome. These actions can refer to, for instance, 'opening up' a project to comments by participants (see 1), which can lead to both interesting improvements and negative comments. Our definition of risk is inspired by Lash, who sees uncertainty and continual questioning as inherent to 'risk culture' and thinks it opens up possibilities to innovation.[114] Also, Stengers' embracing of risk and the qualitative inclusion of risk by Hanseth & Ciborra in ICT systems inspired us.[115]

— by saying that participatory projects are characterised by 'risky trade-offs', risk is redefined as a qualitative part of a participatory project. The term 'trade-off' stresses that risk is not defined by the makers, the objects used in a project or the participants, but by the 'thing': that what is formed between the makers, the objects and the participants.[116] Risky trade-offs are thus described by qualitative actions that makers and participants take, the objects they introduce or change and the inevitable and necessary uncertainties, which are part of a participatory project.

This is quite contrary to the definition of risk as something that is an outside factor that can be objectively calculated and even avoided.

Conclusion

The above framing was a search for a workable definition of participatory projects, which we will use throughout the rest of this book.

Summary

To summarise, our main conclusions entailed:

— that in the fields of art and design, participation evolves via *things*.[117] Participatory projects do not intend to create one object as a form of closure, but rather create a series of 'things' or exchanges between people and objects;

— that *different degrees and intensities of participation* exist.[118] On the one hand, the maker determines to what extent he or she allows (extensive) participation of the participant and thus takes the risk that the outcome of the project differs from his or her original view. On the other hand, as is illustrated by Verba et al., the degree of participation depends on the motivations of participants to share their ideas, to influence projects and to invest their time, money and skills in a project;[119]

114 Lash, 2000.
115 Stengers, 2002; Hanseth & Ciborra, 2007.
116 Storni, 2011.
117 Latour, 2005; Ehn, 2008; Storni, 2012.
118 Arnstein, 1969; Milbrath, 1965; Schäfer, 2008.
119 Verba et al., 1995.

— that *different phases of participatory projects* exist, being project-time and use-time, and that in these phases things are created via different principles. In project-time, the things are often strongly moderated by a group of makers who organise people's participation around temporary objects, with an eye on generating new ideas for future products or works. In use-time, things can be described as participants who organise their participatory exchanges themselves around (a series of) objects, possibly even independently of the original group of makers. These exchanges are, however, regularly facilitated by a kind of infrastructure set up by makers to facilitate this self-organisation.
— that there are different types of *uncertainties*, which are integral and necessary parts of participatory projects. Therefore we defined participatory projects as *risky trade-offs* between maker and participants, with an inherently uncertain and undefined outcome. By using the term 'risky trade-off' we redefined risk — and uncertainty — as a qualitative part of a participatory project.[120] The term also stresses that risk is not only defined by the makers, the objects used in a project or the participants, but by the 'thing': that what is formed between the makers, the objects and the participants.[121]

Combining the above conclusions, we come to our definition of participatory projects.

(1) Participatory projects are characterised by **risky trade-offs** between makers and participants, wherein both parties engage in a participatory exchange, being uncertain about what this exchange might bring.
(2) These trade-offs are '**things**', wherein participants negotiate on objects, like sketches, prototypes, installations or simple comments (often introduced to lower barriers in collaboration between them).[122]
(3) These trade-offs can take place in **two phases** - i.e. project-time and use-time - and can demand more or less strong or explicit participation.

120 In the line of thought of Lash, 2000; Stengers, 2002; Hanseth & Ciborra, 2007.
121 Storni, 2011.
122 Latour & Weibel, 2005; Storni, 2012.

Empirical Section: Risky Trade-offs in Practice

To make the above theoretical reflections more tangible, we now take a closer look at two specific participatory projects. These case studies (i.e. Blast Theory's *Uncle Roy All Around You* and Constant vzw's *Routes and Routines*) were part of a larger research project in which participatory projects were analysed in order to detect how risky trade-offs took place between makers and participants, how uncertainty was defined, integrated or avoided and which 'things' were created.[123] For this purpose, we used 'MAP-it'.

MAP-it is a method and toolkit — developed by the research group Social Spaces — that can be used to analyse the risky trade-offs that take place in participatory projects between people and objects involved.[124] MAP-it contains a background map, stickers and some game rules that assist moderators in structuring the mapping process. Using MAP-it, we gathered participants and makers that were involved in (the creation processes of) participatory projects around the table, encouraging them to address the ever-existing conflicts between visions, ideas, viewpoints, et cetera in an open manner. Several participatory projects — participatory games, interventions, installations, telecommunication tools, et cetera — by different artists and designers were analysed, using the MAP-it method and toolkit. We now discuss two of these projects, being Blast Theory's *Uncle Roy All Around You* and Constant vzw's *Routes and Routines.*

MAP-it is inspired by the framework of the Actor-Network Theory as defined by Latour.[125] Latour stresses that things are complex, that we are 'disabled' to see things in all their complexity and therefore need a prosthesis.[126] Building on this idea, MAP-it is designed as a kind of prosthesis that facilitates collaboratively taking a closer look at things within a participatory project. Since we understand that a thing cannot be displayed completely transparently, MAP-it only allows people to discuss it and collaboratively visualise it, as a possible *representation* of a thing. To stress this subjective character of the method itself but also of the thing that is represented — it is designed in a playful way: people, spaces, objects and relations are all visualised by a set of stickers. Image 3 shows some of these visualisations: colourful stickers that represent straightforward elements ('money' or 'books'), but also more 'risky' components (e.g. 'bombs') in the form of so-called 'risk-stickers'. These risk stickers invite participants to openly visualise their uncertainties in working with other participants in a participatory project. Stickers of the above-mentioned bombs, but also 'likes', 'locks', 'smileys' or 'traffic lights', can be used to express positive feelings and uncertainties in a playful manner. In this way, the risky trade-offs in participatory projects are revealed. The playful character of the method makes the participants more willing to share their opinions and provide feedback, as they see this as part of the game.[127]

123 Huybrechts, 2011.
124 Schepers et al., 2011.
125 Latour, 2005.
126 Ibid.; Latour & Weibel, 2005.
127 Huybrechts et al., 2012.

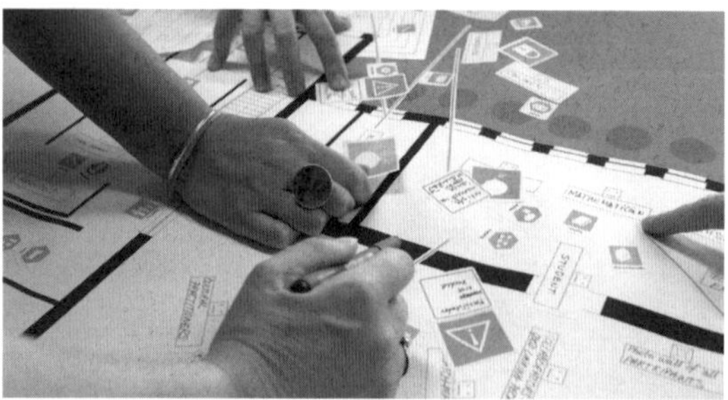

Image 3 **Visualisations MAP-it**

Blast Theory's *Uncle Roy All Around You* is one of the case studies that were mapped (using MAP-it) in order to identify the risky trade-offs and uncertainties involved in (setting up) a participatory project. Additionally, interviews were conducted to gain insights into Blast Theory and its projects. Another mapped participatory project was *Routes and Routines* by Constant vzw. However, we also did a 'live' follow-up of Westenberg's interaction with the participants during the walks, which we discuss below. During the project, we gathered information through observations, interviews and by participating in the creation, the performance process and part of the 'afterlife' of the project. While gathering information, we particularly focused on how the different perspectives of the participants in the project were negotiated and which risks and uncertainties were addressed.

Case study 1: Uncle Roy All Around You

The game, i.e. *Uncle Roy All Around You* (which was

performed three times) is the first case study that we will zoom in on. (see: Image 4) This game aims at finding the fictive character 'Uncle Roy' in the streets of London (UK). Two players — who are random volunteers — have to collaborate in solving questions in order to play the game. One player plays online (in a virtual city, on a computer screen), while the other plays in the actual streets of London (using a mobile device). 'Online players' and 'street players' thus work together to find the office of the mysterious Uncle Roy. When they — eventually — find this office, the two players are invited to make a year-long commitment to each other by exchanging their phone numbers and by promising they will be there for each other when the other player calls. As the game unfolds, players thus move from a game-like world to a real-life environment involving a strange set of social relations.

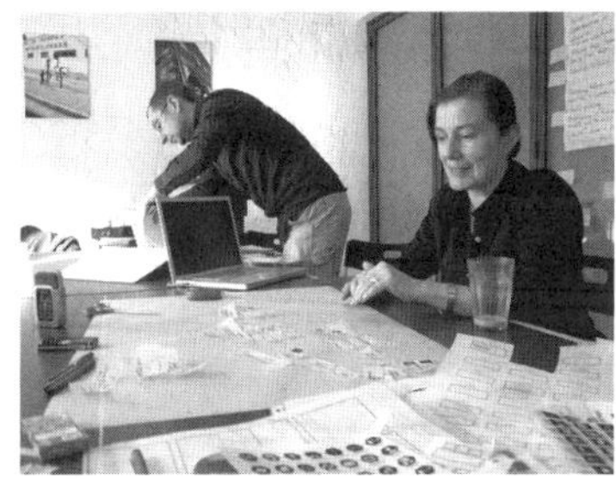

Image 4 **Blast Theory**, Uncle Roy All Around You

Uncle Roy All Around You was created in 2003 by Blast Theory, an art collective based in Brighton (UK) that creates participatory, artistic games and performances in public areas. In the media art and performance scene the collective is known for systematically engaging various participants in (the creation processes of) its projects. They do this, as one of Blast Theory's member states, because: 'otherwise there's nothing at risk, (...), you're not learning and you're not allowing yourself to possibility of really making something fresh.'[128] This was also the case during the creation process of *Uncle Roy All Around You*. During the mapping of the game, the makers visualised how they stepped out of their own comfort zones and worked together with many different stakeholders (a research group with technological expertise, festival organisers, private partners, game players, people in the streets, et cetera) throughout the whole process. Together, they explored how their collaborative insight into art, games, technology and everyday experiences could create a good game experience in which audience members would like to participate. During the mapping, they visualised the uncertainties that they encountered. They expressed how, sometimes, the goals of the partners conflicted with their own goals or the 'languages' or jargons spoken by the participants differed from each other. However, they saw this as a benefit for the project, resulting in new insights and a new language for all partners.[129] The mapping made clear that the confrontation between the technical expertise and the artistic background of the participants functioned as a good driving force for participation. While the technical experts usually focused on creating technologically well-functioning communication systems, the art collective aimed for creating ambiguous and engaging stories that triggered participation. When both parties, however, decided to step back and give up control over how they envisioned the game to be created, the project became really interesting. The technical partner acknowledged that technological communication systems could benefit from ambiguity as a particularly interesting feature for engaging participants. At the same time, the artistic partner learned from the technical partner that there is great value in creating communicative platforms between participants that allow them to collaborate in playing the game. A first 'risky trade-off' that we thus distinguished in Blast Theory's project is the uncertainty coming from the differences between the art collective and participants from other disciplines, which they used as a productive factor in their works.

Blast Theory wanted to offer game experiences that allow as many people as possible to 'speak meaningfully in their own register' and increase participation for all.[130] Therefore, a second 'risky trade-off' that was made by Blast Theory entailed opening up the game to contributions from the 'user' participants by keeping the game unfinished and imperfect, which resulted in uncertainty about participants doing unexpected things in the game set-up. To involve the participants, the team created several unfinished prototypes and tested them in multiple settings to see how participation by and between audience members of

128 Dekker et al., 2010.
129 Ibid.; Huybrechts, 2011.
130 Dekker et al., 2010.

the game could take place. There were a lot of evaluation mechanisms during the creation process. For instance, 'real' public and ten (invited) expert guests tested the overall experience of *Uncle Roy All Around You*. Also, user observations (via video recordings), note taking, evaluations and interviews were conducted. These user tests led to improvements in the interfaces, bug fixing and adaptations in the prototypes. Also, the final mobile game technologies were designed as imperfect communication platforms that required the participant's reflection to complete missing elements. This kind of imperfect technology is not common in the engineering world. In *Uncle Roy All Around You*, the mobile phone interface (see: Image 5) was set up as a map that allowed the street player to communicate with the online player via a live visualisation of her or his trajectory and audio messages. Because of the mobile devices' limited capabilities, the visualisation and the audio were imperfect (e.g. people could record an audio message of 15 seconds maximum). These 'errors' prevented instant gratification, which made the game more exciting to play by forcing the participants to collaborate continuously in gathering clues.

The third 'risky trade-off' in Blast Theory's project was the fact that the game was shared in many ways with various (future, potential) participants *after* the game was played (thus, in use-time). For example, some postcards that were part of the game experience arrived when the game was done, thus triggering participation during people's daily lives. Also, the game

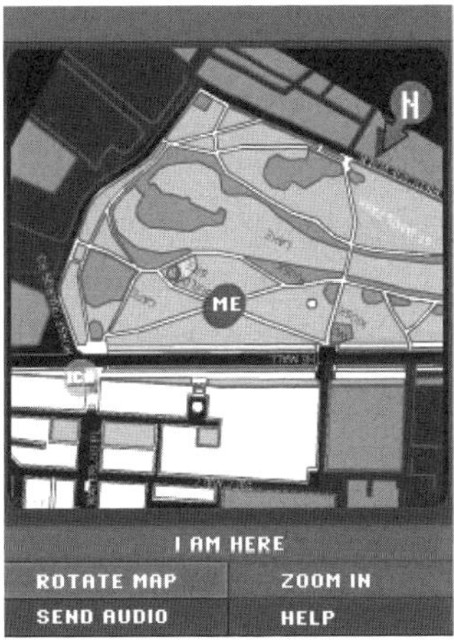

Image 5 Mobile interface Picture by Blast Theory

was opened up to participation in use-time via the publication of documentation (in different formats), such as videos or research papers. The technical partner — functioning in the academic sphere — documented the experience of creating the game via writing research papers that discussed the role of imperfect and uncertain communication platforms in triggering participation. To engage participants in playing the game at festivals, the artistic group documented the game play online via video documentaries. The videos were of various lengths so that they could be used in various ways, e.g. for marketing, explanatory and/or research means. Blast Theory made the videos available although they were not (yet) able to predict in which ways the videos would be used. Moreover, the art collective documented the working process of the game and the raw materials that were used in making it.

The working process of the game — a complex interplay between content and technological triggers — was documented, so it could be repeated by the makers (potentially with new group members) in a different context. They also made copies of all the operating system's libraries and logs data. However, a risk Blast Theory did not dare take was sharing this working process and raw material publicly. External people cannot access the code and hardware that generates the game experience; they thus cannot participate in modifying or constructing the game. Blast Theory explained that it is not that the group does not *want* to share the code, but that it is not their first interest: 'I don't think we're really a group of people who are coding stuff to make elegant pieces of code or make stuff that's reusable. That's not our goal, we're making experiences.'[131] The art collective also feels that sharing is a time-intensive process, which is not prioritized over their artistic goals (see: Image 6).

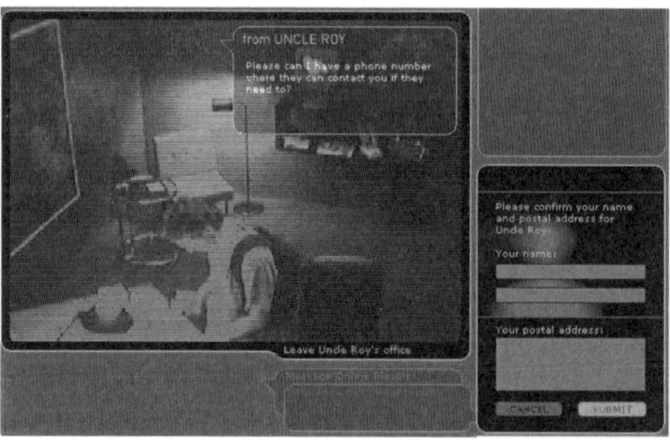

Image 6 **Online interface Uncle Roy** Picture by Blast Theory

The case study of *Uncle Roy All Around* You shows how makers and participants engaged in risky trade-offs on three levels, involving participation with other disciplines, user participants and potential future participants. It illustrates the uncertainties that were involved in these exchanges. The discussions were mainly about how imperfect technologies appear to stimulate participation. At the same time, most participants were not used to create technology and interact with it in this way. Also, uncertainties occurred on the level of how far the makers wanted to go in sharing documentation about the project in order to allow potential future participants to have insight into or even adapt the project to their needs.

Case study 2: Routes and Routines

In this second case study, we discuss the participatory performance project *Routes and Routines*: a series of artistic internet walks through the Belgian city of Hasselt, performed during the exhibition project 'Place@Space' (16.3.08 — 25.5.08) in Z33 — House for Contemporary Art (located in Hasselt). *Routes and Routines* offers a playful approach to serious questions such as: 'Can you "borrow" bandwidth?' and 'how freely can you "walk around" on the Internet?'

The artists involved in *Routes and Routines* engaged participants in the project via an installation

131 Ibid.

(see: Image 7) — situated at the art centre — involving posters, shoes and a database film. The posters displayed in the room were legal documents (by governments and companies), explaining the implications of using technologies in the city space (such as surveillance cameras), the terms of agreement between internet providers and their customers, national and international regulations on privacy, internet access and electronic data traffic. Participants were invited to put on the shoes — equipped with electronics, sensors and recording equipment — in the exhibition room and go outside for a walk. While outside, the participants entered a public Internet space in (parts of) Hasselt, consisting of the temporarily opened-up personal Internet connections of the residents. This public Internet space was explored by the artists and participants throughout the walks. Together, they discussed the significance of technological networks and co-created new scenarios for the integration of technology in the city. To create those scenarios, the participants recorded their experiences during the walks via the equipment on their shoes. The shoes allowed them to register and broadcast live data, visuals and sounds from the walks and also detect technological and digital networks in the city. To stimulate people's imagination in making the recordings, the makers played short audio-fragments during the walk or showed small visualisations about the city and the technologies they encountered. The artists and participants also drove a cart around, containing equipment that allowed the recorded scenarios to be transmitted to the exhibition space. In the exhibition space, people could subsequently experience the scenarios that the makers and participants created about technology in the city in the form of a database movie.

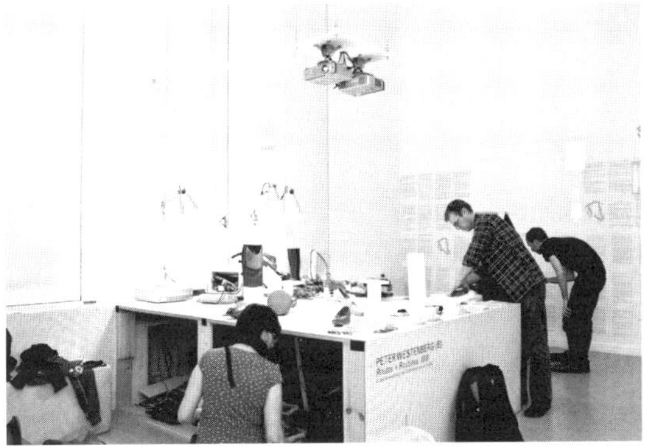

Image 7 **Installation Routes and Routines** photo by Kristof Vrancken

Routes and Routines was created by the non-profit art and media organisation Constant vzw, based in Brussels (BE). The main members of Constant vzw (such as Peter Westenberg and Wendy Van Wynsberghe) come from various disciplines and all have their own networks, backgrounds and perspectives. Members of the core team lead different working groups, to which external people are connected. The group is — among other things — active in the domain of feminism and cyber feminism, alternatives for copyright, free software, digital communication and the culture and ethics of the web. The artistic laboratory of Constant vzw explores the ways in which technological infrastructures, data exchange and software determine our daily lives and — especially — how they can be approached in different ways. The art collective regularly organises gatherings, workshops, events, walks and presentations for and with participants who engage in experiments and discussions. For *Routes and Routines*, Constant vzw collaborated with Z33 — House for Contemporary Art, the city of Hasselt (e.g. policy makers or representatives of the city of Hasselt) and two private companies that managed aspects of the local Internet networks (i.e. Telenet and I-City).

The *Routes and Routines* project started with the makers exploring the technological infrastructure in the city of Hasselt. Constant vzw approached several private and public partners to collaborate in the project. The local technology company I-City offered their experience with local telecom operators (like Telenet) and technological networks to the *Routes and Routines* project. This allowed the artists to make the local technological network public on a larger scale. In addition to that, Constant vzw borrowed a large antenna from I-City to pick up wireless networks. Like Blast Theory, Constant vzw thus collaborated with different disciplines, meaning that the art collective needed to get out of its own comfort zone in order to create an interesting, participatory project. As was the case for Blast Theory, this was a specific risky tradeoff for Constant vzw. During the mapping, it became clear that the partners all had a different vision on the value of open and free technologies and data (within the context of the project). This appeared to be a source of friction between the private companies and Constant vzw. Eventually, this drove the partners to decide to limit their collaboration to an infrastructural exchange, rather than an intense conceptual and technical co-creative activity. Nevertheless, their discussions eventually contributed to a better understanding of the use of technology in the city. (see: Image 8)

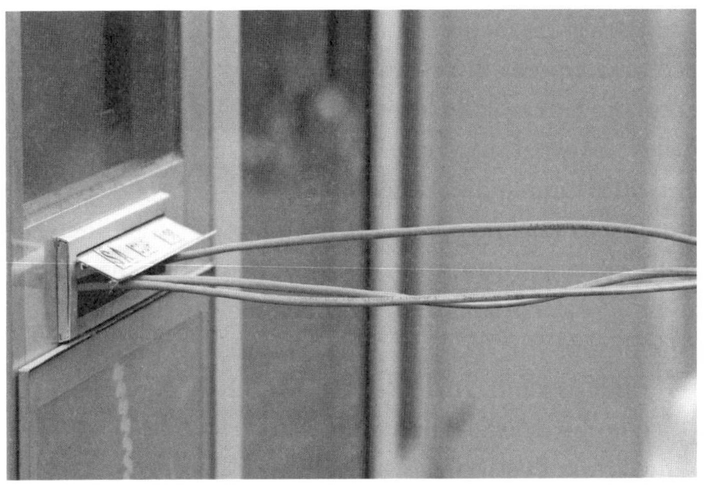

Image 8 **Sharing Internet** photo by Kristof Vrancken

At the same time, potential participants (e.g. local citizens and organisations) were invited to engage in the project at an early stage of the creation process. This was a second risky trade-off that took place within the context of this project. To reach the participants, the artists sent a simple, written letter — besides using other media such as a weblog or postcards — to address the Hasselt community, asking people to participate in the walks and to open up their personal Internet networks for the period of the exhibition. Responding to this letter, one print shop, for instance, proposed to make its Internet cable available through the letterbox, so people could plug in and connect to the Internet from the street. Also, Constant vzw used 'open source' communication tools (in the form of communicative shoes and a shopping cart) to engage with the participants in the project. Open source is a principle and a method of creation via which organisations or individuals provide free access to source materials of a project to a distributed network of people.[132] The participants in *Routes and Routines* — both the technical partners and the other participants — were clearly more comfortable with using communication tools produced by corporate organisations (such as Microsoft). This led them to expect that communication tools always work in invisible and fluent ways. In response to that, Constant vzw deliberately made their open source tools feel 'frayed', strange and rough. Via seams and ragged edges on the technology, they made — as Constant vzw member Femke Snelting stated — the 'breakpoints' of the tools visible to the participants.[133] These breakpoints are the points of connection to other software, hardware, uses and interfaces and can be used to create a deeper understanding of how the technology works. In this way, Constant vzw's tools stimulated the participants to reflect on what these tools are, how they are used and how they can be used in different ways. Thus, the art collective turned the communication tools into an 'uncertain place': a subject of reflection and negotiation. By opening up the tools in such a way to stimulate reflection by the participants, unexpected and uncertain outcomes may arise from the project.

The breakpoints in the tools became particularly tangible in one specific 'thing', namely the participation that was triggered through the electronically equipped shoes that the participants wore during the walk. The way in which these shoes were designed, regularly obstructed fluent walking in order to initiate reflection on technology in the city during a process of communal bonding. The shoes were deliberately made quite 'heavy' in order to slow down the participants in the walking process, thus allowing them to take time to detect technological and surveillance networks in the environment. This means that — as was the case in *Uncle Roy All Around You* — the shoes were created in an 'imperfect' way. (see: Image 9) Another important 'thing' that was created during *Routes and Routines* was the participation evoked via the shopping cart, equipped with a computer, that was driven around by the makers and participants. The cart was a frayed collage of technological material that digitally connected the public space context with the Internet and the exhibition space. Since the content of the cart was carried around openly and was used every time the participants wanted to send their audio-visual material to the exhibition space, it made people conscious of

132 Bauwens, 2007; Tribe & Jana, 2006; Open source initiative, 2010.
133 Huybrechts & Machils, 2010.

the technological connection between these contexts. Additionally, it allowed people to relate to the technology and even play with the relations between the contexts (see: Image 10).

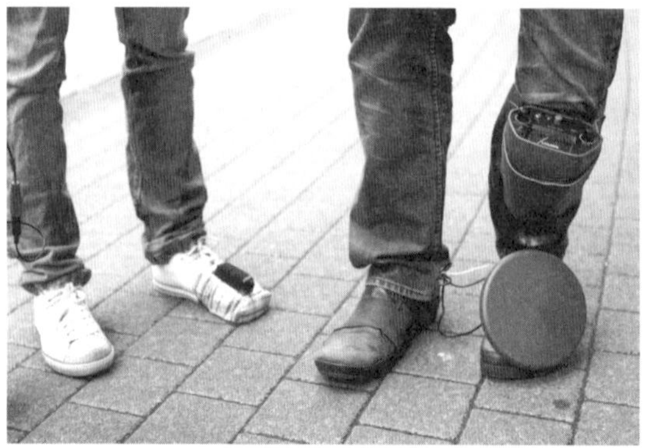

Image 9 **Shoes** Photo by Kristof Vrancken

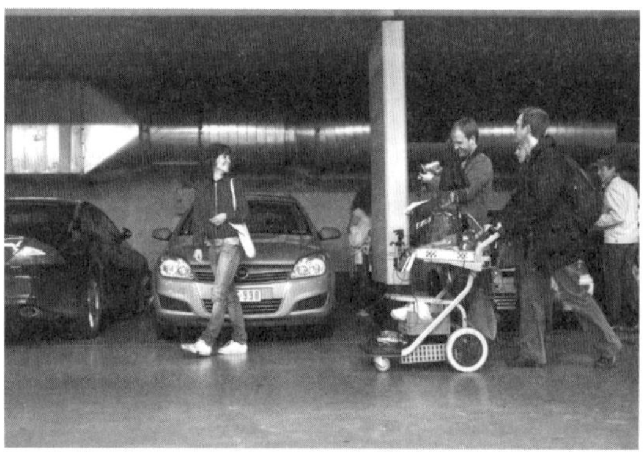

Image 10 **Cart** Photo by Kristof Vrancken

A third risky trade-off entailed how Constant vzw shared technical and meaningful documentation of the project openly, to be reused by others in the future. For instance, the shoes could be adapted by the participants and — depending on the encountered situation — fitted with microphones, mini-cameras, transmitters, antennas and detectors of metal or other materials. Much discussion and reflection was involved in the process of making these shoes adaptable. For instance, discussion arose on how the design of the shoes would be accessible, but at the same time fascinating enough to trigger people's interest in modifying them. The adaptations to the shoes and the manuals or guidelines to create them, but also the other components of *Routes and Routines* — like the walk, the cart and the movie — were shared online. This allowed the project to be redone (and 'remixed') easily by future potential participants.

In this case study, we encountered the same three types of risky trade-offs as in *Uncle Roy All Around You*: between makers and other disciplines, between makers and 'user' participants and between makers and future participants. Especially participation on this first level, i.e. working with other disciplines such as private companies, was experienced as a risky trade-off. There were clear differences in how the different partners approached technology. In working with 'user' participants, it also became clear that there were differences in how technology was experienced. The makers invited the participants to engage with imperfect technologies, which they clearly were less familiar with. This, however, appeared to trigger the participants' curiosity. Finally, future potential participants were invited to comment and reconfigure the project via sharing documentation of the project online.

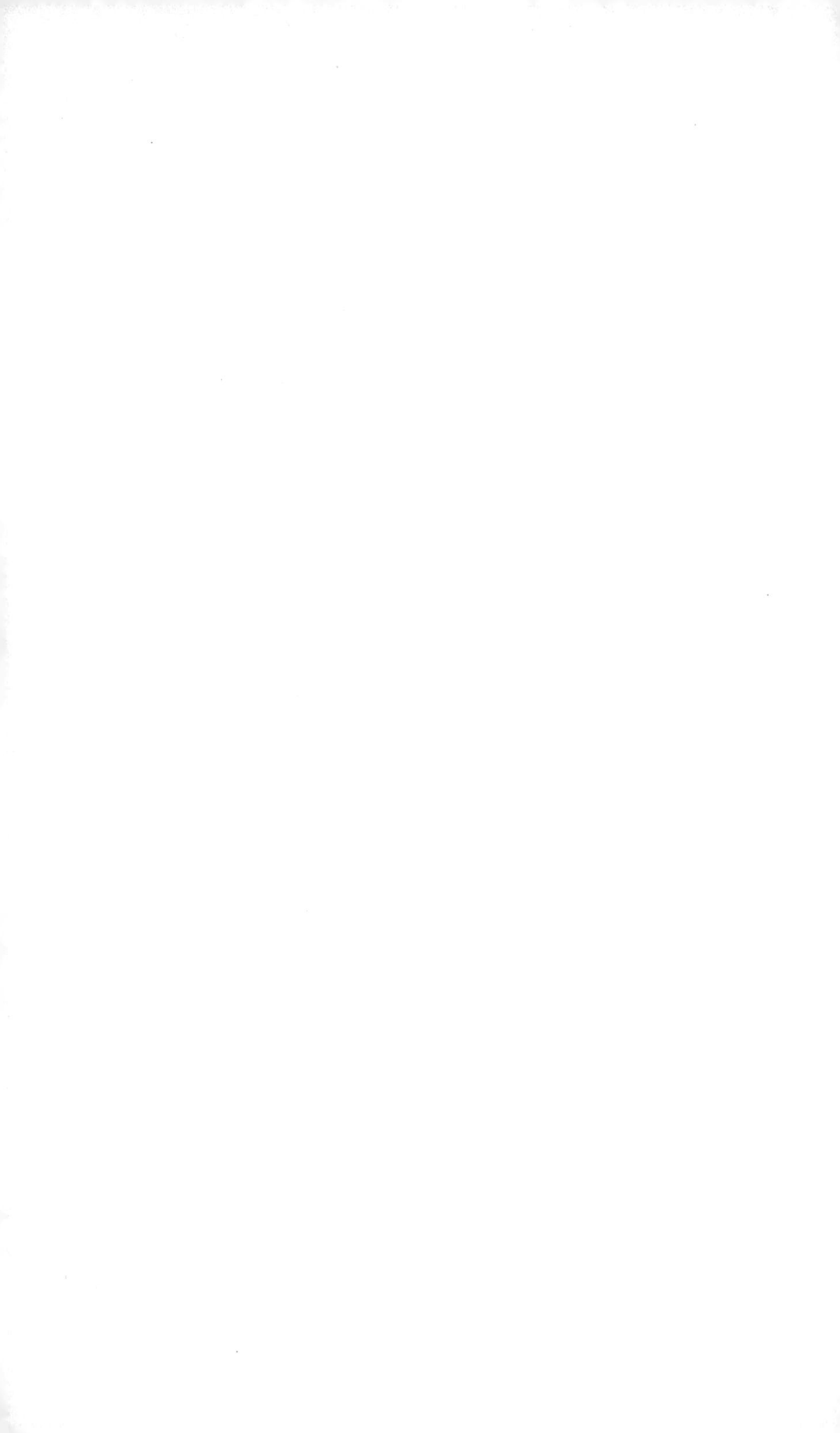

Discussion: Participatory Projects as Risky Trade-offs

We started this chapter by stating that participation remains under-exposed in art and design education and even in professional contexts. By consequence, many makers feel uncertain in the context of participatory projects. We think that this uncertainty is inherent to participatory projects and is also encountered by more experienced participatory artists and designers. However, we also feel that by describing the exchanges that take place in participatory projects, both makers and participants can become more aware of which uncertainties they may encounter.

To describe these exchanges, we first searched for a workable definition of a participatory project. We learned that in the fields of art and design, participatory projects evolve via 'things'.[134] They seldom create one object as a form of closure, but rather create a series of 'things' or exchanges between people and objects. The extent to which these exchanges take place may differ, depending on in how far makers and participants share ideas, influence the projects or invest in time, money and skills.[135] In addition to that, these exchanges take place in different phases, being project-time and use-time, during which things are created via different principles. In project-time, things are often strongly moderated by a group of makers who organise people's participation around temporary objects, with an eye on generating new ideas for future products or works. In use-time, things can be seen as participants who organise their participatory exchanges themselves around (a series of) objects, possibly even independently of the original group of makers. These exchanges are, however, regularly facilitated by a kind of infrastructure set up by makers to facilitate this self-organisation. Different types of uncertainties appear to be integral to participatory exchanges, such as sharing, crossing disciplinary boundaries or negotiating about roles. Therefore, we stated that participatory projects can be characterised by risky trade-offs between makers and participants, with an inherently uncertain and undefined outcome. Through using the term 'risky trade-off', we redefined risk — and uncertainty — as a qualitative part of a participatory project, formed between the makers, the objects and the participants.[136]

The mappings (using MAP-it) and observations brought the complexity of these risky trade-offs in two case studies to the surface, in a way that was collaboratively defined by the participants. The aforementioned 'risk-stickers' — such as 'bombs' or 'traffic lights' — allowed the makers to express their uncertainties in the project. A sticker depicting a 'thumbs up' enabled them to say which uncertainties appeared to be productive. The mappings of the two case studies showed that Blast Theory and Constant vzw engaged in several risky trade-offs in many phases of their participatory projects, which we will now discuss in detail.

134 Latour, 2005; Ehn, 2008; Storni, 2012.
135 Arnstein, 1969; Milbrath, 1965; Schäfer, 2008; Verba et al., 1995.
136 In the line of thought of Lash, 2000; Stengers, 2002; Hanseth & Ciborra, 2007.

Risky Trade-offs, Things and Participation in two Case Studies

In the scheme below, we summarise the risky trade-offs that characterised the case studies *Uncle Roy All Around You* and *Routes and Routines*, several 'things' that came into existence during the project and the various implications for participation:

Risky trade-offs	Things	Participation
1. Working with different disciplines was described as necessary for both projects, but also as being risky, since all participants needed to get out of their own comfort zone in order to participate in the project. In Uncle Roy All Around You, an intense and long-term collaboration was set up between technical and artistic partners.In case of Routes and Routines, the choice was made to limit the collaboration between Constant vzw and a corporate technical partner to an infrastructural exchange, because their visions were too different.	For the diverse disciplines the 'imperfect' platforms/ technologies were a 'new' way of approaching participation.	The uncertainty coming from the differences that arose from the collaborations between the art collectives and participants from other disciplines was used as a productive factor in the participatory projects. The imperfect platforms/ technologies were a source of uncertainty in the collaboration between the different disciplines, but - at the same time - an interesting point of discussion and research.
2. Opening up a project to comments or contributions from 'user' participants was seen as a goal in both of the projects. However, it was also experienced as making a risky trade-off, since it could lead to unexpected and uncertain outcomes.	To mediate the interactions between the art collective and 'user' participants, technologies were designed as 'imperfect', 'frayed' and 'not working fluently'. In Uncle Roy All Around You, the mobile phone interface had limited capabilities, making the visualisation and the audio imperfect. In Routes and Routines, both the shoes and the shopping cart were deliberately created as 'imperfect things'.	These 'imperfect things' or 'imperfect communication platforms' made the participants uncertain, as they were more used to fluently working corporate technologies. At the same time, they attracted people's participation, because the participants were puzzled and triggered to engage more deeply in the project.

Discussion: Participatory Projects as Risky Trade-offs

Risky trade-offs	Things	Participation
3. Handing over the project to a larger group of potential participants that were not immediately involved in the project was seen as a third risky trade-off by the makers. After all, although they were convinced of the potential of addressing unexpected groups of participants, they felt uncertain about how this would fit their defined goals for the project.	Different types of documentation were created and shared to provoke online discussions, sharing and commenting or even recreating the game/performance by participants. Uncle Roy All Around You was documented via the publication of videos and research papers. The technology was created as being flexible and adaptable. In Routes and Routines the shoes could be easily reconfigured, because of their flexibility. Also, the manuals/guidelines to create them were shared online.	In both cases, documentation stimulated participants to engage with the project in the form of discussions and comments. However, some uncertainty existed about how far the project should go in documenting and sharing aspects of the project with potential participants. The flexible, adaptable technology allowed various participants to adapt the technology or recreate it. In Routes and Routines, the uncertainty was related to how the shoes could be designed to trigger adaptation.

The risky trade-offs that both Blast Theory and Constant vzw engaged in with participants, included working with (1) different disciplines (thus, in cross-disciplinary setups), opening up the project for (2) 'user' participants and releasing the project to a larger group of (3) future potential participants that were not immediately involved in the project. Referring to the relation between the participants and the makers, we can thus conclude that risky trade-offs took place on three levels : different disciplines, diverse participants and future, potential participants, all in interaction with the maker(s).

The case studies showed that the art collectives and participants were involved in these risky trade-offs via a process of 'thinging'. As we indicated, Latour, Ehn and Storni state that a participatory project can be considered as a series of 'things' or exchanges between objects and people.[137] In the context of the case studies, we observed that the art collectives introduced several 'imperfect' game elements and technologies, pieces of documentation and flexible technologies to the participants that opened up new forms of participatory exchange between people. We can therefore claim that risky trade-offs on this level were made possible through imperfectness, sharing and flexibility. These three aspects provoked uncertainty, but at the same time lowered the barriers for makers and participants to exchange during the project.

Furthermore, the mappings indicated that the two phases of a project — i.e. project-time and use-time — were associated with different participant groups and more or less strong or explicit participation by makers and participants.[138] Both case studies illustrate that during project-time, especially makers coming from (1) different disciplines and (2) 'user' participants take part in the project. During use-time, the involved participants become uncertain. Furthermore, the intensity of the involvement of makers and participants also differs in the two phases. In project-time, the makers were heavily involved in engaging different disciplines and 'user' participants in the generation of project concepts or materials. In use-time, they focused more on creating an infrastructure — mainly via documentation and flexible technology — around which (3) a group of participants, possibly independently from the makers, could organise their participatory exchanges themselves.

The two phases also each demand different approaches to time, intensity and means. For instance, both case studies made clear that the means are exchanged differently between makers and participants in project-time and use-time. During project-time, the focus was mainly on the 'imperfect things' or 'imperfect technologies' (e.g. the mobile phone interface in Blast Theory's case and the shoes and shopping cart in the case study of Constant vzw) as a 'new' way of negotiating and approaching participation among makers and participants. In use-time, the 'imperfect technologies' — in both case studies — remained important, but were complemented with other factors — such as documentation and flexible technologies — in order for future, potential participants to use and adapt the technologies further.

Discussion

From the above, we can derive that in this first chapter three levels on which risky trade-offs can take place have been discussed. These levels refer to the mutual relations between makers and the participants, being: different disciplines, 'user' participants and potential participants in interaction with the makers. The levels are shown in the scheme below (see: Image 11, in which the different disciplines, 'user' participants and

137 Latour, 2005; Ehn, 2008; Storni, 2012.
138 See e.g. Verba et al., 1995.

potential participants are visualised on the right and the makers on the left). We clearly distinguished these three levels in the two above-mentioned case studies, illustrated how the studied participatory projects take place via these three specific (levels of) trade-offs and described them in detail. Although we briefly touched upon the fact that these trade-offs can be made possible via playing with the 'imperfectness' of technologies, sharing and flexibility, until now we have only superficially zoomed in on how these risky trade-offs take form.

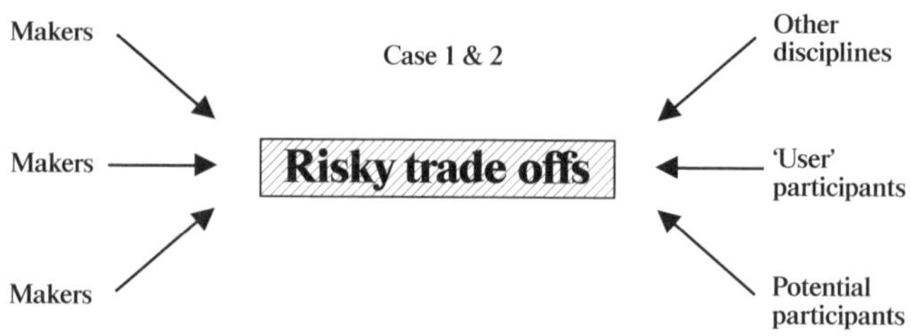

Image 11 **Visualisation of three levels on which risky trade-offs can take place**

In relation to these three aspects, we discovered some issues that clearly deserve more attention and need to be subject of future explorations. In the case studies we described, i.e. *Uncle Roy All Around You* en *Routes and Routines*, we particularly focused on how to engage participants in the participatory project. We noted that other disciplines and 'user' participants are involved during project-time, while potential participants are drawn into the use-time of a participatory project. In relation to the exchanges among these groups, we discovered some issues that clearly deserve more attention.

First of all, Blast Theory and Constant vzw played with imperfect technologies in order to open up their projects to diverse disciplines and participants. Gaver et al. already touched upon imperfect technologies as good drivers for participatory exchange.[139] However, it is something that still requires further research and will also be discussed in more detail in chapter 2. Secondly, the two case studies showed that attempts were made to engage participants who did not participate during the creation process of the projects or in the game/walk, *after* the project. They tended to do this by sharing documentation about the project. This process is continuous; Blast Theory and Constant vzw documented the entire projects and searched for formats to share this with others. Although the art collectives were convinced of the potential of documenting, they felt uncertain about how releasing the project to other participants (besides the ones that participated in the project) would affect the project. Ways of facilitating makers in dealing with this specific uncertainty concerning documentation (e.g. by proposing them formats to share their projects with others and discussing the implications of each format) may be researched and will be discussed in the third chapter. Finally, Constant vzw turned their technologies in flexible and adaptable objects that could be more

139 Gaver et al., 2003.

easily used and changed by participants. They were confronted with several uncertainties in doing so, such as which design would stimulate easy interactions with the technology but also provoke enough challenge to the participants. This aspect as well deserves more research and will also be addressed in chapter 3.

However, although our case studies showed some examples of *which* exchanges take place between makers, different disciplines, 'user' participants and potential participants (being documentation, sharing and imperfect technologies), we did not investigate *how* these exchanges differ between participants. This means that we did not look into how documentation, sharing and imperfect technologies are approached in relation to different groups of participants and disciplines. For instance, the documentation of a project may differ when it is aimed at the participation of different disciplines than when it is aimed at the participation of lay 'user' participants.

In the next chapter, we will discuss further *which* trade-offs take place in participatory art and design projects, specifically during project-time. We will show how most participatory projects in art and design are either situated within a very participant-driven or within a maker-driven approach to these trade-offs. However, we found that the most interesting trade-offs take place when the two approaches are mixed into a hybrid zone: an uncertain third zone that does not belong to one professional expert discipline or a group of participants. Chapter 2 will investigate this concept of hybridity in relation to participatory projects. We will discuss two case studies with a clear hybrid approach. In the context of these projects, we will investigate two main risky trade-offs that take place between makers and participants: via playing with imperfectness (as was already touched upon in this chapter) and making collages.

Mappings

Dekker, A., Huybrechts, L. & Machils, P. (2010). Brighton: mapping Blast Theory. Available at: www.blasttheory.co.uk/bt/work_uncleroy.html and www.map-it.be/mapping-reports/mapping-uncle-roy-all-around-you

Huybrechts, L. & Machils, P. (2010). Brussels: mapping Constant vzw. Available at: www.constant-vzw.org/site/

Chapter II Participation and Hybridity

Liesbeth Huybrechts, Yanki Lee, Selina Schepers & Denny K.L.Ho

Background, Aim and Argument

In this chapter, we look into the ways in which participatory projects are set up in art and design fields. We investigate the exchanges between makers (artists and designers) and participants during the professional creation phase of a project or 'project-time' (as discussed in the previous chapter). In this phase, participatory projects are often strongly moderated by a group of makers who organise people's participation with an eye on generating new ideas for future products or works (this in contrast to the next chapter, in which we will discuss projects where participation is mainly situated *outside* of the control of the makers). We discuss two specific case studies. First, 'Go-for-IT!' (i.e. case study 3) is a participatory art project leading to the realisation of a series of games in public space to involve local youth in an urban transformation process. Second, 'DESIGN.LIVES' (i.e. case study 4) is a design workshop aimed at familiarising design students to work together with disabled and elderly participants.

The field of design has a lot of expertise in participatory work. After all, it has always functioned as a crucial interface between professional domains and (everyday) social worlds. In a text on design, media critic and philosopher Flusser states that — in the 20th century — design started to link artistic and technological culture.[1] He claims that, since then, design is often perceived as a meeting point between the aesthetic, soft and qualitative on the one hand and the scientific, hard and quantitative on the other. Many historical examples illustrate that designers were masters in bridging the gap between artistic and technological culture. For instance, industrial designers like Henry Dreyfuss gave a new life to telephones, trains and other consumer products by investigating their meaning, aesthetics and usability for people.[2] Designers have always looked for ways to connect professional domains, such as the industrial world, with their so-called users, being the people who eventually are going to use, buy or adapt their products. For instance, the Participatory Design movement in Scandinavia in the 1970s played an important role in involving workers in the design and use of computer applications in the workplace.[3] Next to Participatory Design, fields such as Universal Design, Inclusive Design or Service Design adapt comparable, but also slightly different, ways of defining the relationship between the designer (i.e. the maker), other professional domains and the user (i.e. the participant).[4]

Similar to the field of design, that of art has been mixed with other professional domains and with its audience in many ways. Like in other disciplines, the discourse around participation in art became more and more important as the complexity of society increased. In his notes on participatory art, Almenberg searches for the roots of participatory art and ascribes an important role to the experiments by artist Marcel

1 Flusser, 1999.
2 Meikle, 2001.
3 Ehn & Kyng, 1987.
4 As we discussed in the previous chapter, in this text we use the term 'makers' to refer to artists and designers or interdisciplinary creative teams making a project. We use the term 'participants' to indicate people from different disciplines that participate in a participatory project, and (end-)users; Huybrechts & Wilkinson, 2010.

Duchamp and the Dada movement.[5] The Dada movement, for example, was inspired by the idea that the art world was part of a complex whole of societal factors that were responsible for the horrors of World War I. Dada answered to that with so-called 'anti-art': artistic techniques that evoked different, more personal, playful and sometimes participatory ways to deal with art. Examples of such techniques were collages, photomontages and assemblages, which allowed artists to combine elements — like materials, media, et cetera — from different sources. These techniques were open enough to allow input from daily life, thus not being part of the art world.[6] In relation to this, Bourriaud states that later — with the growth of urban culture after World War II — modern cities started to lack space.[7] Therefore, furniture and other daily objects had to become more organised and shrink in size to enable individual mobility and personal interaction. Bourriaud claims that, for many artists, the city became too rigid and appeared to impose certain models of social interaction on people. They responded to this by proposing other forms of social interaction, which aimed for a close relation with the everyday environment, such as performances or happenings.[8]

Participatory projects in art and design thus have a long tradition. From this tradition we learn that participatory projects can be characterised by 'risky trade-offs' between makers and participants, such as the artist and the art audience (see previous chapter). These are called trade-offs since both parties engage in a participatory exchange, being uncertain about what this exchange might bring forth.[9] In the 'Go-for-IT!' project, for instance, the art collective the Patching Zone engaged with students and local youth to co-create ideas, with the intention to engage the local youth in an urban transformation process. The art collective was specialised in making new media installations. However, they were not sure what kind of media installation would result from the participatory process and whether it would meet their expectations.

We would like to point out that the risky trade-offs that we are going to discuss in this chapter should not be understood as 'recipes', determinants or prerequisites for 'good participation'. This is impossible since — as the term 'trade-off' suggests — participatory projects evolve through open-ended negotiations between makers and participants the outcomes of which are uncertain, difficult to predict and to control.[10] Rather, trade-offs are descriptions of interesting practices, that might inspire makers and participants that are or would like to be involved in participatory projects (in the future). We call them trade-offs in order to stress that participatory projects are not limited to producing art or design objects. Instead, they are interactions between people and objects. Art critic Bishop and design researcher Ehn stress that in art and design contexts,

5 Almenberg, 2010.
6 Ibid.
7 Bourriaud, 2002.
8 Ibid.
9 Huybrechts et al., 2012.
10 Ibid.

participatory projects always involve making a central artistic or design medium or material (in the form of theatre, performance or workshops).[11] At the same time, however, they underline that the design or art work is not an isolated artefact, but a project that gathers people around artefacts, often on multiple occasions. To make clear that these projects and the trade-offs that characterise them are exchanges between people and objects, we call them 'things'. The term 'thing' is used to refer to assemblies between people and objects.[12]

While reviewing participatory projects in art and design contexts, we found that there are different approaches to the trade-offs taking place between makers and participants. In both these contexts, similar models have been developed, being participatory and expert approaches to participation. These approaches are visualised in the diagram by design researcher Sanders (see: Image 12).[13] The diagram shows a participatory zone, in which the participant is considered as a partner. It also shows an expert zone, in which the participant is seen as having a more passive role that can be activated. These two models clearly acknowledge the need for risky exchanges between makers and participants in a participatory project. However, they do this in fundamentally different ways.

First, in the model that entails participatory approaches to participation, makers give up a large part of their control over the project to the participants. By doing so, they place themselves in the uncertain position of not knowing what the end result of the project

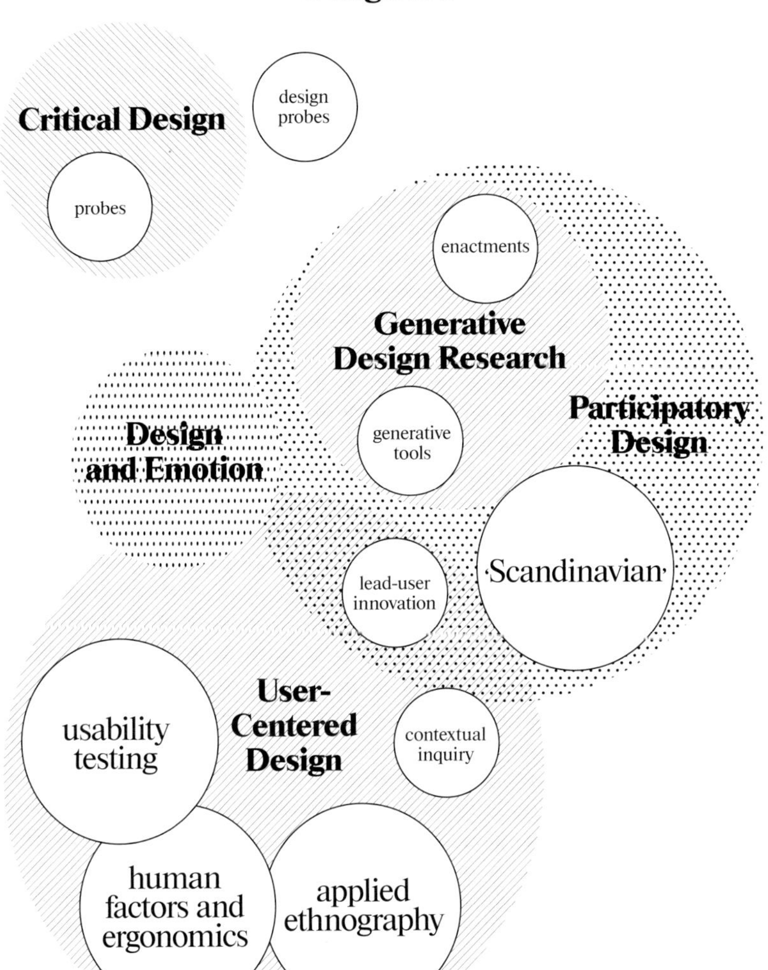

Image 12 **The participatory and expert approaches to participation**
Visualised by Elizabeth Sanders

will be. This first mind set — the participatory or participant-driven approach — is built on the risky trade-off of giving up a large part of the maker's autonomy in favour of other participants in a project. Van Erven states that this can be considered as a hard-core approach to participation, since it stimulates makers to consider the participant as a full partner, or in some cases even the 'leader', in a creative process.[14] It is a reaction to the dominant professional art and design fields, which operate from a so-called ivory tower. Often, this approach is motivated from a political perspective, for instance by stressing the democratic advantages of allowing more impact from (other) participants in a project. Also, the technical advantages of this augmented engagement by participants is underlined, as is illustrated by Ehn & Badham.[15] The confrontations makers have with different ways of working in everyday contexts or other professional contexts can have a radically renewing effect on their familiar approach to the artistic or design process, e.g. on the usage of materials, techniques and concepts. Nevertheless, as authors like Bishop point out, the participatory mind set is often critiqued for solely presenting good intentions rather than producing a real design or artwork.[16] This is often the case when art and design want to be 'something else', like politics, experience, performance or — in short — life itself: a situation that blurs the very boundaries between art and design and non-art and design.

Second, in the model that entails expert (maker-driven) approaches to participation, makers consciously initiate de-familiarising objects or actions that can make participants feel uncertain, with the goal of stimulating them to reflect and work together. The makers deal with the uncertainty that this act of introducing de-familiarising effects may alienate the participants, instead of supporting them in participating. Van Erven describes how this expert — or soft-core — approach starts from the concept of the autonomous artist-designer or maker, who only in a 'second phase' engages the relevant participants in the process.[17] Mostly, the expert mind set produces projects that de-familiarise in order to challenge the status quo perceptions about daily life and to stimulate participants to engage differently in their daily context. We say 'mostly', because parts of the expert mind set — of which user-centred design is an example — approach daily life from a very functional viewpoint and, thus, do not aim for de-familiarising (see: the above-mentioned diagram by Sanders). On the contrary, these parts aim at finding familiar solutions for familiar problems to guarantee a time-efficient creation process. Nevertheless, in this chapter we mainly discuss the expert-based models, using de-familiarising approaches, which can be found frequently in Participatory Art contexts and in so-called Critical Design domains. The advantage of this

11 Bishop, 2012; Ehn, 2008.
12 By, for instance, Latour 2005; Latour & Weibel, 2005; Storni, 2012; Ehn, 2008.
13 Sanders, 2008.
14 Van Erven, 2010.
15 Ehn & Badham, 2002.
16 Bishop, 2012.
17 Van Erven, 2010.

approach is that it can lead to fresh, inventive and even innovative approaches to a problem, project or context. The disadvantage of this approach is that it sometimes presents a rather narcissistic answer to the issue of participation — since it is rather expert-driven — in which participation is confronted with the possible problem that art and design remain in their ivory towers and may become detached from people's needs or desires. By consequence, they could continue to be limited to quite conventional or 'mainstream' art and design production processes.[18]

The art and design literature has made clear that both the participatory and expert models and their typical forms of risky exchanges have great value for participatory projects. However, many authors on art and design agree that participatory projects can only realise their full potential by combining both models.[19] The goal of this second chapter is to explore — via a literature study and two case studies — how the risky trade-offs typical for both models are combined in a participatory project. We show that the risky trade-offs in participatory projects that combine both models can be described via the concept of 'hybridity'. Specifically, we explore the concept of hybridity as a third model, i.e. a hybrid approach — or mind set — to participation.

To sum up, in this chapter we elaborate on the following aspects: the concept of hybridity (p. 104), the participatory mind set or participatory approaches to participation in art and design fields, several subfields in participatory art and design and the specific risky trade-offs that makers in the participatory mind set deal with (p. 107), the expert mind set or expert approaches to participation in art and design fields, several subfields oriented at activation and de-familiarisation and the specific risky trade-offs that makers in the expert mind set deal with (p. 121.) and two case studies with which we provide more insights into the risky trade-offs that makers and participants engage with in hybrid participatory projects (p. 137). We conclude with a discussion on hybridity as a fruitful concept to describe participatory projects, leading the way to chapter 3 (p. 163).

18 Ibid.
19 E.g. Bishop, 2012; Trienekens & Postma, 2010; O'Neill, 2009; Sanders, 2008.

Framing

The Concept of Hybridity

Hybridity is a concept to describe participatory projects that are situated on the border between a participatory and expert-based approach, as can be seen in the visualisation by Sanders, which we have slightly adapted (see: Image 13).[20] We believe that this hybrid mind set offers an interesting perspective on how makers and participants engage with each other in participatory projects. This model starts from the idea that the freedom to generate ideas from an expert position needs the borders of ideas brought in by the participants and the other way around. This idea is based on research in the field of design and HCI, where — for example — Ljungblad & Holmquist stress that, in the creative process in which everything is possible and that has no boundaries or borders, creativity has nothing to build on.[21] We think it is useful to create boundaries that do not limit but instead nurture creativity. Examples of this are boundaries between the expert artistic view in relation to technological, political or social goals in participatory processes or between the maker and participant.[22] Confirming this idea of the fruitfulness of a border region, Bourriaud and Muller state that participatory projects ideally grow out of hybridity, instead of homogeneity.[23]

This concept of hybridity has been explored by Bhabha — an expert in post-colonial studies — and ethnographic researcher Clifford.[24] Bhabha explains hybridity by stating that the border or boundary region between two domains or spaces — in this case,

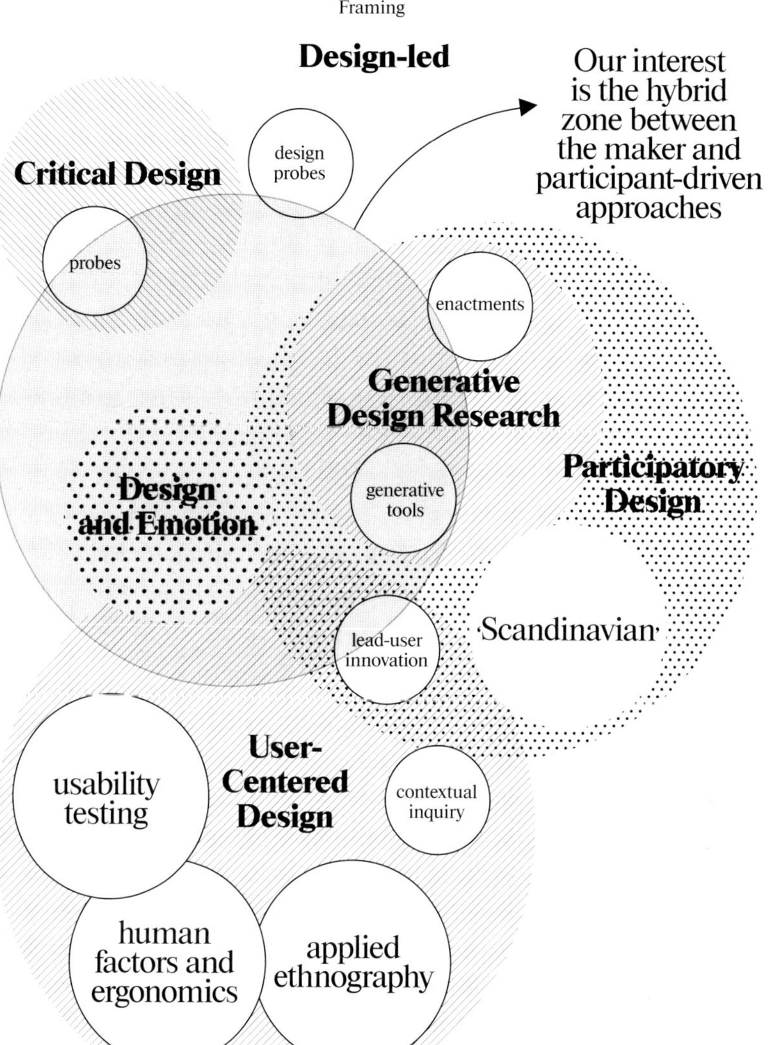

Image 13 **The participatory and expert approaches to participation, as visualised by Sanders, supplemented with a depiction of a third, hybrid model to participation.** Adaptation by Andrea Wilkinson

the participatory or the expert mind set — is a region of overlap or hybridity: it carries traits of both domains. He refers to processes of colonisation, in which people negotiate between their own traditional culture and the culture of the colonisers, producing a new, hybrid culture. Clifford situates hybridity between 'routes' and 'roots'. He uses the metaphor of travel and mobility (routes) in contrast to the fixedness of place (roots). Routes can escape from the context of culture as a homogeneous whole and loosen its constellation of common senses, Clifford states. Routes and roots can meet each other in different zones of contact. To explain when these zones of contact can be called hybrid, he distinguishes between two kinds of museums. The first type of museum extracts objects from their context in order to include them in a different story: the local community enters into a larger nationalistic narrative, imposed by the coloniser. When objects in a museum's display do not refer to the role they play in the lives of people, they are only hybrid because we perceive them as 'out of place' or as being taken out of their original context. The second type of museum makes objects subordinate to the context by focusing on the story of the local population. In both these cases, the experts or the participants are privileged and no real border region is created. According to Clifford, hybridity should emerge from negotiations between the two parties — experts and participants — and between objects, contexts and people, instead of from pulling them apart. In both the definition of Bhabha and that of Clifford one can imagine that the various things that are created in participatory projects take the form of zones of contact between domains, roots and routes. However, Clifford makes clear that not every zone of contact is hybrid. They are only hybrid when the experts from the one side and the involved objects and the participants in a certain context from the other side are taken into account.

Based on the works of Bourriaud, Muller, Bhabha and Clifford, we call the third model — situated in-between the expert-based and the participatory model — a 'hybrid model of participation'.[25] To gain a deeper understanding of this concept of hybridity in relation to participatory projects, we now discuss the participatory and expert-based approaches to participation in more detail.

Participatory and Expert Approaches to Participation

Via an overview of the literature, we want to gain more insight into how makers deal with the risky trade-offs that are typical for the creation phase — or project-time — of participatory projects. There appear to exist two dominant models: participatory, and expert approaches to participation. These two models do not propose a dichotomy, as is the case between what, for

20 Sanders, 2008.
21 Ljungblad & Holmquist, 2007.
22 Van Erven, 2010.
23 Bourriaud, 2002; Muller, 2002.
24 Bhabha, 1994; Clifford, 1997.
25 Friedman, 1988.

instance, Rancière calls autonomous and heteronomous art, referring to art that wants to be acknowledged as an independent discipline and/or space in society versus art that wants to dissolve in society.[26] In both models, autonomous and heteronomous forms of art and design are already intertwined, since in both approaches the maker and the participants are crucial. However, the maker and the participant play different roles. One approach puts more focus on makers who treat their participants as partners and the other approach concentrates on makers who want to activate their participants via a de-familiarising approach. To illustrate this, we first look into the participatory mind set.

Participatory Mindset

The domains of participatory art and design have several subfields that engage participants as partners in participatory projects. As mentioned before, these can be framed in what we call the participatory mind set. The subfields within this mind set have been named differently, like Social or Community Arts and Participatory Design. We explore the literature in and on these subfields to gain understanding of their ways of engaging in participatory trade-offs.

The literature shows us that makers who are engaged in the participatory mind set are mainly focused on creating constructive participation with and between participants while learning from these interactions, rather than on producing friction with the status quo.[27] By consequence, they sometimes suffer from the difficult balance between their social and artistic functions. Art critic Bishop states that in this mind set, the focus is on two aspects — which we identify as risky trade-offs — that may or may not occur together.[28] First, makers relinquish authorship aiming for participation, meaning that they open up their projects to uncertain adaptations by the participants. Second, makers engage with a community, with an eye on participation. This means that their projects are intended to be developed in collaboration with other participants. Here too, the nature of the collaboration is uncertain. In this participatory context, risk is thus defined by the fact that makers deliberately deal with the uncertainty to give up control over their project to other participants and to invest in a temporary or long-term engagement with them, without being certain of the outcomes.

Furthermore, Bishop states that the first aspect — namely makers who take the risk of releasing authorship over a project — is typical for many participatory projects. In the 'de-authored' tradition, the project engages in the uncertain act of relinquishing authorial control. In this mind set, Bishop observes that a project that is created by releasing authorship is regarded as more egalitarian and democratic than a project that is made by a single maker. Bishop also concludes that in this specific approach, projects are considered as more aesthetic when they reflect a degree of unpredictability

26 Rancière, 2010.
27 By, for instance, Twaalfhoven, 2010 and Bishop, 2006.
28 Bishop, op. cit.

and a non-hierarchical social model. Looking at the literature on participation in technical environments, like Human Computer Interaction (HCI) or Computer Supported Collaborative Work (CSCW), one way for makers to relinquish authorship is to disclose the way their works are made. They can open up their work to others via technical documentation or inspiring visualisations.[29] The idea is that a work or project that communicates openness can make people feel less hesitant to engage more actively in it or even adapt or change it (during or after a project). On a technical level, this may lead to surprising changes and maybe even to improvements in the project. On a social level, the open exchange of (aspects of) the project allows participants to gradually engage more in each other's worlds. In general, the outcome of these processes are quite unpredictable since they depend largely on the participants' input.[30]

The second, very often interrelated principle in participatory design and art — Bishop states — involves makers who take the risk of engaging in a community, of addressing a crisis in the community and of aiming for collective responsibility.[31] She states that this principle stems from Marxist thinking, reacting to the effects of capitalism. Bishop underlines that projects that are engaged in the community generally have a strong political goal, namely to enhance people's agency and collaboration in the community. She states that when they are able to restore a social bond through a collective production of meaning and collaborative creativity, such projects are generally perceived as successful by makers. Elaborating on this principle of community building, a lot has been written on the role of art and design in building communities.[32] Furthermore, interesting contributions to this topic have come from authors from the field of Participatory Design or Community Art.[33] We now zoom in on several subfields of participatory art and design, in the context of the participatory mind set we have described above. We also focus on the risky trade-offs that makers and participants in this mind set deal with.

Participatory, Universal, Inclusive Design and Community Architecture

Initially, Participatory Design (PD) was mainly focused on combining different perspectives in the design of software and hardware computer products and computer-based activities. Also, PD explicitly involved participants in institutional settings, such as workers in companies, corporations, universities, hospitals and government. There are many variations to PD, such as 'cooperative design' and 'work-oriented design'.[34] The field is deliberately diverse, drawing on domains such

29 E.g. Vallance et al., 2001; Stallman, 1999; Avital, 2011.
30 Huybrechts, 2011.
31 Bishop, op.cit.
32 E.g. by Wenger, 1998; Kim, 2000; Preece, 2000.
33 On Participatory Design, see e.g. Karasti & Baker, 2008; Merkel et al., 2004; Winschiers-Theophilus et al., 2010; on Community Art see e.g. Bishop, 2012; Braden, 1978; Dickson, 1995; Kelly, 1984.
34 On cooperative design see Greenbaum & Kyng, 1991; on work-oriented design see Ehn, 1988.

as user-centred design, graphic design, software engineering, architecture, public policy, psychology, anthropology, sociology, labour studies, communication studies and political science. Researchers and practitioners of different domains are brought together — but are not necessarily united — because of a shared concern for the knowledge and voice of participants. Every two years, these various groups gather during the Participatory Design Conference (since 1990).

The history of PD is marked by the Scandinavian Collective Design field in the 1970s, strongly related to the workplaces and the history of trade unions. With the advent of computer technologies in the industry, Scandinavian society wanted to protect the workers and employers by designing systems that would 'empower' all parties: machines, workers and employers. Recognising that design and development must be situated in the real, everyday actions of people using technology, Computer Professionals for Social Responsibility (CPSR) was founded in North America in 1981. Collective Design, being the predecessor of PD, is concerned with the engagement of a hybrid set of partners in a design process. Design researchers Ehn & Badham write:

> (...) communities-of-practice where the situated practices are carried out in a direction towards legitimate participation and access to the communal artefacts. Such collective

> design communities can e.g. be communities-of-practice of professional designers, overlapping communities-of-practice between users and designers, or communities of stakeholders including not only designers and users, but also interpreters, jurors and legislators.[35]

Collective Design wanted to design better systems for workplace situations. It wanted to do this in a material way, meaning through technology and through a more service-oriented way, namely via work processes. Today, the focus of PD has extended from the workplace to the performance of people in daily life contexts. Often, everyday activities are studied in their own context with different participants. The participants are seen as experts in their own practices and the makers as facilitators.[36] Also, the fields in which PD operates have extended from ICT to include fields such as product, graphical and architectural design.

In the domain of architectural design, some fields are very related to PD, such as Community Architecture. Flourishing in the 1980s, Community architects were focused on engaging people in, for instance, the design of their apartment building. Well-known architects in this field are Turner, who focussed especially on co-designing with poorer parts of society,

35 Ehn & Badham, 2002, p. 2.
36 Schuller & Namioka, 1993.

and Habraken, who is known for his attention to user participation in home design.[37] Alexander, renowned for his pattern language, was another influence on the Community Architecture movement.[38] Pattern language is a kind of generative language, existing in patterns that are observed to be valuable when building towns or other architectural constructions. These patterns can be used by participants to design architectural constructions by themselves. The patterns had a strong social function and were designed in close collaboration with those for whom the architectural structure was created.[39]

Another important participatory approach in architecture and design fields is Universal Design, which emerged in the United States in the 1970s as part of the human rights movement. This field tries to use a universalising approach that can include almost everyone in the professional design process, especially those with a disability. This means that makers try to take away barriers from or add certain inclusive qualities to a design, while maintaining the design's aesthetic quality. Universal design — or 'Design for All' — has two goals: (1) creating environments, artefacts and experiences that are functional and pleasurable for everybody, including people with disabilities and (2) rejecting the division of people into able and disabled people, thus avoiding stigma. For example, Devlieger et al. discuss that, recently, new ideas about the disability-environment interaction and about the disabled/non-disabled interaction have become common in the field of disability studies, but still need to be fine-tuned.[40] First, the disability-environment interaction means that questions of capability shift from the functioning of individuals to the functioning of the individual's environment (in physical, social and informational terms). Second, 'the disabled/non-disabled interaction emphasizes the temporary and situation-bound contexts of disability. This enhances the interchangeability of the statuses of disabled and non-disabled'.[41] This means that the category of disability loses its grip and is no longer just a static notion. Rather, Devlieger et al. claim, it has also become an instrument of identity, a culture and a way of seeing the world.

The Helen Hamlyn Research Centre for Design at the Royal College of Art (London, UK) represents another interesting variation on PD, called Inclusive Design. In 2005, ten years after the introduction of the Disability Discrimination Act (DDA) in 1995, a formal British Standard (called 'BS 7000-6') for Inclusive Design was launched: 'Design of mainstream products and/or services that are accessible to, and usable by, people with the widest range of abilities within the widest range of situations without the need for special adaptation or design'.[42] Furthermore, Lee wrote that the standardisation of inclusive design processes aims to illustrate to businesses how a systematic approach

37 Turner, 1977.
38 Alexander et al., 1977.
39 Ibid.
40 Devlieger et al., 2006.
41 Ibid. p. 21.
42 Helen Hamlyn Centre, 2007.

to inclusive design can be used in the development of products and services.[43] Inclusive Design focuses on the needs of marginalised, disabled and/or older people in a participant-centred process. Designers intend to grasp the underlying context of people's lives and other social factors, for instance demographic change. Inclusive Design starts from the idea that working with certain groups in society that suffer most from 'bad' design, informs better design solutions for all. Inclusive Design thus involves people as participants in the design process, resisting the 'usability' approach that concentrates on testing with users. Both Universal and Inclusive Design have a lot of affinity with disability studies and ageing researches, both highly interdisciplinary fields in the humanities. *The Disability Studies Reader* gives a good overview of the body of texts produced in this field, discussing terms such as 'normal' or 'healthy' from a fresh perspective.[44]

Participatory Art

Like Participatory Design, Participatory Art also has a rich history. Many terms are used for 'Participatory Art' — as for Participatory Design — like social, engaged or relational art. In 'Artificial Hells: Participatory Art and the Politics of Spectatorship', Bishop prefers the term 'Participatory Art':

> ... since this connotes the involvement of many people (as opposed to the one-to-one relationship of 'interactivity')

> and avoids the ambiguities of 'social engagement', which might refer to a wide range of work, from engagé painting to interventionist actions in mass media; indeed, to the extent that art always responds to its environment (even via negativa), what artist isn't socially engaged?[45]

Versions of Participatory Art, in which the participant is described as a partner in the art project, have been described by authors such as Bourriaud, Bishop or Trienekens & Postma.[46] Especially the French curator and art critic Bourriaud's work on 'Relational Art' gives a very well-known description of these forms of Participatory Art.[47] He talks about exhibition forms, like performances, installations and spaces as relational works, in which makers invite people to participate in a common activity. Bourriaud describes how these works invite people, glue them together in a social in-between space — or what he calls a 'social interstice' — which can trigger new relations (between them). However, he states that it is unclear whether these relations last for a long(er) period of time, since it is not always the intention of the maker and the participants to create a long-term effect. Bourriaud's concept of the relational

43 Lee, 2006.
44 Davis, ed., 1997.
45 Bishop, 2012, pp. I-II.
46 Bourriaud, 2002; Bishop, 2012; Trienekens & Postma, 2010.
47 Bourriaud, ibid.

art work was important in challenging the traditional divisions between artist and audience, by defining the audience as active participants in the creation process of the art work or project. He does not consider the reactions of the audience to the art process as extrinsic, but rather as intrinsic characteristics of the art work. In his view, the meaning of the art project is formed through the interaction with the audience — in a kind of social experiment — and is embedded in the daily human and social context. At the same time, Bourriaud underlines the role of the maker, since he states that — via the relational work — the maker strives for different and new forms of exchange than the current society offers, as it often defines exchange by commercial relationships between consumers, producers and stakeholders. In his definition, makers and participants thus collaboratively propose new ways to live in our society and offer fresh political and cultural social designs. They model 'possible' universes, which are not imaginary or utopian worlds, but have a different time rhythm or scale in relation to daily life and make room for personal and intimate encounters.[48]

Bishop describes two specific forms of Participatory Art — both developed in UK in the 1960s — in which makers treat the participants as partners.[49] In the first form, the artist places her/himself within a company or government body. This form was inspired by the Artist Placement Group (APG), founded by the artist Latham and his partner Steveni. In the second form, the artist takes on the role of facilitating creativity among 'everyday' people and increases their accessibility to the arts. The latter form is generally called the Community Arts movement, which is active in UK, Europe and North-America. Today, many variations on these two models still exist. Within them, the process of engaging with organisations and communities is central and may become more important than the outcome or product.

This focus on relation and process underlines the main risky trade-off in the types of participatory art forms described here: the maker passes a lot of responsibility onto the participants, thereby allowing the outcome of a participatory project to be uncertain. This focus on the art and design *process* — instead of only the outcome — can be interesting, since it may lead to less conventional art and design processes, focusing more on their social character. It can also contribute to an alternative aesthetic judgement of the project.[50] At the same time, this alternative focus might not be the easiest path for makers, since it may become difficult to fit their work into traditional art and design contexts, such as the design market or exhibition spaces that are focused on 'selling' or exhibiting products.[51]

Summary

Based on the above, we can draw some conclusions.

— our literature overview describes how makers

48 Trienekens & Postma, 2010.
49 Bishop, 2012.
50 Explored by, for instance, Kester, 2011.
51 As is stated, for instance, in an interview with Claire Bishop in Barok, 2009.

and participants in the participatory mind set appear to engage in two specific kinds of trade-offs, which entails that they dare to (1) give up a considerable part of their authorship or autonomy over the project and (2) become involved in a thorough way with the participants (e.g. community or organisations);[52]

These trade-offs are:

— on the one hand, described as beneficial for the participatory art or design process, because makers and participants can learn from other approaches to the same context, question or problem situation.
— on the other hand, contributing to the fact that the judgement (more focus on social processes), the outcome (less focus on product) and the context of the project (the market and exhibition context and its focus on products) can become uncertain.
— indeed, an interesting conclusion resulting from the literature reviewed above is that the less autonomously makers work and the more they work with diverse participants, the more the focus lies on the creative process instead of on the 'product' and the more unpredictable and less conventional the artistic or design process becomes. This clearly has both advantages and disadvantages, depending on the viewpoint of those involved in the project. It implies, for instance, that less conventional artistic and design projects can evolve and a

> different aesthetic judgement of the project can be formed, considering the communicative aspects between makers and participants. However, some makers might find it difficult to fit their work into traditional art and design contexts, such as the design market that is focused on 'selling' products.

Within the participatory mind set, we encountered interesting ways to engage various participants as partners in projects. This has clear political and technical advantages. Nevertheless, it is often criticised for being vague about the added value of a designer or artist, inviting participants into a participatory process and not, for instance, a social worker or an engineer.[53] In the second dominant mind set — the expert mind set — the designer or artist is clearly present in the project. We discuss how makers and participants in this mind set engage in very different kinds of trade-offs. Here, makers, as experts, deliberately confront participants with unexpected or maybe unpleasant aspects of daily life to trigger their engagement in a project. Consequently, makers have to deal with the uncertainty that people may be displeased or uninterested in their project. We now discuss this expert mind set in more detail.

Expert Mindset

Sanders explains that makers, active in the expert mind set, want to disrupt the participants' preconceptions

52 As indicated e.g. by Twaalfhoven, 2010 and Bishop, 2006.
53 See e.g. Van Erven, 2010.

about how the world works in order to come to new definitions of projects, products, situations, et cetera.[54] These projects are disruptive and interventionist and seek to provoke participants. Like the participatory mind set, their approach to participation is closely related to the question of political commitment.[55] The discourse around the expert approach to participation can mainly be situated within the field of Critical Design, parts of the domains of Human Computer Interaction and Participatory Art. This approach is oriented at — what Bishop calls — 'activation', desiring to create an active subject that is empowered by the experience of participation.[56] Makers in this mind set hope to create newly emancipated subjects who define their own political and social reality. They often wish to create a causal relationship between the experience of the work and individual/collective agency. The research by design researchers Dorst & Cross shows how this activation process can take place.[57] They describe how many participatory projects try to activate participants by importing elements of default, surprise or friction to disrupt the status quo. As will become clear from the following section, in the literature on expert views on Participatory Art and Design, the process of importing these elements is often called 'de-familiarisation'.

Expert-based Participatory Art

Authors such as Papanek and Gold stress that the element of surprise — created through de-familiarisation — is essential in connecting people.[58] It allows them to approach the other with an open attitude and it opens unopened doors. In that way, the de-familiarising effect can allow and even stimulate co-construction.[59] This is specifically explored in the expert mind set.

The ability of art to de-familiarise and activate is stressed by Shklovsky in his essay 'Art as Device'.[60] Shklovsky wants to prevent the everyday from sliding into automatisation and functioning like a formula. Therefore, he aims at introducing art as a device or technique to make people experience a sensation that is not immediately familiar to them. In this sense, art wants to alter the way people perceive and experience things by turning the familiar into the unfamiliar. According to Shklovsky, playing with length or rhythm and, especially, slowness of perception is the best way to de-automatise the things that are perceived as automatic. Shklovsky thinks that the Russian writer Tolstoj illustrates the workings of art as a device via several techniques. Tolstoj changes the narrator's point of view to one that is difficult for people to imagine, for instance that of a horse. He also uses dialects and foreign languages to shift the reader's perspective.

The French philosopher Rancière addresses the conflict between expert and participatory forms of art by proposing a third way.[61] For him, participation is

54 Sanders, 2008.
55 Bishop, 2006.
56 Ibid.
57 Dorst & Cross, 2011.
58 Papanek, 1985; Gold 2007.
59 Huybrechts et al., 2009; Trienekens & Postma, 2010.
60 Shklovsky, 1917.
61 Rancière, 2002.

possible while also taking a strong expert or autonomous position. Still, by criticising, for instance, Bourriaud, he can be seen as an advocate for more expert-driven forms of participation. He does not believe in the emancipatory power of art works, like they are promoted to the more community-oriented forms of Participatory Art. He feels that art works cannot translate the voice of 'the other'. According to Rancière, the political meaning of art is related to the power of art works to shift and disrupt aesthetic borders via raw, poetic moments or new time-space experiences. These can take on subtle forms, like small changes of perspective (as described by Shklovsky). He thinks that this disruption gives birth to a space for new actors — as political subjects — to claim their right to speak up and create new forms of political subjectivity. Rancière describes art as political, not through its content or message but because it creates new relationships between people and communities. In this perspective, the autonomous role of the artist is important: Rancière sees a partial external position of the artist as a prerequisite for participation. In this he differs from Bourriaud, who does not stress the external viewpoint but rather the connection between people.[62] Bourriaud sees the importance of creating different ways of 'being together' that differ from the status quo but do not necessarily 'confront'.[63]

Perhaps the best known example of how art plays an explicit role in disrupting and stimulating a de-familiar view on daily life from a partially outside viewpoint is the artist Duchamp's treatment of everyday objects as ready-made, in the beginning of the 20th century. The term 'ready-made' indicates that the artist extracts industrial objects from their daily context and puts them in an artistic context, which transforms the object into art. A famous example is Duchamp's transformation of a urinal into a fountain (1917). Turning a urinal on its head is an act of de-familiarisation, which makes it possible to experience its workings or functioning in a different way.[64] Furthermore, writer and theatre maker Brecht was known for experimenting with de-familiarising things. He created 'situations' in theatre, interrupting a smooth narrative by disruptive elements, like a song or an unexpected gesture. This action provokes a kind of montage, causing a break in the identification with the protagonists on stage. Brecht believed that the resulting (critical) distance would put the audience in a situation of action. Via the concept of 'thinking as intervention', he proposed an alternative for 'thinking as an option', which he thought dominated the world of consumer goods. In his 'Short Organum for the Theatre' (1948), Brecht advocates a dramatic art that does not invite people to an illusion or catharsis in an automated 'trip'. He promotes an art that tries to stimulate thinking through pleasure, thus intertwining disruption and pleasure, senses and reason via art.[65] The sociologist Lefebvre calls this situation a 'moment'.[66] According to

62 Bourriaud, 2002.
63 Trienekens & Postma, 2010.
64 Joselit, 2007.
65 Zielinski, 2006.
66 Lefebvre, 1992.

him, dreams, art or poetry create a shift in how people perceive the surrounding space. 'Moments' are 'lived experiences' that people experience intensely, away from the daily routine. These experiences can involve 'the audience' in discovering their role or possibility of action within a given context.

This idea of de-familiarising through critical thinking of Brecht is perceived as much too passive by other authors, who aim to provoke physical engagement of the participants. In response to Brecht, theatre writer Artaud's 'Theatre of Cruelty' promoted going a step further than critical thinking.[67] He wanted to create a theatre that would physically shock the audience through a balanced mix of events, details or light play on stage. Similarly, in many 'happenings' — performances by artists such as Kaprow or the Fluxus movement in the 1960s — the physical proximity between audience and artists was seen as a prerequisite for social engagement.[68] In relation to this, a 'situation' — as defined by the Situationists — was another way to activate people. The Situationists were a group that became active in the 1950s, reacting to a society that was turning into what they considered as a Society of Spectacle. This idea of a Society of Spectacle was conceived by Debord, co-founder of the Situationist International. The Situationists defined a 'spectacle' as a certain way of living that was promoted by a capitalistic society and growing amount of media images, slowly taking over control of all aspects of people's lives. Similar to philosopher Baudrillard, the Situationists stated that people do not see the 'real' world anymore but only the world they are conditioned to see.[69] They considered specialist, disciplinary art as a product of this capitalistic society. Therefore, these artists wanted to create a completely new approach to art that would reach beyond the own art discipline. Their projects were focused on stimulating people to work together in playful ways in order to produce art that was inseparable from everyday life. By doing so, they wanted to provoke a completely new experience.[70] A situation — in the Situationists' sense — intervened in mass media and capitalist life through new ways of physical participatory production. This could be the act of physically wandering — or 'flâner' — through the city or the physical creation of leisure environments and activities. Leisurely, slow walks with a turtle, for example, were ways for the Situationists to address another possible approach to the world than the one dictated by industry and government.[71] Some situations intended to allow people to 'make' their environments themselves and to liberate them from private, social and political conventions and change their social living conditions. For instance, the Situationists — and more specifically artist-architect Constant (Nieuwenhuijs) — worked for years on the construction of New Babylon, which would become a new type of city providing a maximum of self-development for

67 Bermel, 2001.
68 Arns, 1997.
69 Baudrillard, 1994.
70 Vague, 2000.
71 Bishop, 2006; Ross, 1983.

individuals. This — never realised — city would focus on new technologies, while functioning as an environment in which people playfully create by themselves.[72]

The Situationist method was a reaction to the modernistic emphasis on social control. Today, of course, society has changed. However, the images of the 'flâneur', the artist or dweller who walks or allows audiences to leisurely walk the city, continue to appear quite often in contemporary art. Sociologist Bauman indicates that, today, the 'leisurely walk' — problematically — has become a product of capitalistic society as well.[73] In advertisements, the dweller is often represented as the happy mobile phone or iPod user who is persuaded to consume while exploring the city. In our contemporary society it is therefore not easy to distinguish between leisure and control anymore. This example of how the Situationist method lost its power today, shows that no predefined formulas can be applied to create friction with the status quo in society via de-familiarising effects. Both makers and participants involved in participatory projects always have to look for new forms.

Expert Design Field

Many designers have reflected on the de-familiarising qualities of design in a participatory process. In the field of urban design in the 1960s, Lynch stated that cities: '... should speak of the individuals and their complex society, of their aspirations and their historical tradition, of the natural setting, and of the complicated functions and movements of the city world'.[74] He stated that projects that suggest, speak to and invite 'viewers to explore the world' can lead to richer environments and make people feel that they have more impact.

Today, Critical Design has made a clear statement on the qualities of de-familiarisation in activating people. As leading figures of the Design Interactions Department at the Royal College of Art in London, Dunne & Raby play an important role in stirring the awareness of designers to use design in a critical way. They are inspired by critical theory and the vision of Adorno & Horkheimer, stating that the critical power of the arts prevents society from creating commodities.[75] They are convinced that the status quo oppresses society, because it is shaped by agendas of which people are barely aware, such as the politics of gender or economics. They want to react to this by asking expert questions about society, starting from observations of eccentric phenomena in society, triggering discussions about certain subjects and shedding a de-familiarising and radically inventive light on societal and cultural issues.[76] Critical Design is a typical expert approach, since it searches for ways to disrupt daily life in order to activate people. Dunne states that Critical Design wants to 'make us think', engaging people in different, more agent or self-conscious ways and stimulating

72 Van Oenen, 2008.
73 Bauman, 1993.
74 Lynch, 1960, p. 118.
75 Adorno & Horkheimer, 2002.
76 Dunne & Raby, 2001.
77 Dunne, 1999.

awareness around everyday values, practices and perspectives.[77] According to Dunne, Critical Design wants to free artists and designers from the standardised preconceptions about how a design and artistic process proceeds, by creating critical products that introduce provocative statements about the world. Whereas affirmative design confirms present ideologies in society, Dunne & Raby state that Critical Design challenges these ideologies by proposing alternative values. In the 'Placebo Project', Dunne & Raby placed critical objects at people's homes to trigger discussion on the electromagnetic fields that electronic products produce. An example of such an object is the 'compass table[78]. If electronic devices are placed on the table's surface, their electromagnetic fields make the needle of a compass — which is installed in the table — twitch and spin. The 'compass table' offers a different viewpoint on electronic objects and is a conversation starter for electromagnetic fields of daily life products in the home environment. According to Dunne & Raby: 'The objects are designed to elicit stories about the secret life of electronic objects — both factual and imagined. They are purposely diagrammatic and vaguely familiar. They are open-ended enough to prompt stories but not so open as to bewilder'.[79] Critical designers therefore in general de-familiarise a situation in order to invite people to participate in different ways and to think about alternatives for their current situation.

In the field of HCI, Bell et al., Sengers et al. and others (such as Gaver & Martin) have worked with this issue of de-familiarisation as well.[80] For instance, Bell et al. use de-familiarisation in order to open up a new design space for different design proposals for the home: 'because the home is so familiar, it is necessary to make it strange, or de-familiarize it, in order to open its design space'.[81] Also, Sengers et al. have articulated several strategies for Reflective Design, a practice which the authors describe as combining 'analysis of the ways in which technologies reflect and perpetuate unconscious cultural assumptions, with design, building, and evaluation of new computing devices that reflect alternative possibilities'.[82] Sengers et al. propose six reflective design strategies to encourage reflection by participants. A first, important strategy entails that the maker provides for interpretative flexibility, meaning that 'reflective design allows users to maintain control of and responsibility for the meaning-making process. This requires actively building for co-construction of meaning between users, systems, and designers'.[83] A way of accomplishing this, Sengers et al. state, is by actively searching for ways to make the familiar strange. In an experiment, Sengers and colleagues wanted to rethink the known handheld tour of the museum space. They gave the user a voice instead of the curator, while exploring the design of technology in mobile and context-aware

78 For more information on the 'compass table', see: www.dunneandraby.co.uk/content/projects/
79 Dunne & Raby, 2001, p. 11.
80 Bell, et al., 2005; Sengers, et al., 2005; Gaver & Martin, 2000.
81 Bell, op. cit., p. 149.
82 Sengers, op.cit., p. 1.
83 Ibid., p. 7.

computing for art museums. In an experiment it became clear that museum visitors just did not want to speak into a handheld device, because they did not feel they had something valuable to say. Therefore, the researchers changed the familiar conception of the process of active participation. They visualised the users' voice in different ways, by tracking instead of asking their active input, and materialising their behaviour in a museum. These tracks became the subject of discussion by the museum visitors and curators.

Summary

Based on the above, we can draw some conclusions:

— makers and participants in the expert approach to participation also deal with a specific trade-off. This trade-off entails that makers engage participants in a de-familiar situation to trigger participation.[84] We call this a trade-off, because:

— on the one hand, an interpretative or even physical action can be triggered (through de-familiarisation).

— on the other hand, de-familiarisation can also alienate or scare people. Because of the unpredictable reactions of participants, the outcomes of this specific trade-off are always uncertain.

— Bourriaud already suggested that these de-familiarising actions can be an interesting start for a participatory process, but that makers working in an expert mind set do not necessarily create them to be appropriated (in the sense that they can be adopted and adapted) by participants in their daily lives.[85] They often take the form of performative acts or artefacts that live a life in one-time events, books and exhibitions.

Conclusion

To summarise, we can draw some over-all conclusions from our literature review.

Summary

— The overview described that makers and participants:

— in the participatory mind set engage in two specific kinds of trade-offs by (1) giving up a considerable part of their autonomy (or authorship) and (2) involving in a thorough way with the participants;[86]

— in the expert approach are often involved in a trade-off, in which makers engage participants in a de-familiar situation to trigger participation.[87]

— Both approaches have advantages and disadvantages. Many authors have discussed the weaknesses of both the expert and the participatory model as presenting a one-sided view on participation.[88] The discourse within the participatory mind set,

84 See e.g. Dorst & Cross, 2011; Shklovsky, 1917; Bell et al., 2005; Sengers et al., 2005.
85 Bourriaud, 2002.
86 As indicated by e.g. Twaalfhoven, 2010 and Bishop, 2006.
87 See e.g. Dorst & Cross, 2011; Shklovsky, 1917; Bell et al., 2005; Sengers et al., 2005.
88 Such as Bishop, 2012; Trienekens & Postma, 2010; O'Neill, 2009; Sanders, 2008.

for instance, pays much attention to engaging participants as partners in the creation process. However, sometimes makers who are active in this area are accused of focusing too much on the technical and political dimensions of participation while forgetting about the artistic and design specific contributions. The other way around, expert models of participatory projects use the strength of design and art to de-familiarise situations, engaging participants in unexpected ways. Still, they pay little attention to how participants could appropriate the project for their own ends. The authors we discussed make clear that these weaknesses have contributed to the 'bad' reputation that Participatory Design and Art forms often have as being 'elitist', 'unworldy' or — by contrast — 'soft', being 'social work' or 'not art'.[89]

— As a reaction to the described weaknesses of both models, a third model has been developed that can be positioned between the other two. This third, hybrid model — which we discussed above — demonstrates the added value of turning participatory projects into a border or boundary region between two domains, in this case, the participatory and the expert mind set.[90]

In the following empirical section, in which we discuss two case studies of real-life participatory projects, we show that makers who work within this third, hybrid model have developed an expertise in engaging participants in their creative process. They do this by combining the soft and constructive qualities of participatory art and design and their disruptive and de-familiarising characteristics.

89 Bishop, 2012; Trienekens & Postma, 2010; O'Neill, 2009; Sanders, 2008.
90 Bourriaud, 2000; Muller, 2002; Clifford, 1997; Bhabha, 1994.

Empirical Section: Participation in a Hybrid Mindset

As became clear from the first part of this chapter, makers and participants in participatory and expert mind-sets are confronted with various trade-offs. In a hybrid context, however, they deal with the trade-offs that are present in both of these mind-sets, specifically releasing autonomy, deeply engaging with the participants and de-familiarisation. They continuously have to reflect on where the border between the maker and the participant is situated, investigate how important their autonomous position is in a certain context, how far they can go in making de-familiarising statements and how much control they want to have in a project (in what stage of the process). Via the following case studies we discuss which specific trade-offs makers and participants in a hybrid context engage in. As will become clear in the case studies and in the following discussion, the trade-offs that took place in the described hybrid participatory projects were mediated via making collages and via playing with imperfect characteristics. These trade-offs are a combination of the de-familiarising aspects developed in the expert mind set and the aspect of releasing control (mainly in the participatory mind set). In the case of collages (particularly researched by Muller), aspects of both the makers' and the participants' worlds are combined, meaning that the unfamiliar and the familiar are brought together and that each partner releases part of their control over the process.[91] Playing with the imperfect differs from de-familiarisation in the sense that the 'imperfect' is something a maker or participant knows only partially, but is not completely outside of their own familiar experience. Consequently, both the maker and the participants only partially release control over an aspect of a project and are also only partially de-familiarised by this aspect of the project experience. This trade-off has been thoroughly discussed, for instance by Gaver et al..[92]

These risky trade-offs will be discussed via two case studies. Through the first case study, being 'Go-for-IT!', a participatory art project by the Patching Zone Lab, we look into the risky trade-off of collage making. 'Go-for-IT!' has been analysed via an in-depth interview and via extensive e-mail communication with the Patching Zone's director Anne Nigten. Furthermore, the existing documents and web platforms involved in the project were thoroughly analysed. We investigate the second risky trade-off of playing with imperfect characteristics via 'DESIGN.LIVES (設計點生活)': a project that entailed subsequent participatory training sessions for design students. It was studied via an ethnographical analysis by the facilitators of the project, who recorded the exchange of ideas and behavioural patterns after each training session they organised. The units of analysis in both cases were the 'things' created during these trade-offs in participatory projects, referring to the participatory interactions between people and objects (such as prototypes, workshops and performances).

91 Muller, 2002.
92 Gaver, et al., 2003.

Case Study 3: 'Go-for-IT!'

The Patching Zone is a trans-disciplinary innovation lab that is based in Rotterdam (NL).[93] It has strong roots in Media and Participatory Art and also has an educational component: the lab invites master, PhD- and post-doctoral students in practice-based research projects to develop technologies and digital media for social and cultural ends, together with local community members and while being supervised by professionals. One of the Patching Zone's projects is 'Go-for-IT!' which resulted from an assignment commissioned by the Dutch city of Rotterdam in which a large process of urban transformation was planned, in the neighbourhood of Feijenoord. The city wanted to engage the rather socially vulnerable local youth of 6-18-year-olds in the co-creation of the public (city) space. The goal of 'Go-for-IT!' was to create more space and understanding for local youth and, additionally, more intergenerational interaction.

In the beginning of the project, the participants were asked to collaboratively make 'objects', being media products. The goal of making objects together is to create a form of trust between the participants, eventually leading to the creation of a media product, being a video, a website, a mobile application or a game, that would strengthen the engagement of youth with the larger urban transformation plan. Since the participants' backgrounds were so varied, it was difficult for them to find a common object they all liked. This led to a difficult negotiation process. Some of the participants liked making video clips, while others preferred drawing, or playing games. To make these objects while negotiating, director Anne Nigten proposed to use the methodology of 'Process patching', developed by the Patching Zone.[94] In this methodology, objects function as a trans-disciplinary zone, weaving viewpoints and practices of diverse participants together in the form of collages. Nigten states that in 'multidisciplinary' zones, everyone works from the perspective of their own expertise. In 'trans-disciplinary' collaborations, people work together in a way that is new to all participants. Nigten thinks that this degree of unfamiliarity makes everybody equally responsible for the process and its outcome(s). This trans-disciplinary zone resembles what we call hybridity, an uncertain third zone that does not belong to one professional expert discipline or a group of participants, therefore leading to a feeling of shared ownership.[95] Together with her team, Nigten introduced various collage-like techniques to increase the collaborations between participants from different backgrounds and ways of working. She combined de-familiarising experiences, such as working together with diverse participants in the project, with the use of unfamiliar technologies in order to invite the participants to bring their own experience and knowledge to the project.

In answer to the question of the city of Rotterdam, the Patching Zone started the project by situating their

93 The Patching Zone, 2010.
94 Nigten, 2006.
95 Muller, 2002.

lab in the neighbourhood of Feijenoord. Here, they gathered a team of professionals, students and community members: young and old, girls and boys. Within the team there was a good balance between theory and practice, expertise domains and different personalities. Subsequently, the team undertook a series of workshops — in and outside the lab — in which they experimented with media and technologies (such as online videos, 'wearables', mobile communication devices and games) that could allow youth and other local inhabitants to interact in a more profound way. The Patching Zone's vision was that by gaining experience in dealing with media, people become more involved in their local environment and society as a whole.

In a first stage, the team of professionals, students and community members started to explore what the local youth liked and what they did in their daily lives in the neighbourhood. This meant that they handed over their control over the project to the participants in order to provide content to the project. While doing so, the Patching Zone's team lived in the neighbourhood themselves and observed the day-to-day activities of the locals. Based on several ethnographic observations that the team conducted, a workshop on mobile phones was organised. The Patching Zone observed that mobile phones were already omnipresent in the studied neighbourhood and were the main tool for communication within it. The team made this local expertise and their own technological knowledge into a collage and experimented with making a game in which mobile phones were used to read QR codes (i.e. 'Quick Response' codes, matrix codes that can be read by the camera of a mobile phone and by a QR code reader). In the resulting game, the local youth had to find the printed QR codes to discover clues in several, specific locations. The game failed to attract significant engagement by the participants, which was mainly due to the fact that the software needed for reading the QR codes did not work on all brands of mobile phones. By consequence, this first 'thing' in the project was a disappointment for the team of the Patching Zone. They had even anticipated this problem by providing more than 20 software packages for mobile phones during the workshop. They were therefore well aware of the diversity in the neighbourhood. The focus in this workshop was fixed on an object that was frequently used in the neighbourhood. However, it underestimated how differently participants — coming from various cultural backgrounds — dealt with such an object.

A second workshop focused on discovering how the youth perceived living in the neighbourhood. To achieve this, the Patching Zone took the risk of placing the responsibility of making into the hands of the young participants. They gave them cameras and montage courses to make and edit short videos in which they narrated their dreams about the neighbourhood. Video was a format they were not familiar to express themselves with. This made the outcome of the videos (and the process of making them) difficult to predict.

The resulting videos were gathered on a website. To motivate the youth to participate, it was intended that the best videos would be awarded at the Digital Dreams Festival. In this way, the expertise of the creative team in making videos was passed on to the young people to help them express their own expertise (i.e. their knowledge of their daily practices and the local environment). At the same time, the youth gave their expertise back in the form of the stories about the neighbourhood. In this way, a second hybrid 'thing' was created, being the video platform (or website) as a site where a collage of expertise and knowledge between makers and participants was shared. On the platform, the multiple, mutually unfamiliar perspectives of the local youth on the urban environment were gathered.

Observations of the ways in which local youth interacted with each other in the streets and of the videos, inspired the creation of another hybrid 'thing': the exchanges between makers and participants around a game prototype. The Patching Zone observed that in the local youth culture, basketball — and especially dribbling — was an important social activity. Since the Patching Zone wanted to combine the strengths of the local youth with the team's expertise in making games, the lab designed a digital game that invited the local youth to dribble by using their feet. Additionally, the team integrated game rules from digital game culture (such as the automatic registration of scores or feedback from the environment), which was different from the game played by the local youth in the streets (see: Image 14). The game prototypes were developed using a basic software template. The template allowed the makers to design demonstrators of games and applications in various, flexible ways. In this way, the prototype could be easily adapted to correspond to how participants were playing the game. This means that the Patching Zone designed the software in such a way that it could be adapted to uncertain and unexpected outcomes. To see how the local youth would participate in the prototypes, the Patching Zone organised an event in a sports centre during which they observed the local youth as they played digital dribble games. This inspired the team to design new prototypes.

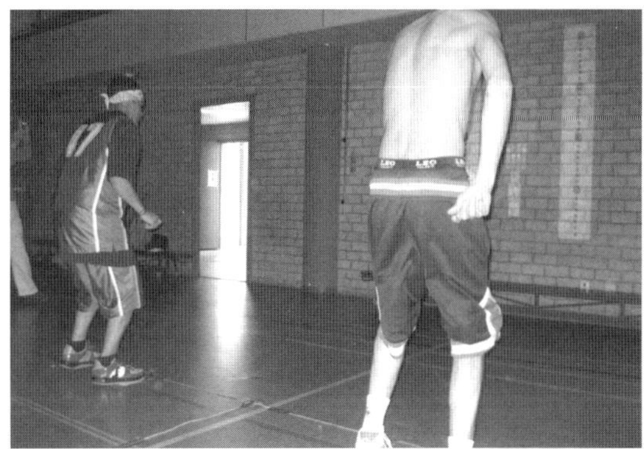

Image 14 **The local youth is playing the Patching Zone's dribbling game**

The next hybrid 'thing' that was developed was a version of the game prototype triggering new types of interactions between makers and participants. This particular prototype focused on creating a game environment in the streets of Rotterdam: the 'natural habitat' for the youth to dribble. The game was a collage between the digital game and the physical street. The Patching Zone experimented with bringing a new type of game into the streets that was familiar to everybody, but unfamiliar to this specific context. More specifically, they adapted an existing, popular game for a public space context: 'Tic-Tac-Toe'. This folk game is usually not played in urban environments, but on paper or on a screen. The game rules are simple: on a three by three grid, players add crosses and circles until they have three crosses or three circles in a row. The Patching Zone translated this game to the context of the project, by turning it into a multiplayer game in a public space. In a first prototype, the team designed a grid of 9x9 (an adaptation of the original 3x3 grid) with chalk on the pavement, using cardboard boxes instead of circles and crosses. This low-tech prototype allowed the makers to observe how people participated in the game and which kinds of participation it triggered. They observed that — because of the strange insertion of a folk game in the streets — many local inhabitants gathered in the streets. By allowing the locals to play the game themselves, new knowledge on the role of these types of games for participatory ends was generated. Every single inhabitant played the game in his or her own, personal (and, for the Patching Zone, unexpected) way: younger kids mostly laid down boxes as quickly as possible, while the older people played more tactically and also removed boxes. At the same time, the Patching Zone noticed that, because both young and old people were familiar with the folk game, interaction was generated between them (see: Image 15).

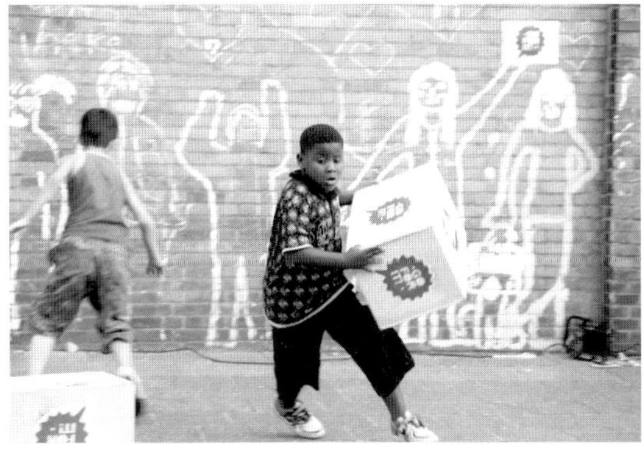

Image 15 **The inhabitants are playing with boxes, as a variation on the folk game 'Tic-Tac-Toe'**

Based on the previous experiments, in which several collages were made combining the media and artistic expertise of the Patching Zone's team with local expertise, a final series of games to trigger participation by the local community was created (see: Image 16). These games were constructed via LED lights and sensors that were integrated in the tiles of the streets in the form of the above-mentioned Tic-Tac-Toe game. People could log into the games via their mobile phones. Next, they could start dribbling on the tiles that would provide interactive feedback via the LED lights. In the end, four different games were installed in the streets for a year. Each one focused on different skills that were observed during the experiment with the cardboard boxes, such as speed or elegance. In this way, the simple game of Tic-Tac-Toe, that allowed intergenerational interaction, was combined with the first, technical dribbling prototype, specifically aimed at the local youth. The four games were obvious collage-like hybrid zones, combining diverse social worlds in urban games that were at the same time familiar and unfamiliar to the participants. This status of the game made the participants slightly uncertain about what was expected of them, which also made them feel curious about the game and stimulated them to start an interpretative and physical action. At the same time, many aspects of the game were familiar to them, such as the skills that had to be used or the act of dribbling.

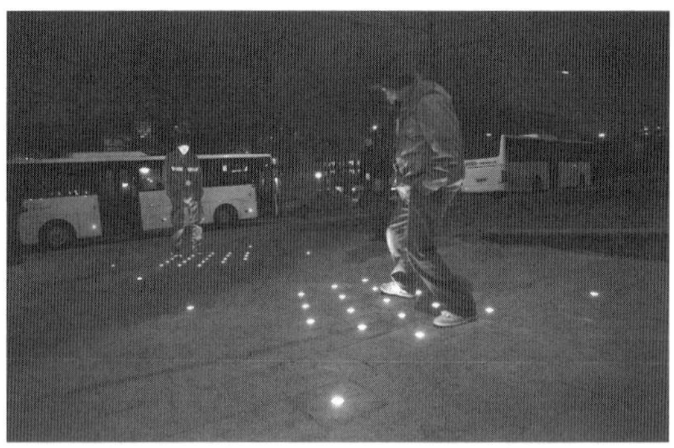

Image 16 **The final 'Go-for-IT' games**

Moreover, the Patching Zone concluded that the final game should not have a very strict set-up, but should leave room for personal appropriations. However, although this flexibility appeared realistic during the creation process, it proved to be otherwise afterwards. The games were difficult to program, integrate and sustain in the streets for local community members and thus required continuous professional advice. Since this professional expertise could not be provided constantly, the games were only installed for the period of one year. In this sense, the games mediated the conversations between makers, youth and other local community members in an urban transformation process, which was the main assignment for the Patching Zone Lab. However, the 'thing' that was the result of the participatory activity remained a temporary set-up.

To summarise, the Patching Zone combined information that was already present in the community —local practices, ideas, desires and knowledge — with unfamiliar elements in several 'collage'-like games. On the one hand, they introduced aspects into the community from an expert position, such as their idea of playing a folk game or their experiments with making videos with the local youth. This appeared to trigger the engagement of the participants, invited them to talk about their expectations of the city (through the videos) and stimulated them to exchange with different groups in the city (old and young). On the other hand, during the creation process, the team also released control and opened up the game prototypes for adaptation by the participants. The participants did not use the games as they were intended and made them into their own, new games. This became clear in the try-out of the Tic-Tac-Toe game, in which people of different ages played the game in different ways. This creative game play inspired the makers to make several versions of the game.

Case Study 4: 'DESIGN.LIVES'

The second case study we present is 'DESIGN.LIVES *(設計點生活)*', a project that was launched in 2009 by a design researcher and a sociologist. The project provided training and experience for young people on how to design participation for social inclusion as well as on how to design their own lives. This is a form of Inclusive Design and it has a strong link with Participatory Design. The founders of 'DESIGN. LIVES' renamed Participatory Design to Design Participation(s). By doing so, they stressed raising awareness of social inclusion and teaching it through design practice. The main aim of the first 'DESIGN. LIVES' Lab in Hong Kong in 2009 was to inspire potential and novice design students to experience the Inclusive Design process in a shifting social context. The lab was part of the Hong Kong Design Centre's outreach programme — called Discover Design — for getting young people to experience design. The participants included students from both the secondary schools in Hong Kong and first year design students from a university in China. A group of creative partners consisting of disabled and elderly people from Hong Kong was formed to be active design partners in the lab. A group of volunteers with backgrounds in either design or social sciences from a local university in Hong Kong served as facilitators.

The lab's design was somewhat complicated, since there were two levels of participation. The first level was the collaboration among novice designers (i.e. the youth from Hong Kong and those from the mainland of China). The second was the collaboration between the active design partners and the novice designers. Via this large diversity of participants, the lab organisers increased the hybridity, but also the uncertainty, of the participants and thus the need for them to negotiate. It appeared to be difficult to determine the appropriate way of arriving at shared objectives and designs, even though each group was guided by a facilitator. To decrease the uncertainty that resulted from such difficult collaborations, the workshop adopted the Cantonese language to facilitate the communication for both educational and executive purposes.

Specifically, eight design teams were set up, each consisting of one disabled or elderly active design partner and approximately ten to fifteen student designers, accompanied by a facilitator. In order to prepare the high school students and college freshmen with the necessary knowledge about what they were expected to do, the first day started with presentations on design in general and on Inclusive Design. Next, the students were divided into groups and, subsequently, introduced to their design partners and facilitators. To exchange ideas among the group members, the groups were provided with a template consisting of different questions. The template served as a general guideline made by the makers/experts in order to govern the design process. On the second day, the workshop started with a critique session during which the participants played the role of critics, asking challenging questions about their initial design ideas (based on the template). This critique session was followed by another round of discussions and the formulation of a concrete design plan for the rest of the workshop. In the last presentation session, all groups presented their hybrid ideas, inspired by the makers' guidelines and the participants' critiques. The best design was awarded, while another group with a good representation was also appraised.

The participants were asked to construct an 'object' together, being a product, an idea, etc. They negotiated, exchanged ideas and viewpoints and shared their different and diverse orientations in order to come to a final output. In this case, the participants — coming from diverse cultural contexts and being novice designers and active design partners — found it difficult to obtain a good object through which they could communicate and share thoughts. This offered an opportunity for the workshop organisers to examine the hybrid nature of participatory design, namely the need for the co-creation of an object for discussion and communication, the hybrid nature arising from participants with different cultural and social backgrounds and the inherent tensions among them.

While observing the novice designers' orientations and performances in the lab, the organisers discovered that the willingness of the student designers to listen to the active design partners (disabled and elderly people) was associated with the students' interpretations of the designers' roles. At the outset, most student designers chose interviews as their preferred form of interaction. They interviewed their active design partners in order to identify 'problematic' situations that they though would require interaction with the designers. For example, two young male students already had specific ideas of design as having a clear procedure, well-defined clients' needs and product orientation. They saw themselves as experienced, having won several awards. By consequence, they were too focused on practical difficulties and identifying wishes and (almost exclusively) wanted to arrive at solutions that would 'assist' the design partner. This format of interviewing eventually did not lead to risky exchanges between makers and participants or to the production of hybrid things. Rather, it put the expert/maker in a dominant position. For instance, in one group, the 84-year old active design partner Granny T. was fed up with the novel designers, who kept asking her about the problems in her everyday life. The novel designers asked Granny T. questions such as 'What is most inconvenient in your everyday life?' and 'Do you have any regrets about things that you haven't done yet?' Granny T.'s response was brief: 'Everything is just fine'. Understanding the experiences of the participant was clearly informed by pragmatic problem-solving thinking. The old-versus-young relationship was replaced by an experts-versus-participants relationship (see: Image 17).

The situation changed once Granny T. informed the novice designers of her medical appointment, which she had that particular afternoon. The designers

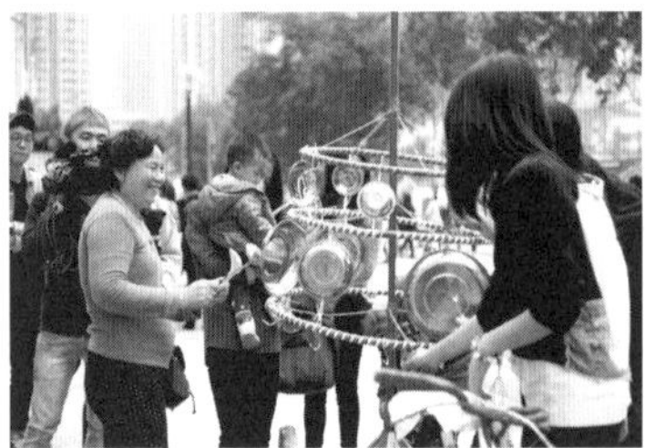

Image 17 **The novice designers are working together with elderly, active design partners** Photo by Meng Lau

decided to accompany her to the nursing home where she lived. This was the moment of the disruption of the existing relationship. Granny T. became a 'tour guide', bringing the novice designers to the Underground and to the nursing home, introducing them to the internal design of the nursing home, et cetera. Granny T. was no longer an active design partner, but a tour guide. This led the novice designers to question their own role within the project, which resulted in feelings of insecurity. In this sense, 'DESIGN.LIVES' experimented with shifting roles and also with changing the views of the makers and participants in the project.

Also, during the intensive workshop — before accompanying Granny T. to the nursing home — the participants were situated in a classroom-like environment, equipped with formal conference facilities. Shifting from such a formal place to an open space (on the way there) and finally to the unfamiliar interior of the nursing home — which they had no perfect knowledge about — had a positive impact on the students' experiences and interactions with Granny T. It was a long journey from the workshop venue to the nursing home where Granny T. lived. The students appeared to be relaxed, as soon as they left the lab environment. They clustered in small groups, excitedly chatting about irrelevant topics along the way. When entering the nursing home, the student designers quickly seemed to shift back to a 'working' mode and started taking pictures everywhere, as if they were reminded of their task by the special facilities installed in the building and the particular spatial arrangement there. The shifting of spaces had a positive impact, but from time to time the de-familiarising experience became too much. Students were overwhelmed by this place they had only imperfect knowledge about and started behaving noisily and excited. At the same time, the large group of student designers was such an unusual sight for the elderly residents that some of them even sat at their bedroom doors, staring silently at the 'invaders'. Granny T. introduced the students to her neighbours, by emphasising several times that they were her granddaughter's friends. She did not mention a word about the workshop event. The objective of this journey was meant to observe the ways in which Granny T. managed her life in the nursing home. However, the new experiences of visiting a nursing home appeared to be surprising to the novel designers. They had no previous experience with such a living place, neither physically nor psychologically. It was evident that the student designers did not realise that they were welcomed into Granny T.'s personal space. They kept chatting and making loud noises, even in the narrow corridors. They did not hesitate to enter Granny T.'s tiny bedroom, as one normally would when entering the personal space of someone else. The students continuously missed the experiences disclosed by perceiving the space. After their visit, they conducted a group discussion about design opportunity identification in the common room of the nursing home, while Granny T. sat silently in the same room by herself. No one felt any inappropriateness, since the students considered themselves to be designers who were 'on the job'. This small space, where every member was present, accentuated the literal alienation that was going on. So far, it had reached the peak of user-exclusion, which is against the ethos of participatory design. After the visit, Granny T. never participated in the workshop again. In this sense, it became clear that creating an imperfect situation in which designers and participants are positioned in unclear roles or unfamiliar spaces can lead to uncertain outcomes. In the aforementioned case of Granny T., the students were not able to find the right balance between makers' and participant's needs in this imperfect situation.

However, another group's practice in the workshop showed the promising result of playing with imperfection in a project. This group presented a cheerful game that every participant enjoyed, including their active design partner B.: a young girl who has a hearing impairment and is a lip-reader. Being close to B. during the workshop, the students found that she was passionate for life and possessed a keen sense of colour. Her stories struck a chord with the students, since they had similar aspirations for fun. Here, B.'s personal account provided the data for the designers to capture the unique individuality of B. The following was drawn from the notes jotted down by the facilitator of this group:

> In order to understand her better, they tried to discover what B.'s strengths were and also asked her why she liked to do it. Finally, the students discovered B.'s interest in art, drawings, and photography, and understood that these activities could help her to express her inner feelings. B. loves photo-shooting, because a colourful world to her is equivalent to musical rhythm (as she could not hear music).
> (Field note, B.'s Group).

The facilitator made use of the personal description by B. as a way to place the designers in a role they did not know perfectly, namely having a hearing impairment. The facilitator encouraged the student designers to connect with B.'s bodily experiences:

> B. is very sensitive to colour. I asked the students if they knew the reasons. I asked them to imagine being under water, almost incapable of hearing

> anything, and see if they could find that images are much more prominent. So I asked them to cover their ears and walk for a distance in order to feel from the user's angle, to put their feet into the user's shoes.
> (Field note, B.'s Group).

Tapping into the other's bodily experience like this brought together seemingly incompatible frames of reference — that of the students and of the active design partner — into a hybrid experience. The facilitator's tactic was to place the students in a context that they were not perfectly familiar with, in order to generate brand new interpretations of situations, experiences or viewpoints and a rich understanding of the participant. Consequently, the outcome of the exchanges between the students and B. emerged as a game, as a kind of translation from music to action. At the final presentation, the group performed a silent piece of music. A 'conductor' translated the melody of a song into gestures that were supposed to be signals conveyed to the 'musicians'. Musicians (including B.) lined up and each held two transparent bottles filled with water in various vivid colours. Under the direction of the conductor, they shook the colourful bottles in different bodily movements with a unique rhythm. Upon finishing the game, the group eagerly asked the audience whether they could feel that it was intended to be a music piece. Apparently, active design partner B.'s unique experience had been translated through a synaesthesia attempt. This was achieved — empathetically — through student designers' entering B.'s experience of music. The access to this experience was aided by immersing them into a situation they did not know perfectly, namely having a hearing impairment, which stimulated them to become involved in something that B. knew very well: the imagination of colours and rhythms. This risky trade-off, in which makers and participants exchange experiences, brings two parties into a new site: a soundless world with music, in which objects (the colours representing different tones) bring a both familiar and unfamiliar experience to all participants (see: Image 18).

To sum up, we can state that during the 'DESIGN.LIVES' Lab in Hong Kong in 2009, a hybrid zone was deliberately created between makers

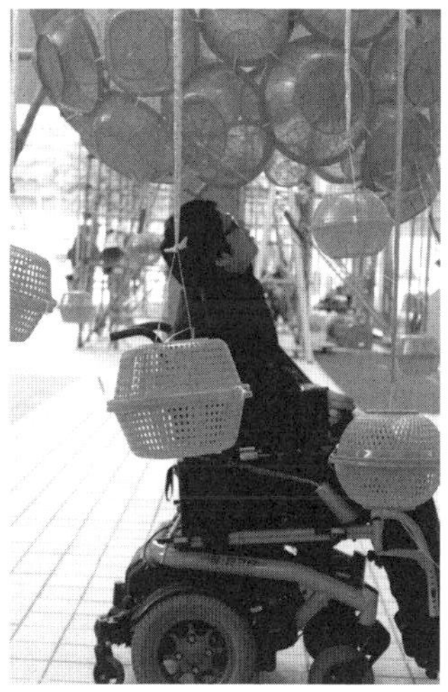

Image 18 **The game, as created by B. and the novice designers**
Photo by Paula Dib

and participants through playing with the imperfection of roles and contexts. The uncertainties of the makers and participants, resulting from this imperfect situations, were deliberately played with in order to enhance the need for negotiation between both parties via continuously balancing between partnership and de-familiarisation in the participatory process. In the 'DESIGN.LIVES' projects, this imperfection referred to the lack of clear roles, institutional arrangements or briefing processes of the participants before the commencement of the activities and the shifting of familiar contexts. These imperfect experiences forced the student designers and participants to communicate in order to figure out what they could and should design 'with' and 'for' the active design partners. At the same time, the participants were true partners, since they were invited to take leading roles in guiding the students through their personal world, literally as a guided tour or via a bodily performance.

Discussion: Hybridity in Participation

As we have illustrated, most participatory projects are either situated within a participatory approach or within an expert approach. In the first approach, participation takes form via the risky trade-off of makers who release control over the project or engage participants closely in the project. In the second approach, makers de-familiarise situations to activate participants. However, different authors — although often using a different vocabulary — state that participatory projects can be best situated between these two mind-sets, in a hybrid zone.[96] Participatory projects are then an uncertain zone and do not belong to one professional expert discipline or a group of participants, but strive for a feeling of shared ownership. This concept of hybridity has been thoroughly explored in Participatory Design and in HCI.[97]

As the two case studies showed, interesting risky trade-offs can take place between the makers and participants in hybrid participatory projects. In the case of 'Go-for-IT!' and 'DESIGN.LIVES', these trade-offs, the people and objects that were involved, but also the contexts in which the 'things' took place, were placed in an uncertain relationship with each other and were then opened up for reflection. The hybrid zone that is typical of hybrid participatory projects is built on a great deal of — sometimes deliberate evoked — uncertainty for makers and participants. This uncertainty is mainly about who is in control of which part of the project and about how open or provocative the projects can be. Risky trade-offs often manifest themselves in what Raley calls 'tactical behaviour', referring to 'the intervention and disruption of a dominant semiotic regime, the temporary creation of a situation in which signs, messages and narratives are set into play and critical thinking becomes possible'.[98] When reflecting on the three participatory models, it became obvious that risky trade-offs can be defined in different ways. In the expert model, the risky trade-off is defined by participants (tactically) entering in the abstract world of the professional designer and artist (e.g. in the form of a lab-like setup or an installation). In the participatory model, professionals (tactically) enter the world of the participants (e.g. in the form of a participatory game in public space). In the third, hybrid model, the trade-offs are multidirectional (see: Image 19).[99] The makers, with their expert viewpoints, relate (tactically) to the participants and to the other disciplinary expertise. Of course, this also works the other way around: the participants relate (tactically) to the abstract world of the makers. Via this risky interchange, participants recombine elements of both worlds in a continuous chain of hybrids.

These 'risky' trade-offs became clear in the case of 'DESIGN.LIVES'. In the workshop with B., the first step in the exchange was taken by the girl with the hearing impairment when she told the novice designers about her experiences. The second initiative was taken by the professional who asked the students to step into

96 E.g. Bishop, 2012; Trienekens & Postma, 2010; O'Neill, 2009; Sanders, 2008.
97 For instance, by Muller, 2002.
98 Raley, 2009, p. 6.
99 Lee, 2008.

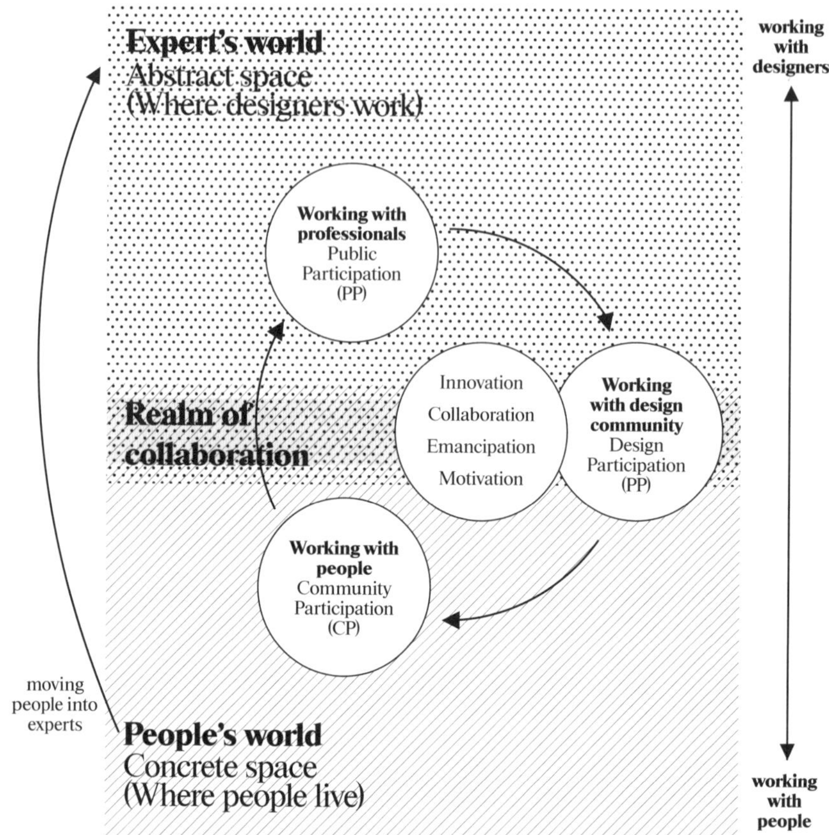

Image 19 **Multidirectional trade-offs in the third, hybrid model**
Visualised by Yanki Lee, adaptations by Andrea Wilkinson

B.'s shoes (representing a world unfamiliar to them). A third step in the exchange was taken by the students, when they presented their colour game to the professionals. A similar trade-off took place in the case of 'Go-for-IT!'. First of all, the Patching Zone team immersed themselves into the environment of the local youth to grasp their world and the local youth told their stories via video. Then, the lab introduced a prototype of a dribbling game in the Rotterdam community, which triggered new types of interaction between participants. Conversely, the different participants engaged with the game in ways the Patching Zone did not intend and could not predict. For example, the younger children focused on other, different types of game play than the older children did.

In the case studies it also became clear that participants often felt uncertain when these risky trade-offs, for instance initiated by experiences with imperfect roles, took place in a specific project. Gaver et al. argue that it is important to take into account that some people — for instance, when they expect clarity and consistency — are more easily surprised than others and their reactions can differ considerably.[100] Some people can react in a passive way to a de-familiarising experience, while others may engage with it intensely. Therefore, an on-going assessment of the trade-offs took place by both makers and participants in each project or project phase of the case studies. This continuous uncertainty and assessment places participants and makers in a demanding situation, in which they are supposed to interpret a situation and contribute by sharing their opinions. Gaver et al. state that this has a clear advantage: 'by impelling people to interpret situations for themselves, it encourages them to start grappling conceptually with systems and their contexts, and thus to establish deeper and more

100 Gaver, et al., 2003.

personal relations with the meanings offered by those systems'.[101] Hybrid things thus create a situation of interpretative flexibility. 'Interpretative flexibility' is a concept derived from the SCOT methodology (or Social Construction of Technology), developed by Bijker et al..[102] The interpretative flexibility of a thing refers to its quality to generate different or alternative meanings for different social groups, like makers of different disciplines, professionals and amateurs, journalists, et cetera. This means that not only the ways in which people think or interpret projects are flexible, but also the ways in which projects are designed. There is not just one possible — or best — way of designing a project.

We observed that projects gain a hybrid character via two main forms of risky trade-offs: (1) making collages and (2) playing with the imperfect. We now discuss these two risky trade-offs and illustrate their workings by referring to the two above-mentioned case studies.

Collage-making

The first form of risky trade-offs between makers and participants we are going to discuss and that contributed to constituting a hybrid zone in the observed case-studies, took the form of collage-making. The term 'collage' is inspired by Muller's finding that 'things' in participatory projects — like people gathered around games, maps, story probes or prototypes in a certain context — are often constructed with in-between qualities.[103] This means that they are created in collage-like ways, mixing elements from various domains, disciplines and contexts in one 'thing'. 'Things', then, form an in-between zone, a 'gluing element' or bonding agent that gathers disparate people, objects and contexts, stressing collectivism and shared ownership.[104] At the same time, it is a marginal space, carrying traits of previously disconnected or incompatible fields or discourses that do not belong to (one of) the participants. In that way, every role or discipline (engineer, end-user, artist, human scientist, et cetera) is deliberately put in an uncertain position and on a similar level of learning and interpretation, since the totality of the thing is unfamiliar to all. By consequence, 'things' introduce various conflicting uses and meanings of elements that are negotiated by the participants.

In relation to this collage making, we observed — particularly in the case study of the Patching Zone — the following three things. First, we noticed that collages were made by putting *objects* in unusual contexts or by adding new functions to them in order to challenge their expected goal(s), thereby turning them into a collage of realities.[105] In this way, objects or aspects of objects were combined and placed in relation to each other. For instance, in the case of 'Go-for-IT!', the dribbling game played in the streets for years eventually became a digital game. It was thus given a new form and different functions, such as keeping scores of

101 Ibid., p. 233.
102 Bijker, et al., 1987, pp. 44-46.
103 Muller, 2002.
104 Bourriaud, 2002.
105 Gaver, et al., 2003.

the participants while dribbling in a digital way. The game was also clearly a collage of the expertise of the local youth (i.e. dribbling), the creative team (i.e. game technology) and folk culture (i.e. Tic-Tac-Toe).

Second, we noticed from the case study of the Patching Zone that *participants*, previously unfamiliar with each other, were brought together. The project, composed of the interactions between heterogeneous participants, was a team-work based activity. Different types of makers, artists, designers or engineers, worked together with heterogeneous community members. Clearly, this differs from projects that involve heterogeneous end-users only.[106] As has been shown in relevant literature, heterogeneous makers bring different knowledge, skills and expertise into the creation process and finally shape an innovation.[107] Moreover, as Bucciarelli has pointed out: 'in most cases today, it is the business of groups of individuals who, if they are to be effective, must know how to discuss, deliberate and negotiate with others if their individual proposals and claims are to be taken into account and have meaning'.[108] Thus, the participatory project in which the Patching Zone was engaged was conceived as a series of emergent processes in which teamwork — with loads of interaction and communication exchange — was central. In particular, the interaction between the various makers and local youth was full of conflicts and surprises.

Third, we found that — especially in the case of the Patching Zone — two or more very different *contexts* were connected. For instance, the artistic media lab was situated in a neighbourhood. The lab was located there, in order to get a long-term intermingling of the expertise of the professionals and students with the local community. In this way, the Patching Zone was able to come to a conversation about the urban transformation process in the neighbourhood. Another example from the Patching Zone's case is how the local youth was asked to make videos and present them at a festival. They entered the unfamiliar context of video making and presentation and linked this to their own context by narrating about their neighbourhood.

Playing with the Imperfect

While Muller stresses that hybrid things can be seen as a collage of elements from different contexts, Gaver introduces a second risky trade-off between makers and participants that can contribute to the hybridity of participatory projects.[109] His research points out that makers and participants can create things as being imperfect, unfinished or — as Gaver calls it — 'ambiguous', never imposing solutions or roles. Imperfect things can take on the form of inaccurate sensors, inexact mappings, low-resolution displays or insecure roles for participants. They encourage participants from various backgrounds to supplement these objects or roles with their own scepticism, interpretations or appropriations and to develop new values and goals for them. This imperfection thus

106 Dalsgaard, 2008; Tomico, et al., 2009.
107 Chen, 2005; Cross & Cross, 1995.
108 Bucciarelli, 2002, p. 220.
109 Muller, 2002; Gaver, 2003.

also contributes to the first trade-off of collage making.

In this context, we observed — especially in the above-mentioned case of 'DESIGN.LIVES' — the following three things. First, we noticed that *participants* were given roles that they did not control perfectly, outside of their expert position, in order to provoke their uncertainty. However, to prevent people to feel alienated or not interested in the participatory process, participants were explicitly made part of a co-creation process in which they could further define these imperfect roles. In the case study, the alternative definition of roles and confrontation of roles between the participants, made the participants suddenly feel incomplete and this motivated them to search for their renewed role in the project. In 'DESIGN.LIVES', the facilitators' studies of the performance of the participants indicated that the understanding of the makers' and participants' roles in the design process slowly unfolded. During the workshops, the students often assumed a quite conventional conception of their role as designers (as creators, helpers and experts). Often, the identity of 'problem solvers' emerged fairly soon during a workshop, especially when designers carried out a design process which was understood as a process of problem-solving. Correspondingly, the participants' identity as 'problem-carriers' was also established and reinforced through the ways in which they function merely as the 'end-users', which eventually became their designated role. The formation of the new co-creation relationship only happened when alternative identities were perceived and earned through supporting roles in experiences such as — in this case — the participant as co-creator. Various empathising experiments were done, such as putting oneself in the shoes of somebody with a hearing impairment, to try out alternative identities. As Finlay suggests: 'empathizing is not simply about putting oneself in the other's shoes. Instead, one has to leave behind one's own context and understandings to imaginatively project oneself into the Other's situation in an attempt to see the world through their eyes'.[110] In this case, this particular tactic did not only allow students to understand the feelings of being in a soundless world. It also included the active design partner in a participatory way into the exploration of the kinds of activities that they all would enjoy together.

Second, we noticed from the case study of 'DESIGN.LIVES' that *objects* took the form of imperfect set-ups, prototypes, probes, games or open-ended technological systems that allowed participants' mutual evaluation and construction. These set-ups, et cetera, stressed incompleteness and artificiality and were anything but smoothly working.[111] According to Kluitenberg, a cryptic text message, a blurry picture or a low voice can provoke frustration but also stimulate people's imagination, their need to fill in gaps or to gather clues about how things work.[112] In the case of 'DESIGN.LIVES', this was illustrated by the musical

110 Finlay, 2005, p. 13.
111 Zielinski, 2006.
112 Kluitenberg, 2008.

performance without sound. This 'imperfect' musical performance stimulated the performers and the audience to address new senses, such as touch and sight. It enabled makers and participants to think about what potential 'not hearing' can bring and to engage in new collaborations, informed by this experience.

Third, we found that essential aspects of a *context* were made absent or made extremely explicit. Taking the risk of playing with the imperfection of contextual experiences, with the aim to stimulate participation between the makers and participants, became obvious in the case of 'DESIGN.LIVES'. For instance, the experience of travelling to the nursing home provided insight into the fact that the student designers' performance was affected by the changed contextual experience. The student designers also experienced a changing of context, when they covered their ears and walked a short distance in order to experience the world in the way B. does. In this way, the participants used B.'s bodily experience to learn from her and from each other. This type of teamwork resulted in an unexpected outcome, which was illustrated by the (music/action) game that the student designers and participants created.

Discussion

We discussed that hybridity is an interesting concept for describing participatory projects, since it gives attention to the worlds of the makers and the participants as well as to the uncertain space that participatory projects are. We reflected on two hybrid participatory projects and looked into the trade-offs that took place between makers and participants. Instead of completely releasing autonomy or authorship over their projects or — on the one hand — engaging closely with the community and — on the other — de-familiarising, makers (on the left side of Image 20) and participants (on the right side of the image, shown below) in hybrid participatory projects came to interesting exchanges via collage-making and playing with imperfection.[113] These two trade-offs are visualised in Image 20.

While these two trade-offs illustrate how makers and participants can set up participatory projects together, they can never function as 'recipes', determinants or prerequisites for successful participatory projects. In every project, it is a challenge to find the right balance between what each maker or participant brings to a 'collage' or what level of imperfection is fruitful for participation. The cases clearly show that this balance often depends on the contexts in which the projects are developed and on the people and objects included. For instance, one team of students participating in the 'DESIGN.LIVES' project became alienated when elements of imperfection were introduced into the project. This was not productive to participation. More specifically, the unfamiliarity with the contexts that they were introduced to contributed to uncomfortable and even inappropriate behaviour. However, in another team in which students were immersed in a role they were not perfectly familiar with

113 See e.g. Dorst & Cross, 2011; Shklovsky, 1917; Bell, 2005; Sengers, 2005.

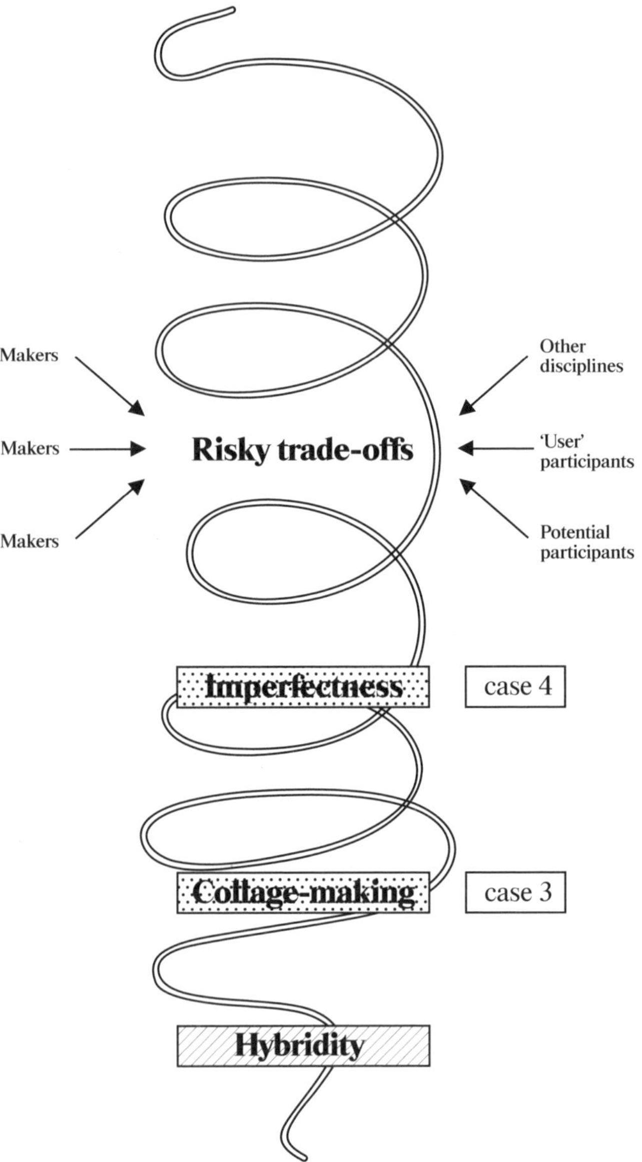

Image 20 **Visualisation of hybridity and the trade-offs of collage-making and playing with imperfection**

(concerning not being able to hear), this led to interesting exchanges between makers and participants. Therefore, it would be interesting to compare experiences of makers and participants in participatory projects, in which the trade-offs of collage-making and playing with imperfection are experimented with.

To conclude, we want to stress that hybridity is only one of the concepts that describes the particularity of participatory projects. As, for example, Schäfer indicates, in a digital age participants do not necessarily need to collaborate closely with the original makers of the participatory projects they engage with.[114] For instance, many examples of online communities exist in which participants self-organise their participatory exchanges, with little support from the original maker(s). Such communities exist, for example, around the open source 3D printer RepRap which allows participants to print objects in 3D and build their own printer. In the next chapter we will deal particularly with participation *after* the professional creation process. In this so-called 'use time', makers can release their projects into the world, for the participants to appropriate them and further develop them (maybe even independently or outside of the original project context). The idea that participants can continue projects by themselves sheds a different light on participatory projects. In the next chapter, we will describe this through the concept of generativity.

114 Schäfer, 2010.

Chapter III
Participation and Generativity

Liesbeth Huybrechts,
Cristiano Storni &
Jessica Schoffelen

Background, Aim and Argument

In this chapter, we look at a series of participatory projects in order to continue our discussion on participation in art and design. Particularly, we focus on projects wherein participation occurs with little input from the initial maker(s) (the term we use to refer to artists and/or designers), who — initially — started the project(s). We refer to three examples of participatory projects: 'l'Artisan Electronique' (i.e. case study 5), 'Touchatag' (i.e. case study 6) and the 'Arduino' prototyping platform (i.e. case study 7). In different ways, these are platforms for people to discuss, appropriate and adapt new media tools, building — often in unexpected ways — on the work of their original makers. 'L'Artisan Electronique' offers a platform for 3D printing, while 'Touchatag' is a platform for attaching digital information to everyday objects. Arduino provides a platform for making interactive products or installations.

In the first chapter, we learned — especially from literature in the political, media and cultural discourse — that participatory projects can be characterised by risky trade-offs between makers and participants.[1] In the 'l'Artisan Electronique' project (that we will discuss later), for instance, these trade-offs take place between the makers who originally started the platform for 3D printing and the designers, technological experts and amateurs suggesting or making improvements to this platform online. The makers benefit from the participants' adaptations to the platform, since it leads to improvements. However, they also deal with the uncertainty that these adaptations do not correspond to their initial intentions with the platform.

Furthermore, the three case studies in this chapter are described not so much as pieces of technology with specific functions, but rather as assemblies of people and objects where the participating elements mutually define and shape each other. We call such assemblies 'things' (as discussed and defined in the first chapter). In these 'things' makers and participants participate in collaborative but also competing activities around certain topics, issues, contexts, et cetera, such as a concrete technical question that the original makers of the 3D platform 'l'Artisan Electronique' might have. 'Things' assume a relational understanding of agency.[2] This means that all the elements (such as the makers, the participants or a technical question) characterising the discussed projects have a potential impact on the participatory process. None of these elements should therefore be understood as determinants — or prerequisites — of certain forms of participation. Participation is not caused by putting certain specific 'recipes' in play. Rather, it is a process that is open-ended, emerging and difficult to predict and control, in which makers, participants and their concerns and objects intersect. The outcomes of the risky trade-offs that makers and participants engage with are therefore always uncertain.[3]

These trade-offs can be appreciated in two key moments — project-time and use-time — and can

1 Such as Arnstein, 1969; Milbrath, 1965; Schäfer, 2008; Dreessen et al., 2011.
2 Storni, 2012.
3 Huybrechts et al., 2012.

demand, more or less, strong or explicit participation.[4] In the previous chapter, we focused on project-time. As we discussed, in project-time, things are often strongly moderated by a maker or group of makers who organise people's participation with an eye on generating new ideas for future products or works. 'L'Artisan Electronique', for instance, was initially mainly driven by some specific questions that the original makers shared online in order to generate ideas to answer them. In use-time however, things are mostly self-organised via a group of participants, often independently from the makers, with an infrastructure to organise their participatory exchanges themselves. Over time, participants started making their own 3D platforms that were inspired by 'l'Artisan Electronique' but no longer directly connected to these specific questions. In this chapter, we concentrate on what happens after the initial design input from the makers.[5]

We are specifically concerned with the aspects of projects that trigger and sustain on-going participation. In chapter 2, we already argued that participatory projects can be described as being hybrid. Based on anthropological literature, Participatory Design and Art literature and Human Computer Interaction literature, we concluded that hybridity in participatory projects can be described through risky trade-offs between makers and participants, in which they realise exchanges by making collages or sharing or adding to imperfect characteristics.[6] The term 'collage' refers to the fact that via continuous interaction between makers and participants, they produce a space that contains elements brought in by all of them. This creates a zone of potential conflict, mutual learning and exchange and results in projects that do not belong to one 'stakeholder' but to everyone. A collage is not entirely symmetrically co-constructed. Sometimes the makers produce quite predefined projects that are rather intended to provoke small or pre-planned contributions by the participants or the other way around. For example, the 3D platform was initially more driven by the makers' ideas and specific problems. In chapter 2, we also observed that hybridity in participatory projects is characterised by makers and participants who exchange imperfect (aspects of) projects, with which we mean that the project is unfinished, 'frayed' and still open to interpretation and contributions by other participants. For instance, 'l'Artisan Electronique' was not created as a finished 3D platform, but was shared online with clear technical problems and questions.

Looking at the overview by Muller, hybridity is described in association with makers' and participants' experiences of the project phase of participatory projects, in which makers are still heavily involved.[7] However, with the increasing adoption and pervasiveness of new media, and concerns about,

4 Ehn, 2008; Huybrechts, 2011.
5 Ibid.
6 For anthropological literature: Bhabha, 1994; Clifford, 1997; for Participatory Design and Art literature: Muller, 2002; Zielinski, 2006; for Human Computer Interaction literature: Gaver et al., 2003; Sengers et al., 2005.
7 Muller, 2002.

for instance, democracy, empowerment or sustainability, many areas in art and design have shifted their perspectives on participation. They became increasingly concerned with participation after the project-time, so in use-time. Following this new trend (in which ICT plays a key role), new products, services and systems allow 'participants' to create for (and by) themselves, even independent from the original makers. In many cases, there is, or is no longer, a line to be drawn between makers and participants. In this new emerging tendency, the traditional divisions between production and consumption seem out-dated. Illustrative cases, such as Wikipedia, the growth of digital Do It Yourself (DIY) and Do It With Others (DIWO) communities and experimental forms of collective arts and activism, show a myriad of different, often unforeseen possibilities of fostering, enabling, facilitating and affording different forms of participation. This enabling of participation in use-time can be described with the term 'generativity'.[8] Generativity results from makers who engage in the uncertain exchange of releasing control over a participatory project after the creation process, handing it over to many uncertain participants and contexts. In this chapter, we further investigate this concept in order to distinguish the risky trade-offs that are involved. Generativity, as a concept, is closely related to hybridity. Also, generative projects are often highly hybrid, collage-like and imperfect. The other way around, collages and imperfect projects are open to unexpected contributions. Hybridity and generativity can therefore be considered as two sides of the same coin. In this chapter, we first look into the concept of generativity. Starting with a general description, we then focus on manifestations of generativity in (computer) design and art. More concretely, we distinguishe between approaches that discuss generativity from the maker's point of view on the one hand and from the participant's point of view on the other hand. We also zoom in on an approach that detaches generativity from the maker or participants and rather emphasises the role of the duration of a project. Next, we present three case studies of participatory projects — being 'l' Artisan Electronique', 'Touchatag' and Arduino — and reflect on how they have tried to enable generativity in practice. Finally, we put the reviews of the literature and practices together and present a framework for generativity in which we discuss three trade-offs.

Framing

The Concept of Generativity

The term generativity was first coined in 1950 by psychoanalyst Erikson.[8] He describes it as a strength that comes through caring for others and producing something that contributes to the betterment of society, namely 'the interest in establishing and guiding the next generation'.[9] A review made by Avital & Te'eni illustrates how generativity is used in other fields.[10] Chomsky introduced generative grammar to refer to the rich structure of language that is capable of generating infinite configurations and expressions.[11] Moreover, Schön uses generativity in relation to metaphors that we use to change our perspectives on the world and, by doing so, to constantly reconstruct our social realities and actions.[12] Similar, Gergen introduces the idea of 'generative capacity' to explain the human capacity to challenge assumptions, transform our social realities and rethink our social actions.[13] Zandee focuses on 'generative inquiry' as a form of questioning, which produces new knowledge by distancing ourselves from assumptions and existing paradigms.[14] Kornberger & Clegg discuss generative buildings as undefined spaces that allow its inhabitants to interact freely and enact their ideas in creative ways, by re-defining and using the space in surprising ways.[15]

Zittrain and Avital & Te'eni describe generativity as an important feature of participatory projects in information systems.[16] Van Osch & Avital explain how generative systems can enable distributed communities of online participants to engage collectively in bottom-up processes of creation and innovation.[17] They introduce design considerations for these systems to create this collective generativity, stating that systems should be engaging, evocative, open and adaptive. The authors claim that an engaging system is playful, affective and exciting in order to encourage people to participate, explore and tinker. They define a system as evocative when it challenges people to explore new perspectives, insights and actions, evoking reflexive dialogues among members of a community or users of a system. They see a system as open if it is transparent and accessible, promoting negotiations and encouraging free and collective use, sharing, modification and evaluation of information. Finally, they describe it as adaptive, or flexible, for a heterogeneous group of users in a variety of contexts, if it allows producing complementary features in order to meet new or unanticipated needs.[18]

Zittrain also sees generativity as a basis for participatory innovation.[19] He defines it as a system's capacity to produce unanticipated change, based on unfiltered contributions from various participants. More concretely, Zittrain speaks of a pattern of generativity

8 Erikson, 1950; Avital & Te'eni, 2006; Zittrain, 2008.
9 Erikson, 1950, p. 231.
10 Avital & Te'eni, 2006.
11 Chomsky, 1972.
12 Schön, 1979.
13 Gergen, 1994.
14 Zandee, 2004.
15 Kornberger & Clegg, 2004.
16 Zittrain, 2008; Avital & Te'eni, 2006.
17 Van Osch & Avital, 2009.
18 Ibid.
19 Zittrain, 2008.

that consists of four phases: (1) it begins with a technology that is created for fun and/or for profit. (2) the (incomplete) technology's blueprints are shared. (3) these blueprints and the technology are made modular (meaning that the tools to make content are transferred, rather than the content itself) to welcome contribution and improvement. (4) finally, a technical infrastructure can be set up that is owned in a partially structured and distributed way to facilitate unexpected tinkering by participants.[20] This distributed character removes some legal and business practice barriers that are related to central and unanimous control by an institution. Zittrain optimistically describes how generativity allows participants to refine the technology as it spreads, leading the technology into new markets, where commercial or public organisations can help to package and refine the technology for even more people. To illustrate, Zittrain uses the Apple II computer as an example of such a generative system that invites people 'to tinker with it'. By contrast, he does not consider the Apple iPhone as being generative:

> ... the iPhone comes pre-programmed. You are not allowed to add programs to the all-in-one device that Steve Jobs sells you. ... [T]hose who managed to tinker with the code to enable the iPhone to support more or different applications, Apple threatened (and then delivered on the threat)

> to transform the iPhone into an iBrick. The machine was not to be generative beyond the innovations that Apple (and its exclusive carrier, AT&T) wanted.[21]

Media researcher Lovink criticises Zittrain for limiting generativity to some products.[22] He suggests that it is not the product, but the interest of hackers in opening up the product that turns technologies into generative constructions. This critique underlines that generativity is always a multidirectional process that can never be controlled by the makers alone and is thus always a trade-off. The idea that participatory projects are trade-offs is also supported by the fact that Zittrain grounds his pattern of generativity on what he calls the 'procrastination principle', implying that most problems confronting a project can be solved by others later on.[23] It is driven by two assumptions. The first assumption refers to the modularity of a project, which makes it endlessly adaptable, preventing it from becoming optimised for one use only. The second assumption is based on trust in the participants who use and configure the project. Zittrain explains that many critics question the value of taking the risk to engage in a project that is only partially planned, measured, controlled and accounted for by its makers. Zittrain replies:

20 Ibid., p. 19.
21 Ibid., p. 2.
22 Lovink, 2008.
23 Zittrain, 2008.

> Imagine planning but not yet executing Wikipedia: "Won't people come along and vandalize it?" One response to that question, and to the others like it that arise for an idea as crazy as Wikipedia, would be to abandon the idea; to transform it so much in anticipation of the problems that it is unrecognizable from its original generative blueprint. The response instead was to deem the question reasonable but premature. The generativity that makes it vulnerable also facilitates the tools and relationships through which people can meet the problems when first-round success causes them to materialize'[24]

Zittrain acknowledges that generativity — which is typical for many participatory projects — involves many uncertain factors. Nevertheless, he also underlines that makers and participants have to trust in an interesting outcome in order to realise innovations. A better understanding of this concept of generativity can contribute to this trust. Therefore, we will now shed more light on generative practices and uncover some of its realities in the domains of participatory art and design.

Summary

In this introduction to the concept of generativity, we have learned that:

— generative projects enable distributed and varied participants to engage collectively in bottom-up and partly structured processes of creation and unexpected change.
— generative projects have some interesting qualities, such as openness, adaptability, evocativeness and engagement,[25] as well as shareability, modularity and distributed ownership.[26]

Generativity and Participation: a Review of the Literature

In this section, we discuss design and art literature that is concerned with a series of issues reflecting the notion of generativity and participation in use-time. We review how a participatory project can support makers in releasing control and handing a project over to other participants. We look into how allowing participation after the creation process challenges the traditional divisions between creating and using. The first body of work that we discuss draws on literature in various design research fields dealing with new technologies: Human Computer Interaction, Computer Supported Cooperative Work and Participatory Design, with some reference to innovation and media studies. The second review discusses new design and development practices linked to the growing area of digital Do It Yourself, Do It With Others and hacking

24 Ibid., p. 241.
25 Van Osch & Avital, 2006.
26 Zittrain, 2008.

practices in digital media. These practices are also reflected in the areas of contemporary art and activism and have recently been brought to the attention of the afore-mentioned design fields. Finally, we review some work in the area of participatory and public art with a particular focus on so-called 'durational art' or art that wants to endure longer than an eventful participatory moment.

Human Computer Interaction, Computer Supported Cooperative Work, Participatory Design

Concerns about active and creative participation in use-time are not new in design fields — such as Human Computer Interaction, Computer Supported Cooperative Work and Participatory Design — and in some innovation and media studies. In general, this literature deals with how a maker can release control and how design can be made less predefined and more open for uncertain contributions by participants (such as their modifications of the design).

Some of these studies reflect on practices that emphasise a more active role of the participant (in the outcomes of a project), like appropriation. In general, these studies all challenge a strong separation between makers and participants. For instance, Moran introduces the notion of 'Everyday Adaptive Design' and argues that participants' everyday adaptation in the use of interactive systems should be regarded as a form of design itself.[27] Dourish calls this 'appropriation', by which he not only refers to the capability of design to be adapted (i.e. customisation) but also to the practice of participants adopting design in their daily lives.[28] This notion of appropriation has been applied to many different technological devices, such as copiers, ubiquitous computing, mobile phones, self-monitoring devices or, more recently, objects in domestic environments and Latino car design (which Eglash et al., call 'vernacular' engineering).[29] The concept of appropriation is influenced by phenomenological approaches in the HCI field and by work in the field of Information Systems.[30] Also, a series of user studies in Media Studies and Science and Technology Studies have further contributed to the establishment of the notion of appropriation and the idea of the social shaping of technology.[31] These studies show that there is no single force, but rather there are multiple forces that can shape technology.[32] Appropriation has also been discussed in light of the notion of 'domestication' by arguing that participants 'tame' a new technology, which goes through various stages before being incorporated into everyday life.[33] This body of literature contributes to makers' consciousness about their projects being

27 Moran, 2002.
28 Dourish, 2003.
29 Copiers: Wagner & Balka, 2005; ubiquitous computing: Lemhachheche, 2005; mobile phones: Carroll, 2002; Carroll et al., 2003; self-monitoring devices: Storni, 2009; objects in domestic environments: Wakkary & Tanenbaum, 2009; Latino car design: Eglash et al., 2004.
30 Suchman, 2007; Winograd & Flores, 1986; Ciborra, 1992; Ciborra & Hanseth, 2000.
31 MacKenzie & Wajcman, 1985/1999.
32 See also: MacKay & Gillespie, 1992.
33 Silverstone & Hirsh, 1992.

used in unexpected ways by participants, outside of their control and raises awareness that makers can even support this behaviour.

Other studies refer to what the design itself affords and how it can enable active participants, referring to concepts ranging from accountability to knowing how (affective modelling). Looking more specifically from the perspective of the design and the designer, many authors have reflected upon the design qualities that support participants in appropriating the design. For instance, Dix — in his essay on 'Design for Appropriation' — believes that projects that want to stimulate appropriation have some qualities.[34] They allow interpretation, provide visibility of their functioning and meaning, support people in designing new elements by being 'pluggable' and 'configurable' and allow participants to share and learn from modified projects. In CSCW, MacLean et al. addressed this issue by putting forward the notion of 'user-tailorable systems' that support participants in tailoring or modifying a design.[35] Henderson & Kyng describe this as 'continuing design-in-use, which means that designers search for ways to enable participants to further elaborate the design of their system during use.[36] The authors argue that this is important since it is impossible for makers to foresee all the possible contexts of use during design. Therefore, Henderson & Kyng stress that systems should enable people to 'tailor' (besides: use) the design. For instance, 'use' can be illustrated by participants modifying a font in a word document and 'tailoring' by modifying the default font for all new documents. Therefore, tailoring becomes somehow linked to the depth and duration of the modification, affecting future uses. Robinson coins the notion of design for unanticipated use, putting more emphasis on certain provisions ('affordances') of design that allow a group of participants to work on common objects in collaborative settings.[37] He refers to some provisions, such as the predictability of the design, the ability of it being discursively articulated, present to the peripheral attention and providing an overview of the work. In this research strand, design projects that allows active participation are also called 'pliant systems'[38] or they are compared to clay, designed to be pliable or malleable.[39] Here, projects are therefore seen as increasingly appropriable systems.

This same line of thinking was further developed when the idea of ubiquitous computing — entailing computer technology becoming omnipresent, invisible and embedded in everything — was put forward.[40] In this area of research, concerns were expressed about whether the participants should be able to act upon these ubiquitous solutions that seemed to be disappearing. To discuss the ability of people to act upon technology, Weiser et al. developed the idea of 'seamful' ubiquitous computing solutions.[41] Seams, like in clothing,

34 Dix, 2007.
35 MacLean et al., 1990.
36 Henderson & Kyng, 1991, p. 221-224.
37 Robinson, 1993.
38 Harris & Henderson, 1999.
39 Bødker, 1999.
40 Weiser, 1991; Norman 1998.
41 Weiser, 1994; Weiser & Brown, 1996.

allow people to see how a technology is composed and provide them with an opportunity to act upon it. Chalmers et al. suggested that these seams (and scars) can represent interesting, interactional features that allow participants to appropriate the technology, acting like a sort of interface.[42] In this research strand, there seems to be a general agreement that increasing the designer's accountability for his or her design — for instance, via making the function and meaning visible through showing seams — can benefit the ability of the participants to appropriate the design.[43] Dourish & Button introduce this idea via a 'technomethodology', referring to artefacts that account for their functioning to users.[44] Similarly, in discussing the contribution of feminist studies (a perspective concerned with questioning traditional models of authority), Bardzell mentions the quality of self-disclosure.[45] He sees this as the extent to which a designed artefact renders visible the way in which it interacts with participants as subjects. In this regard, he pleads for a re-education of the (participant's) perception against the background of a narcotisation of perception operated by more traditional 'fixed' design.[46]

Although traditionally concerned with the agency and the active role of participants at project-time, Participatory Design research has also become concerned with the agency of participants in use-time. Approaches are formulated by, for instance, Fisher et al. who call for new roles for makers and participants in so-called 'Meta-design'.[47] Meta-design refers to a process in which participants become co-creators, not only at project-time but also after that (throughout the whole existence of the system). Fisher et al. formulate some essential qualities of Meta-design projects, such as being flexible and evolving and therefore not completely finished prior to use. Also, these projects are made possible partly by users and are deliberately created for evolution. Therefore, they are open and underdesigned, providing a context against which cases can be interpreted, so that 'owners of problems' are allowed to create solutions themselves. Interesting is that Fisher et al. underline that — rather than via accountability or 'knowing what' — Meta-design is made possible via 'knowing how', being an affective model or 'embodied interactionism'.[48] This affective model provides participants with opportunities, tools, and social reward structures to extend the system to fit their needs. Addressing these aspects, Fisher et al. formulate a series of challenges for Meta-design, one of which underlines the need for makers and participants to create a new, integrated design space, in which they bring together both the technical and the social conditions of certain design projects. Also, Kanstrup states that makers should emphasise the, partly unconscious, negotiations, inquiries and engagements by participants with the logics and

42 Chalmers, 2003; Chalmers & Galani, 2004.
43 See e.g.: Robinson, 1993; Randell, 2004.
44 Dourish & Button, 1996.
45 Bardzell, 2010.
46 See also: Spiekerman & Palles, 2006.
47 Fisher et al., 2004.
48 Ibid., pp. 5-7.

expressions of the design, beyond its functionality.[49] She argues that this prevents that only a small elite of leading users or domain experts are stimulated to keep on participating.[50]

Questioning the traditional asymmetry between 'professional' design and 'lay' users, Meta-design asks for an explicit reflection on the political and emancipatory role of technology and design, which has been taken up by recent studies in the HCI field.[51] In this context, DiSalvo et al. explore robotics in lay community settings, discussing participants' critical engagement with this technology in the 'Neighbourhood Networks Project'.[52] The authors show how people who are less experienced with technology are not necessarily passive with regard to technology but rather are able, interested and willing to critically engage with what is usually perceived as 'being for experts'. Drawing on another important contribution by DiSalvo, Le Dantec discusses a co-design project aimed at democratising the design process with those who live in the margin of society (in this case, a community of urban homeless).[53] He, too, illustrates the proactive attitude of participants. DiSalvo's more recent contribution on 'Adversarial Design' further examines the ways in which a technology design can account for and provoke the political.[54] With his adversarial design, he describes designed objects that talk about contemporary political issues, values, beliefs, desires and power structures, provoking a reaction from the people who use or see those objects. This 'adversarial' discourse brings us to a second part of this review, which is about a renewed attention to practices of Do It Yourself, Do It With Others, hacking practices and social innovation practices linked with Web 2.0 platforms and open-source projects.

Summary

We reviewed a series of concepts about generativity and participation in use-time in fields such as HCI, CSCW, PD and some innovation and media studies. Several of these studies put a lot of focus on the **activities of the participants** in the project that contribute to generating participation in use-time. The way they describe these activities appeared to be strongly related to the amount of control the makers risk to give to the participants, allowing them to adapt[55] or appropriate the project.[56] This literature increases makers' consciousness about the fact that participation is possible in their design, in unexpected ways, outside of their control. It also raises awareness of the fact that they even can support this behaviour. Other literature refers to the **provisions** of the design itself and how these can enable active participants. These studies generally reflect upon the design qualities that support participants in appropriating the project. Instead of calculating the risk for unexpected or unintended use of a project, these studies show

49 Kanstrup, 2012.
50 Björgvinsson et al., 2010.
51 E.g. DiSalvo et al., 2010; DiSalvo et al., 2009.
52 DiSalvo et al., 2009.
53 Ibid.; Le Dantec, 2010.
54 DiSalvo, 2012.
55 Moran, 2002.
56 Dourish, 2003; Dix, 2007; Silverstone & Hirsh, 1992.

how the uncertainties about how participants will, for instance, perceive, use, alter or repurpose the project, can be regarded as qualities of the design. We now summarise these described provisions of design that support participants in appropriation and that can contribute to the generative quality of the design:

— according to the studied literature, to enable participation in use-time, makers and participants embrace the uncertainty of making the project **accountable**. The accountability of the project[57] refers to projects that self-disclose their functioning and meaning to the participant ('knowing what').[58] Projects that account for their functioning and meaning give participants the opportunity to appropriate the project, in ways that are difficult to predict for its original makers. In the literature, a lot of attention is paid to making the functions of a project accountable. However, less attention is paid to making meaning accessible. DiSalvo's recent book on adversarial design describes how makers can create projects talking about what they 'mean' to people, accounting for their relation to contemporary political issues, values, beliefs, desires and power structures and provoking a reaction from the participants.[59]
— furthermore, the studies indicate that makers and participants can also provide an insight in *how* their project can be used to increase its generative qualities. This affective model of 'knowing

how' provides participants with opportunities, tools and social reward structures to extend the project to fit their needs, making room for their conscious or unconscious negotiations about the design's expressions and logics.[60] The main uncertainty dealt with here relates to how makers can make their projects less predefined, and more stimulating and open to unpredictable negotiations by participants. Some authors suggest that seamful, tailorable, pliant or modular designs can contribute to this affective modelling by participants.[61] These notions seem to account only for modelling a project's functionalities. However, they can also be applied to the more conceptual level of a design, referring to the modelling of its meaning, for instance.

— finally, we learned that design can afford ongoing participation in use-time. As we already stressed at the beginning of this text, we do not see the described aspects as 'recipes' or prerequisites. Also, we do not see them as strictly separate. Although we noted a distinction between 'knowing what' and 'knowing how' in the reviewed literature, we do not see these as two entirely separate forms. Trying to enable 'knowing how' — by providing tools or a setting for affective learning

57 Randell, 2004; Dourish & Button, 1996; Bardzell, 2010.
58 Robinson, 1993.
59 DiSalvo, 2012.
60 Fisher et al., 2004; Kanstrup, 2012.
61 MacLean et al., 1990; Weiser 1994, 1996.

or negotiations, for instance — is often very related to stimulating 'knowing what', by articulating a design's function. For instance, by making the 'seams' in a technology visible, a project accounts for how it is made. At the same time these seams can show how participants can model the technology in a new form.

Hackers, Open-Source and Do It Yourself/Do It With Others

In this second section, we review a series of studies that describe the blurring of boundaries between makers and participants in a similar way, but focus more on the perspective of participants. Starting with computer hackers in the 1960s, we discuss some key studies in the area of open-source and conclude with an appreciation of the revamped areas of (digital) Do It Yourself (DIY) and Do It With Others (DIWO). These domains break with 'traditional' models that focus on authorial control and formal management of projects and dare to embrace more open and free standards, flexibility and creative reconfiguration. This radical choice of putting a lot of control in the hands of the participants challenges many uncertainties that makers of participatory projects are confronted with.

To explore the evolution of how participants began to play a more active role in (e.g. software design) projects in use-time, we start with the activities of computer hackers and, more precisely, with the new values that the hacker ethics brought about.

Rheingold's *The Virtual Community* and Levy's *Hackers* describe how the hackers ethic expanded along with, for instance, the growth of the Internet, the MIT computer lab, the transition from large mainframes to powerful personal computers, garages in the areas of San Francisco and Seattle (where young inventors explored new futures) and the establishment of Silicon Valley.[62] The practice of releasing authorial control — in the form of opening up projects for participants and by stating, for instance, that software and derivative work should be free and shared — is very important to the hacker ethics. With the hacking metaphor, Galloway et al. look for deeper forms of participation and suggest a new model — called 'Design for Hackability' — for makers to think about participants.[63] Unlike tailoring — reasoning from the perspective of the maker — 'hacking' resonates with the idea of appropriation as it concerns the possibility for the participant to reclaim ownership of a project or re-purpose parts or all of it. This idea of hackers survived after 1992, when the Internet was opened up to companies and became a major market place largely dominated by corporate and profit-oriented interests. The hackers idea survived thanks to the birth of open-source movements, artistic activists, as well as the later explosion of the so-called Web 2.0, DIY and DIWO. Also, the first copy-left licenses,

62 Rheingold, 2000; Levy, 2010.
63 Galloway et al., 2004.
64 Hartmann, 2006; Nissenbaum, 2004.

developed by Richard Stallman and others, played a key role in this.[64]

In this context, research on free and open-source software (as discussed in the first chapter) enriches an area where traditional models of production are discussed or even criticised. The open-source development model has especially been adopted by computer programmers around the world since the early 1980s and gained recognition in commercial contexts in the 1990s.[65] The LINUX open-source operating system must be the best-known example of an open-source system.[66] Instead of commercially produced values, free software supporters focus more on the political and social values of openness, such as its potential for people to work together in a more easy way or its potential for governments to only use publicly owned information systems.[67] In this context of open-source and free software, hacker ethics explore the more *horizontal* ways of exchange between makers and participants and its potential for participation in use-time. Wark for instance, contrasts the intellectual property of proprietary designs and large software corporations (via restrictive licenses) with the communal character of open innovation in user communities.[68] In his *Hacker Manifesto*, he discusses that people today are alienated from their production and consumption, meaning that they seldom know how and why their consumer goods are produced and what their value is. Himanen focuses on the ethic of labour, differentiating between the Protestant ethic — based on formally free work and scientific management

— and the hacker ethic, based on free and unstructured work.[69] Similarly, Hannemyr contrasted the Tayloristic and rigid organisation of work in software development — i.e. traditional waterfall labour models — with hackers' practices in which development phases — such as 'implementation' and 'maintenance' — are gradually transformed into an on-going, all-encompassing and sometimes perpetual 'hacking' phase.[70] Also, Raymond in his well-known The *Cathedral and the Bazaar*, discusses how FLOSS (Free Libre and Open-source Software) dismisses the idea of hierarchical, managerial and top-down development models in favour of horizontal, bottom up and distributed development that results in high quality software.[71]

Recent studies of open-source technologies and Web 2.0 technologies emphasise their ability to support *sharing* between people, which contributes to the generative qualities of projects. The open-source development model works via continuous reworking of concepts, products and services by sharing. Sharing means that the items (content, software, hardware, et cetera) are made publicly available to anyone who wishes to use or modify them for their own purpose. Stallman, to whom the open-source development model is often attributed, proposed that open-source

65 Bauwens, 2007; Open-source initiative, 2010.
66 Vallance et al., 2001.
67 Stallman, 2008.
68 Wark, 2004.
69 Himanen, 2001.
70 Hannemyr, 1999.
71 Raymond, 2001.

software should provide specific qualities to developers and users, namely the freedom to run the software (for any purpose), to modify it and to (re)distribute copies of the original or modified versions of the software.[72] Besides sharing source code, (digital) blueprints of the hardware construction or step-by-step instructions of the making processes of the project can be shared.[73] Items can be shared in the form of 'patterns', providing a language that is more abstract than a notation or programming level to make a project understandable and stimulate makers to be more explicit about decisions. 'One of the great things about patterns is that they take them out of the realm of vague intuition. The shared vocabulary facilitates designers to communicate, document, and explore design alternatives'.[74] Patterns, instructions or blueprints take some time and experience to make, but they enable makers to communicate about a project, for which they are valued. These sharing practices require active participation of makers and participants[75], allowing them to learn from each other's knowledge and practices and permitting the appropriation or reproduction of this knowledge and practice for other goals and groups.[76] Open-source literature suggests that this may lead to better quality, reliability, flexibility and lower costs.

Technology 'guru' O'Reilly defines Web 2.0 technologies as series of internet technologies and services — like YouTube, Flickr, Facebook and so on — that make easy sharing accessible to 'everybody'.[77] Instead of being concerned with implications for makers, this body of literature praises how new media support new ways to rethink and broaden the notion of exchange between participants. Also, Von Hippel discusses user-led innovation, arguing that leading users — sharing their practices — might be extremely important to innovate products in the market.[78] Possibly, they become self-manufacturers themselves.[79] This thinking has grown exponentially and is even becoming a key marketing operation for large corporations. In it, the participant's adaptations are seen as a form of innovation-in-use, creating a new use value for a given technology. A similar idea is that of the 'Pro-Am revolution' — or the user innovation revolution — that draws on a series of fortunate examples, in which participants played a relevant role in the establishment of a technological innovation (e.g. the design of a mountain bike by the appropriation of traditional bikes by extreme-sport amateurs).[80] Indeed, an increasing number of neologisms address the new roles for people acting at the intersection of consumption and production, design and use, such as the concepts of 'prosumers', 'prod-user', 'users as everyday innovators' or 'users as empowered users'.[81]

72 Vallance et al., 2001; Stallman, 1999.
73 Avital, 2011.
74 Gamma et al., 1995, p. 395.
75 Fisher et al., 2003.
76 Bauwens, 2007; Tribe & Jana, 2006.
77 O'Reilly, 2005.
78 Von Hippel, 2005.
79 Ibid., see also: Gershenfeld, 2005.
80 Leadbeater & Miller, 2004.
81 Prosumers: Toffler, 1980; Tapscott & Williams, 2006; prod-user: Bruns, 2008; users as everyday innovators: Haddon et al., 2008; users as empowered users: Pierson et al., 2010.

Hacking is certainly not limited to computers but extends to a whole series of activities reflecting the idea of tinkering with technology and doing 'bricolage'.[82] An entire new movement of active users redesigning and repurposing all sorts of everyday, mundane objects has started to populate the Internet. This is contributing to the more recent explosion of DIY and DIWO practices, now linked with Web 2.0 platform and online communities (sharing 'how-to' advices).[83] In this context, we also witness open-source communities traditionally concerned with software extending to hardware, in which physical prototyping, tinkering and bricolage platforms are developed, based on the principle of FLOSS. DIY and DIWO practices underline the value of *flexibility* of projects in order to generate participation in use-time. Different approaches to this flexibility have been accounted in literature, looking at how new waves of 'digital artisans' engage with different types of technology and media. In this context, the notion of script has been used to distinguish between different socio-technical systems: proprietary systems with fixed scripts and a tendency to homologise the users (e.g. by using restrictive licenses), Web 2.0 platforms with more flexible scripts enabling different forms of participation (which, however, is still limited to the business model of those owning the infrastructure) and open-source and DIY with open scripts where design and use interpenetrate each other (e.g. with the help of online forums or copy-left licenses), enabling different levels of participants' engagement.[84] These models produce a series of new innovation practices, such as hacking and jail breaking but also remixing and repurposing. These new practices are starting to characterise the innovation landscape in new media. From these practices, new actors emerge, such as consumer associations, NGOs, prosumers, ad-busters, home-brewers, hackers, digital artisans, smart mobs, open communities, and so on.[85]

In addition to this flexibility, DIY and DIWO stress the value of participants who *reconfigure* projects in creative ways. In an extensive survey among DIY and DIWO communities, Kuznetsov & Paulos consider the value of creativity (in which the physical and the digital are integrated), and of sharing and learning (through iterations and distributed feedbacks), to be more important than profit and social capital.[86] In the field of new media, Lievrouw studies how oppositional and activist new media, such as culture jamming, alternative computing, mediated mobilisation and indy-media, challenge the cultural domination of media and information industries.[87] She argues that the on-going re-configuration of technology and remediation of contents characterising these communities should be taken seriously by design disciplines concerned with participation. Writer and media artist

82 See e.g.: DelFanti & Söderberg, 2012.
83 Buechley et al, 2009.
84 Storni, 2009.
85 Ibid.
86 Kuznetsov & Paulos, 2010.
87 Lievrouw, 2006.

Ramocki also describes how hackers performing DIY practices creatively repurpose consumer goods and intellectual properties by recreating the information and material present in our society into something new.[88] They do this in order to demonstrate how the creative process can be perceived and handled differently from the 'traditional' media industries. These hacker ethics can thus enable new and unexpected forms of participation and interactions between participants, practices and materials.

Summary

Engaging with forms of participation in the line of hacker ethics, DIY and DIWO indicate that makers allow the participants to take the project into their own hands. This implies that the project deliberately remains highly uncertain and unpredictable. We distinguish two valuable characteristics in this body of literature that appear to be quite similar to the two elements we mentioned in the earlier part:

— we discovered that the engagement in horizontal relations of *sharing* between makers and participants is closely related to the afore-mentioned idea of accountability.[89]

— the discussed practices stressed flexibility and offered participants opportunities for creative repurposing.[90] This idea stretches the concept of modularity (mentioned above) to more open ways of recombining and repurposing materials, media or concepts.

We can state that hacking, DIY and DIWO practices explicitly question authorship — more so than in the field of HCI, for instance — of creative work by handing over power to the participants. However, the notion of authorship remains an important issue, even though some distance is taken. In the following section about durational and media arts we place this notion of authorship into a renewed context.

Durational and Media Art

Instead of authorship, some participatory projects especially emphasise time or duration. By doing so, they intensely relate to the idea of on-going participation.[91] In this overview, we discuss some authors in the domain of participatory art and media art who have stressed that makers must pay more attention to the aspect of time — or duration — in participation to enable a project to generate on-going activity.

In the 1970s, Lynch criticised the focus of participatory and public art practices on the space of participation.[92] He states that the artist should create a 'time-place', in which the time that is spent in a place becomes more important than the owner of a work or the space in which it takes place. As Philips argues, progressive participatory art invests time in a certain community in order to relate with it.[93] Also, Kwon's influential book

88 Ramocki, 2007.
89 E.g. Wark, 2004; Himanen, 2001; Hannemyr, 1999.
90 E.g. Kuznetsov & Paulos, 2010; Lievrouw, 2006.
91 As discussed by e.g. Hannemyr, 1999.
92 Lynch, 1972.
93 Philips, 1992.

One Place After Another: Site-Specific Art and Locational Identity is a critique on the place-focus of participatory art.[94] Kwon talks about an obsession with place and considers 'new genre public art' as an alternative. This is a form of 'socially responsible' public art and a community-based practice since the 1960s. It engages intensely with the people on site, involving direct communication and interaction over an extended period of time. Lynch, Philips and Kwon define participatory art as more than an 'event' at a specific moment in time, that is experienced *en masse*.[95]

To address this different form of participatory art, art theorist O'Neill introduces the term durational art:

> If duration involves being together for a period of time with some common objectives, then durational praxis is the specific quality of a new mode of relational and participatory practice. ... By taking account of participation with art, and in art, as an unfolding and longer-term accumulation of multiple positions, engagements and moments registered in what we account for as the artwork, then we may be able to move beyond the individual participatory encounter of an eventful exhibition moment.[96]

O'Neill considers participation as on-going, sometimes discordantly experienced and enacted by the participants.

It allows the formation, dispersal and reformation of temporary active communities.[97] According to O'Neill, durational art works approach participation in two important ways. Firstly, these works criticise the fact that in the art field most discussions around participation revolve too much around what happens between the participants and the artists through the art work, i.e. the space of art. Durational projects think beyond triggering participation with 'the participants' via the art work. They want to engage various agents, not only the art audience but also commissioners or people living in the neighbourhood, to co-produce. O'Neill also stresses that the question of *what* is created is less important, since there are no prescribed outcomes. Secondly, durational art encourages new participants to be formed beyond the initial participants. This is made possible via makers and participants who spread the narrative of a project over time. In that sense, durational art not only invites more types of participants, but also stimulates the outgrowing of the (heterogeneous) group of initial participants. In this way, the work transcends its immediate relations in time, place and people involved. Projects are translated and extended into the future, through the artist's work and the resident initiatives that endure beyond the project's lifetime or in art discourses. The focus is therefore on the work's duration, namely art's goal to leave something behind that could not have been anticipated. It aims at generating

94 Kwon, 2002.
95 Lynch, 1972; Philips, 1992; Kwon, ibid.
96 O'Neill, 2011.
97 O'Neill, 2009; ibid.

participation, also after the artist has left the project site. Then, participation becomes more than a form of co-production. It becomes an end product in itself.

A similar goal of participation as an end product is stressed in the domain of interactive media art. Fisher et al. point to the fact that much interactive art aims for collaboration and co-creation.[98] The authors define interactive art as a form of Meta-design, in which an original design is proposed as a context that participants can co-create and manipulate at the level of code, behaviour, and/or content. This enables them to perform meaningful activities. Interactive media art allows participants to be active participants in the creative process and to share this creativity beyond the realm of professional artists. Consequently, interactive art is not about sharing the object, but rather the tools of art. In this way, interactive art creates conditions for the on-going process of interaction.[99]

The literature on Participatory and Media Art sheds a new light on participatory projects, by focusing on its duration. Some, albeit small hints were given about how time may become an interesting focus for participatory projects, instead of its participants or products. Reading the above literature suggests that maybe the central risky trade-off that makers and participants engage in when paying attention to the duration of their projects, is letting go of control, allowing other participants to repurpose the project and risking that they will use it in unforeseen or even contrasting ways, *deviating* from the initial meaning or purpose of the project.

Summary

The discourse in the participatory art field stimulates us to shift our focus from *who* is in control, the maker or the participant, to the more uncertain factor of *time* that is spent together in a space.[100]

— O'Neill coined the term 'durational' to describe this approach to participation.[101] He defines participation as an end product in itself and as a form of co-production.
— Fisher et al. point to the fact that interactive arts also pay a great deal of attention to this durational aspect of participatory work, not by sharing an end-product but by sharing the tools with which participants (co-)create.[102]
— We can state that, by letting go of the locus of control and authorship, the notion of uncertainty comes to the foreground. Makers can distance themselves from the control question and explore participation as what happens over time. In this sense, makers explore a territory that is often not so familiar to them, questioning how to involve in long-term engagements with partici-pants, setting up short-term interventions that are repeated on different moments with different participants or leaving it all up to the participants by trading tools with

98 Fisher et al., 2004.
99 Ibid.
100 Lynch, 1972; Philips, 1992; Kwon, 2002.
101 O'Neill, 2011.
102 Fisher et al., 2004.

which they can do whatever they want, whenever they want.

Conclusion

As we have shown, there seems to be a growing interest in the emerging areas of participation at use-time and the intermixing of roles between participants and makers. In different ways, the review of the literature raises new issues and opens up new spaces to reflect on the idea of participation (especially in the context of generativity and its implications for participatory projects). Since we wanted to link the concept of generativity more clearly to the field of participatory art and design, we explored this literature in depth. Although these bodies of literature come from different fields of practices, they all contribute to our understanding of generativity in participatory projects.

After reviewing the literature, we can distinguish some interesting risky trade-offs that take place between makers and participants in generative, participatory projects.

First of all, makers and participants engage in the risky trade-off of *sharing* their (contributions to) projects more or less openly with each other in order to facilitate appropriation. This act of sharing makes a project vulnerable, since others can copy or rework it in positive or less positive ways. However, this also appeared to stimulate participation. HCI, PD and CSCW literature pointed out that sharing can be made possible by making a project accountable, showing its functions and meanings (*what*). The hacker ethics showed that sharing was often a means to rethink traditional forms of authorship and development and a way to stimulate mutual learning and collaboration in flat, small-scale, interventionist, activist or larger distributed and open-ended settings.[103] We saw that literature mainly emphasised the sharing of functionalities of projects. The role of sharing of meaning, however, deserves and has gained more attention the latest years.

Second, the literature described that sharing was often supported by allowing participants to affectively model the material that is shared (*how*). This can be done via offering participants not only functional and meaningful information about a project, but also opportunities, tools and social rewards. In this line of thought, we learned that makers and participants engage in the risky trade-off of making their projects *modular* to enable further (although unpredictable) affective modelling.[104] They do so by releasing their product as being mouldable, seamful, unfinished and under-designed. DIY, DIWO and hacker practices shed light on the fact that the agency of participants in modular systems is increased via highly flexible systems that allow creative repurposing.[105]

Finally — as illustrated by the literature on durational art — makers and participants in generative participatory projects engage in a project that needs close

103 See e.g. Hannemyr, 1999; Raymond, 2001.
104 See: e.g. Kuznetsov & Paulos, 2010.
105 E.g. Lievrouw, 2006.

attention to the *time-aspect* of participation, instead of to the space or the product of participation. However, the literature remains rather vague about how makers can address this aspect of time. In this context, we learned two things. First, we saw that that these projects put forward participation as an end product, rather than as a pre-described outcome. This means that makers and participants allowed projects to evolve over time and allowed new and unexpected participatory communities to arise. Second, makers and participants handed over projects to new groups of (temporary) participants in on-going, often discordant projects. Learning about these two aspects, we question if it is this time-aspect that is a key risky trade-off in participatory projects, besides sharing and modularity. Maybe the central risky trade-off is that makers and participants let go of control, allowing other participants to alter or redesign the project and risk they will use it in unforeseen (possibly contrasting) ways, *deviating* from the initial meaning or purpose of the project. We discuss this concept of deviation in the following case studies.

In the following section, we discuss some real-life case studies that provide more insight into the three risky trade-offs — enabling generativity — that we distinguished in the literature overview (i.e. sharing, modularity and 'deviationism').

Empirical Section: Participation in the Wild

In this empirical section, we describe three projects to illustrate how generativity is initiated between makers and participants in real-life participatory projects. By doing so, we explore the three trade-offs from within practice. All participatory projects were discussed as a series of 'things'.[106] This means that we focused on the specific assemblies that took place between people, mediated by objects. In every project, these assemblies took place in different moments in time: sometimes one thing followed another, sometimes they took place parallel to one another, sometimes the original makers were involved, sometimes not, et cetera. First, in the case study of 'l'Artisan Electronique', we especially focus on how the project explored the trade-off of sharing to allow participation in use-time. Second, in the 'Touchatag' case study, we discuss the modular character of the project in stimulating generativity. Finally, in the case study of Arduino, we highlight the aspect of deviation in the trade-offs between makers and participants and how this contributes to the generativity of a participatory project.

The descriptions of the first and the third case studies — respectively of l'Artisan Electronique and Touchatag — are the results of (1) a collaborative mapping of the projects with the participants that were involved in the making of them. This was performed via the aforementioned mapping method and toolkit MAP-it, developed by the research group Social Spaces (see chapter 1). Also, (2) a series of interviews and follow-up e-mail conversations, as well as (3) an online review of the projects via official websites and the surrounding conversation and exchanges in related blogs and social networks were carried out.[107] The description of the second case study (Arduino) is based on the following empirical materials: (1) a number of open interviews with some of the original developers of the Arduino board, (2) a review of Arduino material available online (including the official Arduino website and forum and the websites of other similar microcontrollers (Boarduino, Freeduino, et cetera), (3) some of the most popular online forums where Arduino is discussed and the relevant discussions about the interlinks between the Arduino project and its community of users.[108]

Case Study 5: l'Artisan Electronique

The design project l'Artisan Electronique (see: Image 21), by the design collective Unfold, revolved around open-source hardware (DIY/DIWO) principles. Open-source hardware refers to physical artefacts that are designed and shared in the same manner as open-source software (see p. 206). The project's goal was to create an open-source 3D printer that allowed people to mould pottery in a digital way and print it. Resembling the classic pottery wheel, it made use of a laser technique that scanned people's hand movements. The moulded

106 Latour & Weibel, 2005; Storni, 2012.
107 E.g. www.unfoldfab.blogspot.be/, www.bitsfrombytes.com and www.touchatag.com.
108 E.g. www.slashdot.com, www.wired.com, www.make.com and www.ponoko.com.

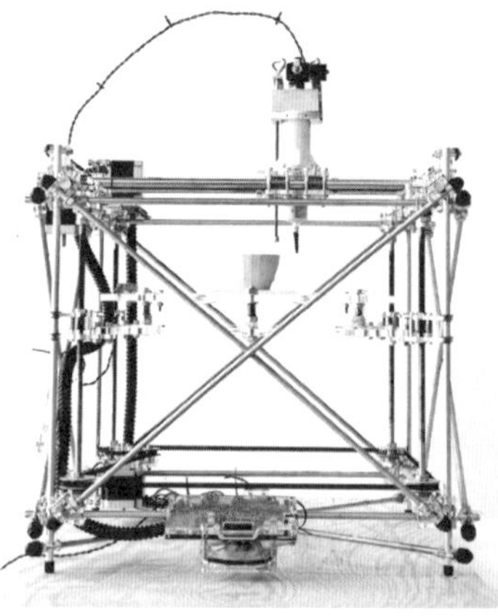

Image 21 **3D printer** Photo by @KristofVrancken /Z33

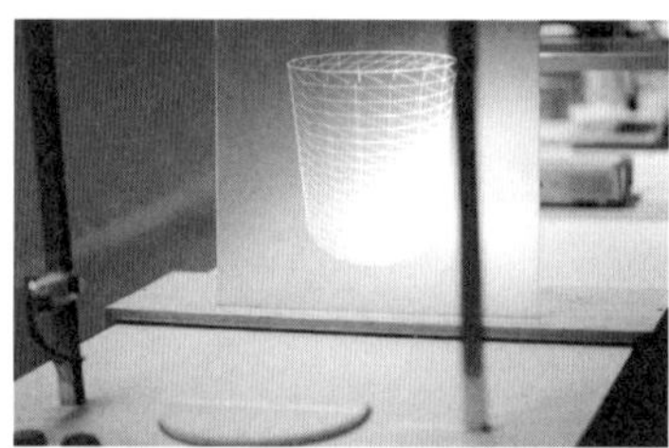

Image 22 **Pottery disk** Photo by @KristofVrancken /Z33

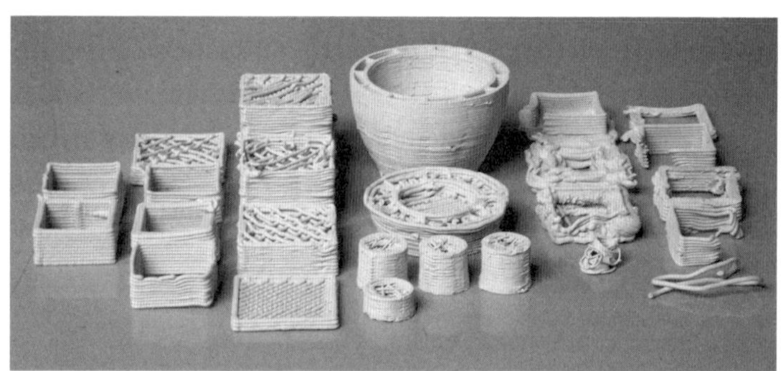

Image 23 **Clay forms** Photo by Unfold

pot was visualised on a computer screen and if visitors felt that they had made a successful design, they were able to 'save' it or, if they were not satisfied, to 'reset' it. Saved models were sent to a modified open-source 3D printer, placed in several exhibition settings, to print the models in clay. The making process of the printer was documented online on the project weblog (see: Images 22 and 23).

The mapping of the project showed that Unfold felt that 3D printing did not enhance the makers' or participant's creativity, due to the generally limited engagement that they could have with the printer and the limited possibilities in working with different materials. They felt that the 3D printers that are available on the market mostly facilitate mass production instead of personal creativity (what they promote). Usually, people send a digital model to a designer, a 3D company or science lab, to print the model. This typically happens in a material way — often in plastic — on large, complex industrial 3D printers. Even if 3D printers can be bought, manufactured and used by participants themselves, which is often facilitated by the open-source model, they do not allow much more than printing an object in plastic. Therefore, Unfold wanted to enhance the open-source RepRap printer's potential to creatively design in 3D. The RepRap printer is inspired by the recent evolutions in the domain of open-source hardware and more specifically of 'FabLabs'. Neil Gershenfeld was involved in conceptualising these so-called Fabrication (or Fabulous) Laboratories for making production tools, developed by MIT, available to students. The FabLabs promise people to be able to 'make (almost) anything'. People gather worldwide and online around the machines, knowhow and objects that are created in a FabLab.[109] An example of an open machine in the FabLab is the 3D printer RepRap (Replicating Rapid Prototyper), an idea by Adrian Bowyer. It can be produced with parts that people can buy in a Do It Yourself shop. Once built, the printer can print the parts for a next, new RepRap printer. People share their knowledge on and experiences with the printer and the changes they have made to it online.[110] Since Unfold was interested in extending the RepRap's potential, rather than building the RepRap themselves, they used an open-source printer building kit: the RapMan version 3.0. This kit allowed them to build the printer much quicker since the needed parts were already gathered in a €1000 DIY package, delivered in a box. The design collective bought the kit from 'Bits from Bytes', a manufacturer of affordable 3D printers and printer toolkits based on the RepRap project.[111]

The kit allowed Unfold to concentrate fully on extending and modifying the printer and making several improvements to it. More specifically, Unfold wanted the printer to refer to old ceramic techniques. The design collective wanted the 'feel' of moulding to be present in the interaction with the 3D printer. They wanted to provide an alternative to what it usually prints in commercial use, i.e. plastic. At the same time, they cherished the printer's digital character, since it added quality to the process of moulding clay. The produced clay forms were so small and detailed that they could not have been manipulated by hand (see: Image 23). To combine both qualities — the old technique and the digital character — Unfold wanted to enhance the 3D printer with an interface that would enable people to model clay in a digital way. For this reason and because of other challenges they were struggling with, Unfold engaged in the risky trade-off of sharing their development process (enhancing the printer's qualities) early on in the process with a larger online community. Their goal was to exchange ideas and practices around the issues they were working on, knowing that this could lead to both interesting as well as negative comments and adaptations. To share the project, Unfold made it accountable via providing different forms of documentation. They blogged quite intensely about the process of building the printer on their own website. Well-written manuals but also conversations (online and offline) on blogs, community sites and in exhibition spaces made the printer and its specific elements more transparent. In the documentation that Unfold created, people could read and experience how the constructions were made, which aspects needed to be improved and how they could contribute to and work with it.

109 Gershenfeld, 2005.
110 RepRapWiki, 2013.
111 www.bitsfrombytes.com.

This act of sharing appeared to trigger a lot of valuable contributions to the project. Via e-mail, events, forums, blogs and chat, a series of negotiations took place with technical experts, designers and amateurs. By making the project public, several elements quickly became matters of concern that were resolved collectively. During the mapping, it became clear that especially the exchange between several people in order to solve issues concerning air pressure and clay paste were an important 'thing' in Unfold's project. The 'Bits from Bytes' online forum became a place of exchange in this quest and even offered to be a sponsor of Unfold's project by providing material. Also, the research into an interface that could allow people to 'mould' clay became a 'thing'. Via a small Belgium-based RepRap user group, which Unfold co-founded and used to document aspects of their making process, a colleague designer expressed his interest in finding a solution together with them. Together, they came up with a digital pottery disk, making use of a laser that scans hand movements and projects the resulting design on a screen (see: Image 24). Not only the elements that allowed for printing and moulding clay but also the way in which the printer — as a whole — was manufactured, became an object that stimulated exchange between people. The designers created the printer as an unfinished design, clearly showing seams between its components. They did this so it could easily be deconstructed and remixed by the participants. The printer was conceived as an assembly, consisting of components that were obviously brought in from various perspectives. They made clear that not only the artistic and design related viewpoints but also the engineering or end-user's perspectives, the older technique of ceramics and the newer discourse around open-source 3D printing were present in the creation process of the printer. To experience the printer as a whole, not only the online documentation but also the physical set-up of l'Artisan Electronique enabled participation. Several exhibitions and fairs offered participants the possibility to see and use the printer themselves and make their own pottery with it. Participants could mould clay via the digital interface, push the save button when they were happy with the design displayed on the screen and see how their personally made pots were printed and displayed or documented in a physical cabinet in an exhibition room.

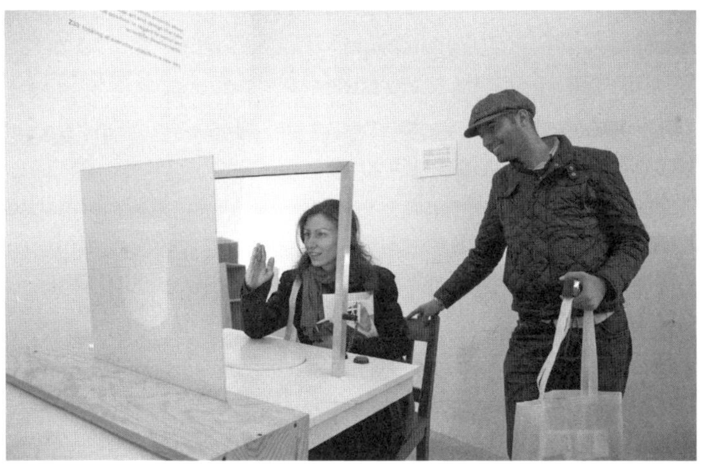

Image 24 **Moulding clay** Photo by @KristofVrancken/Z33

From this, we may conclude that sharing was a key element for Unfold. They engaged in this risky trade-off with various people, dealt with some important questions and gained interest for and discussions about their project. Via sharing, Unfold thus aimed for interesting contributions to their project but also embraced the uncertainty coming from an (international) audience taking over parts of their project and using it for their own ends. During the mapping (see: Image 25), it became clear that Unfold even tried to document some of the uses of their project by other participants, supporting these uses and participating in them. For instance, on their blog, Unfold documented how an Israeli student used some of the knowledge created during their project to build his own ceramic printer. 'Eran graduated this June with a fantastic, massive 80x80x80 cm darwin style printer that prints porcelain in a continuous way using a commercial moineau pump and a refilling plunger type extruder he developed'.[112] They tried, and still try, to keep the participants' appropriation activities alive via a thorough strategy of sharing. This strategy also forms the basis of deviations on the l'Artisan Electronique project, such as the example of the Israeli student. We explore this aspect of deviation further in 3.3.

Case Study 6: Touchatag

Touchatag is '… a starter kit and some client software', through which '… you can program your own RFID tags so that they can do anything you want them to do.

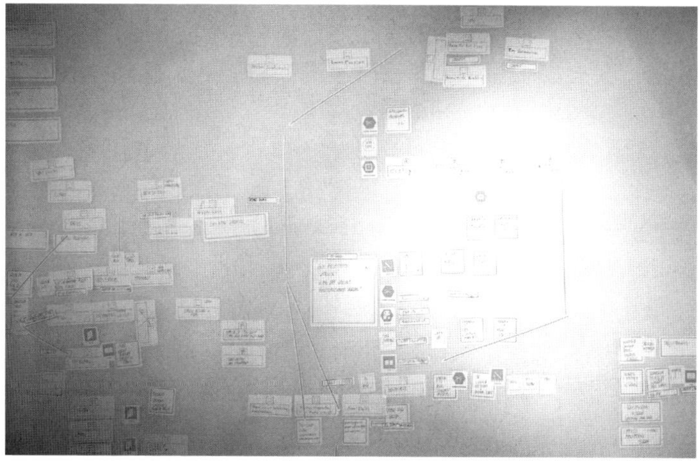

Image 25 **Mapping Unfold**

They can launch an application, deliver you to a URL ...'[113] The kit contains a small RFID reader (Radio Frequency Identification, comparable to a very small computer) and RFID stickers (see: Image 26). This RFID, integrated in a sticker, can contain digital information. The sticker can be stuck on an object, e.g. a book, and can be scanned and read with an electronic device, e.g. a mobile phone. On the screen of the mobile phone a short video may appear with an interview by the author of the book. One of the important challenges of the Touchatag project was to find out how this toolkit — once it was launched on the market — would engage end-users to participate in finding new, creative applications for it and in sharing their creations online.

112 Unfold, n.d.
113 Touchatag, n.d.

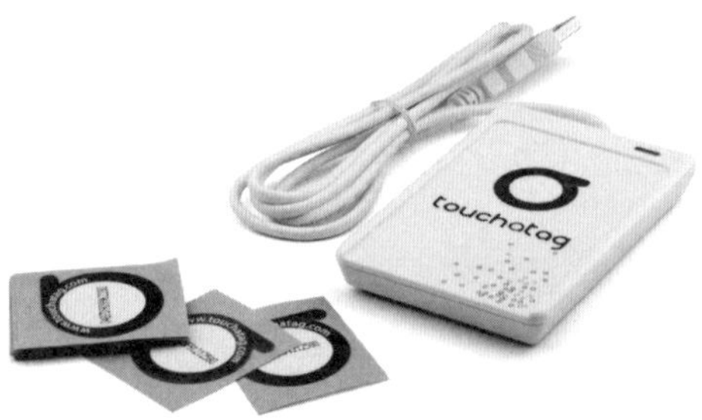

Image 26 **Touchatag, toolkit**

Touchatag results from a large-scale telecommunication project by Alcatel-Lucent. The project team included designers, engineers and human scientists. The team gathered around the issue of creating a playful telecommunication toolkit that allowed people to make things talk (literally). They hoped that 'talking things' could enable a different form of communication between people — instead of, for instance, a classic telephone call — and stimulate participatory creative work between various people. From the start, this project aimed for long-term participation. Therefore, the creative team explicitly started co-creating the tool with various groups of participants in order to answer their needs. During a long period of time, several 'things' were created between makers and participants. For instance, the project team of Alcatel-Lucent allowed participant groups to create their own urban game or digital diary, using a prototype version of the kit. This enabled the team to evaluate the ways in which people would appropriate the toolkit.

When the toolkit was finished, the team became involved in the risky trade-off of handing over control of the product to the online participants. On the one hand, they did this — comparable to the Unfold case study — via several strategies of sharing in order to trigger the community to discuss and use the toolkit. On the other hand, they made the tool modular by offering tools to participants that enabled them to reconfigure it, with a flexible but not completely open script.[114] The RFID stickers could be placed on any object or surface and their content and interactions could be reprogrammed on both Microsoft Windows and Mac OS X platforms. An application was also available for Linux platforms, although unsupported by the company. The modular toolkit aimed at enabling participants to personalise the toolkit. However, at the same time, the Touchatag project team was aware that they were making a risky trade-off by only approaching participants with some technical expertise or interest. Nevertheless, they did their best to engage a larger group of participants. For instance, Touchatag created a website on which they challenged online participants to experiment with the toolkit in successive 'things'. They set up a contest for creating an urban game with the stickers, which triggered many experiments. They also documented the creative experiments by participants with the toolkit on the website, in order to inspire other participants. Even though the Touchatag toolkit

114 See: Storni, 2009.

was released under a protective copyright licence of the company, the application was creatively repurposed in unexpected ways on many other platforms, beyond the company's control. For instance, although the company intentionally designed Touchatag as a commercial electronic 'wallet' or as a toolkit to create games, the designer @Hugobiwan created a very low-tech tool for architects to design collaboratively via the Internet. He placed the RFID stickers on foam miniature bricks that could be physically moved by, for instance, one architect in Belgium and another in China. He made an application that could visualise these 'tagged' bricks and their movements in a digital, online environment (see: Image 27). Also, hacker communities used the toolkit to hack the Amsterdam OV chip card to enter public transport for free. We believe this underlines how generative projects always develop in multidirectional ways between participants and the makers.

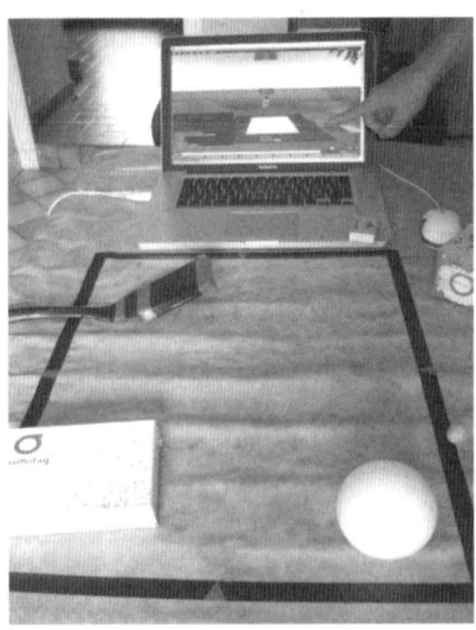

Image 27 CC-by Marie Amelie Subile, mixed reality @Hugobiwan

For a long time, Touchatag sold the hardware with protected software. However, the company decided to end their activities because Alcatel-Lucent — not the Touchatag brand — 'began providing mobile wallet and mobile marketing solutions to mobile network operators. This is the market we are currently engaged in and will continue to serve, this means we cannot support touchatag anymore'.[115] With the idea of stopping the service, the organisation referred more freely to other possible software that could work on the hardware platform:

> your hardware will continue working but our service will not work anymore. We have seen many of you using our hardware with software like libnfc and processing, so we are confident that the majority of you will be fine. For those that do not run their own application or service, there are some alternatives available that you can use with your touchatag hardware. You could try out iotope.com. This service is as close as you can get to the touchatag service. It is still in the early stages, but you can already use your old touchatag weblink apps with it.[116]

115 Touchatag, n.d.
116 Ibid.

Stopping the Touchatag service illustrates how participatory projects are a continuous negotiation between makers and participants. In this case, the makers lost their interest in the project. The future will tell if the Touchatag project can survive without the makers' continuous challenging of participants via their website.

As was the case in the l'Artisan Electronique case study, the Touchatag project illustrates that even though makers want to put more responsibility into the hands of the participants in order to stimulate them to create projects that deviate from their original ideas and concepts, these projects still require a lot of time investment from the makers. This investment is often made without the certainty of return in the sense of ideas or financial gains. The case of Touchatag (see: Image 28) also shows how risky trade-offs between makers and participants can take place by making a project modular. The original makers did some research into how their toolkit could be made modular by experimenting with how participants would appropriate it. The participants often used this modularity in unexpected ways, by creating applications that stretched the borders of what the makers thought or even wished that participants would do with the toolkit. This aspect of makers and participants having deviant expectations and making deviant uses of the same tools or platforms is dealt with in the next case study concerning the Arduino microcontroller.

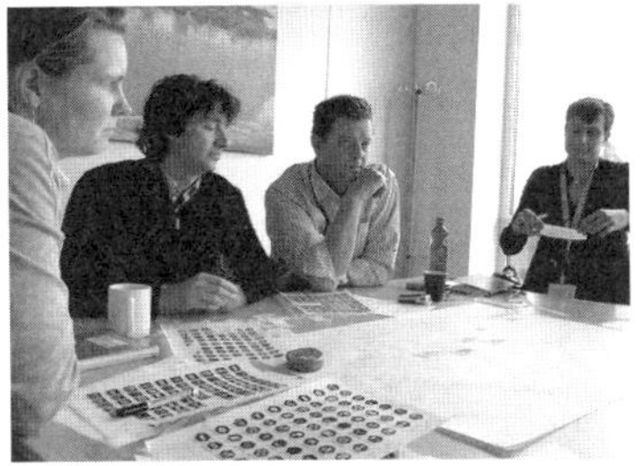

Image 28 **The Mapping of Touchatag**

Case Study 7: Arduino

Arduino has gained wide visibility in the field of Interaction Design and Media Art and in supporting communities of DIY enthusiasts, hobbyists, digital artists and hackers. The Arduino is an open-source electronics prototyping platform based on flexible, easy-to-use hardware and software. It is intended for anyone who is interested in creating interactive objects or environments. On Arduino's official website, it is stated that the Arduino is an open-source physical computing platform based on a simple microcontroller board and a development environment for writing software for the board (see: Image 29).[117]

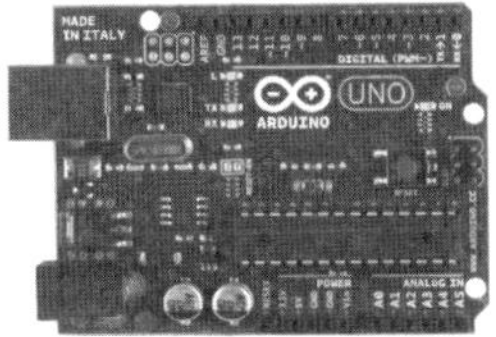

Image 29 **Arduino Uno Front, Creative Commons Arduino**
Pic http://arduino.cc/en/uploads/Main/ArduinoUnoFront.jpg

117 www.arduino.cc.

The Arduino was invented in an Interaction Design Institute in Northern Italy concerned with teaching and educating design students (with different, not necessarily technical, backgrounds) in new emerging fields of design, intersecting with computer science and engineering (e.g. tangible computing, mobile and ubiquitous computing). The teachers were facing the problem that available programming boards for tangible computing were expensive and based on not widespread, often difficult to learn programming languages. Moreover, available boards were difficult to adapt as they were protected by copyrights. Massimo Banzi, one of the teachers of the module in tangible interaction, said:

> We already work with Processing a lot. At that time Processing was limited to visual animations. When dealing with tangible and real-time interaction we had to use another language. One day we asked ourselves: "Why not to have Processing to generate programs for our hardware too?"[118]

A specific module for the Processing language was implemented so that students would not have to learn another language to program hardware in their tangible real-time interactions design works. One student (Hernando Barragán) had already started to develop a prototyping board (called 'Wiring'). On this initiative, the original concern with enabling the design of tangible interaction was translated into an even simpler board. This board was perhaps less powerful than the 'Wiring' or the more traditional ones, but easier to use, open-source and compatible with the processing programming environment. In a few weeks — thanks to a series of collaborations among some volunteers in the Italian design institute — the first board was ready. It consisted of a series of ports for inputs from sensors (for motion, light, proximity, et cetera), a series of output ports connected with whatever actuator is used (motors, lights, computer devices, et cetera) and a central processor (a micro-controller chip) with a flash memory where written code (written in Processing) could be stored.

Along with this first series of prototypes, workshops with students and interested design teachers were organised to gather interest and test the board. Early prototypes were given away to teachers for free in order to explore the possibility of adopting the Arduino for their classrooms. In a few months, the Arduino board gained widespread popularity in design institutes all over Europe and within many DIY communities feeding on the phenomenon of open hardware. Hobbyists from all around the world suggested changes and improvements to the programming language, to the software and also to the physical board. People used Arduino to build their own robots, amateur UAVs (Unmanned Aerial Vehicles), music electronic gadgets and interactive systems. Expert users published

118 Storni, 2008.

their projects while inexperienced users took advantage of the many step-by-step tutorials available on the Internet. Also, companies and magazines contributed to the distribution of the Arduino. The firm Botanicals, for instance, developed an Arduino-powered device that monitors houseplants and indicates when they need to be watered. Interested people can buy or, obviously, make the device themselves. Makezine.com inaugurated an Arduino section by introducing the board as the best all-around centrepiece to a modern electronics project and by listing step-by-step tutorials on how to build nice gadgets with the Arduino. Also, Ponoko.com — one of the biggest DIY technology websites — sells Arduino-based products along with a series of add-ons to the board. The Arduino could not have taken off without all this (human) support. Since the initial development of the Arduino, its original developer has been in continuous contact and collaborating with a growing global community of Arduino enthusiasts. This led to the development of different versions fitting different purposes and design settings. For instance, for those projects intending to use the Arduino to build wearable computing solutions, a lighter and smaller version of the board (called 'Lilypad Arduino', see: Image 30) was developed to be embedded in clothes and different types of fabric.

However, apart from the (human) support the Arduino received, its generative qualities appeared to be strongly related to the openness of the project for deviant uses. Not all the versions of the Arduino can

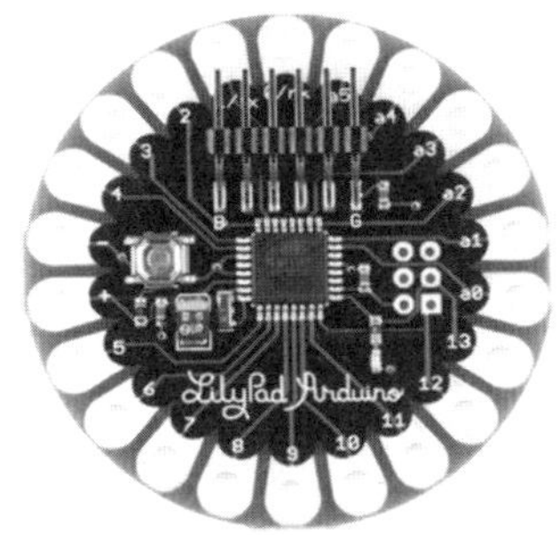

Image 30 **Lilypad Arduino, Creative Commons Arduino**
Image snapshot website, http://arduino.cc/en/Main/Products

be considered as being part of the Arduino family, in the sense of sharing the same development environment, set of licenses and brand. It should be said that, first of all, the Arduino itself branched off of a previous board (the Wiring) that was more difficult to use and more expensive. Second, the Arduino produced a series of separations in its early adoption between adopter (cooperatively adopting and sharing improvements of the board) and critics (competitively proposing alternative boards). Indeed, it is incorrect (and reductionist) to conclude that the design of the Arduino board and its characteristics (open design, available schematics, availability of accessible online tutorials, et cetera) simply enrol users and other elements in a cooperative whole that represents an ideal instance of collective participation in a design. Participation might not necessarily be about a collaborative effort to build something together. Indeed, it can also manifest itself as a sort of competitive separation that, instead of creating sharing and cooperation, creates divisions or 'deviationism'. It is true that the Arduino board — as a design associated with other inscriptions such as licences and other tools — also divides participants. Some early Arduino users, for instance, were not happy with the schematics provided on the website (which are not the traditional PCB files). They felt that making a compatible board was 'not easy' (enough) and users had to reverse-engineer the original Arduino board. Other users asked for more computational power or expressed their needs for different types of microcontrollers. The following extract of a discussion in a popular online community where technological innovations are promoted and discussed, illustrates these controversies:

> Don't forget the Arduino official homepage [arduino.cc]. It's simple, very hackable, Mac and Linux-compatible and it's a true free/open-source design, so they don't have a monopoly on it and you can buy compatible boards from other sources or DIY!

Three hours later, SuperBanana replied by contrasting YA_python and wrote:

> Actually, it's not an open-source design; Arduino is an actively protected trademark and they do control who manufactures it, because they

> won't release the files necessary to manufacture the circuit board. Without them, you cannot (easily) make a compatible board; you have to reverse-engineer it. Which is precisely what some people, fed up with not being able to make their own Arduino boards, went and did. Freeduino, *is* actually free and open-source (and compatible) and they have specifically said that people are welcome to use the Freeduino name. All Arduino proves is that people will slap "free" and "open-source" on just about anything, and there's no shortage of people who will parrot it.

A few hours after a new comment popped up from someone from the MAKE site who refuted the claim made by SuperBanana:

> ...what you're saying is not accurate. i'll do my best to address your comments. 1. Arduino is open-source, anyone can make them and they released all the files. just check the site you'll see all the downloads, if you can't find them email me. 2. the *name* is trademarked, this is likely the confusion. you can make Arduino clones all you want in china, you just can't call them Arduino. just

> like you can make other versions of Firefox but you can't call yours Firefox.

(YA_Python_dev, Friday October 24, 'do not forget the ARDUINO!!!').[119]

Licenses appeared to be key in allowing deviations on the original board. The schematics and design files of the Arduino board are released under the 'Attribution share alike 3.0 Creative Commons' license, under which anyone is allowed to produce copies of the board, to redesign it or even to sell boards that copy the design, without paying a license fee to the Arduino team, or asking their permission. In an extensive article on open hardware boards, *Wired* provided a provoking description of this aspect:

> You can send the plans off to a Chinese factory, mass-produce the circuit boards, and sell them yourself - pocketing the profit without paying the creator a penny in royalties. Arduino developers won't sue you. Actually, they are sort of hoping you'll do it.[120]

However, in order to republish the reference design, the original Arduino group has to be credited. By tweaking or changing the board, the new design automatically uses the same or a similar Creative Commons license. This ensures that new versions of the board will equally be without fees and open to future modification and redesign. The language used to program the microcontroller is borrowed from Processing, an easy FLOSS programming language originally intended for graphic design. The language has been extended by the Arduino team with a particular module in order to deal with microcontroller physical boards. The Arduino's integrated development environment to write the code and flash it into the board, is a piece of software released under the GNU GPL license, embodying a copy-left clause that gives participants the right to change and distribute the software, provided that new enhancements are released under the same licence.[121] The Arduino website, where a collection of code examples from the user community is growing on a daily basis, is also released under Creative Commons allowing free use of all the scripts, code and tricks posted by partici pants. Moreover, as spin-offs from the design of the original Arduino, a whole new series of projects (e.g. 'Freeduino' (see: Image 31), 'Sanguino' and 'Pinguino') emerged based on the actual modification of the board. These projects embody a separation from the original collective and create environments for the birth of new alternative routes for the development of similar boards. In some cases, these deviations and separations might also occur as an effect of the board reflecting different ideologies and understandings of users, in other words through creating interesting controversies.

119 Hardware Slashdot, 2013.
120 Thompson, 2008.
121 GNU, 2013.

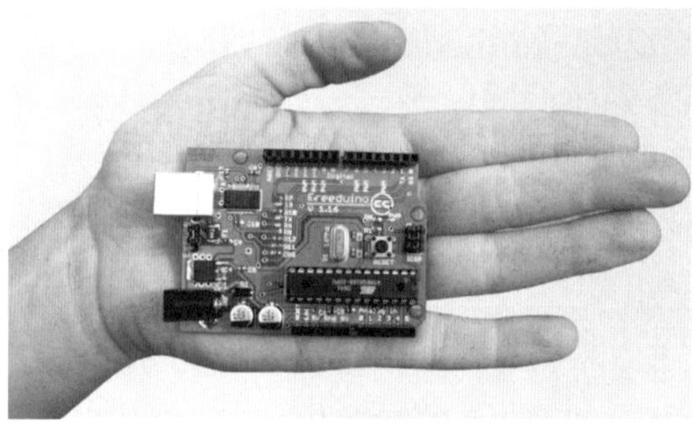

Image 31 **Freeduino, Wikicommons**
http://upload.wikimedia.org/wikipedia/commons/f/fc/Freeduino_hand.jpg

Our first reflections in the literature overview mainly pointed to the importance of time in generative projects. However, as we indicated, this time factor was quite vaguely described. The Arduino case study made clear that the possibility of a project to evolve over time and to be taken over by participants is related to the allowance of deviations in a project. We now clarify this aspect of deviation in the following discussion.

Discussion: Generativity in Participation

In projects that aim at triggering on-going participation in use-time, the two discussed concepts of generativity and hybridity seem to go hand in hand. The first is thoroughly discussed by Muller and by us (see chapter 2) and describes how participatory projects are an uncertain, hybrid zone.[122] As mentioned before, this zone is created by makers and participants through making projects together as collages, carrying imperfect characteristics. These are stimulating factors for makers and participants to interpret things together. In this chapter, we have focused on how makers and participants can support the generativity of projects. In this context, we referred to projects in which participants continue to participate, even without a lot of support from the maker(s) of a participatory project.

The three case studies that we discussed investigated the ability of a project to generate participation in use-time. From these case studies we may conclude that this generativity is mainly built around three types of trade-offs taking place between makers and participants: (1) making a project shareable (as we saw in the case of the l'Artisan Electronique), (2) modular (the Touchatag case) and (3) embracing deviations (the case study of Arduino). Two things are important to mention here. First, in relation to our proposed relational understanding of participatory projects, we do not see these trade-offs as 'recipes' or prerequisites that determine generativity. Second, as we mentioned, we propose to make the aspect of 'time' as discussed in our literature overview more concrete and translate it to makers and participants who allow deviations to occur in the project. We clarify this in the following sections where we describe the three risky trade-offs that emerged in the studied projects.

Shareability

As our literature overview and case studies show, makers and participants who aim for generating ongoing participation engage in the risky trade-off of sharing aspects of their projects with each other. Some of the authors we discussed made clear that making projects accountable for their functions and/or meaning can make participants more conscious about their rationale.[123] When sharing a project, this aspect of accountability is important. The hacker ethics also makes us understand that sharing can be a means to rethink traditional forms of authorship, by stimulating mutual learning and collaboration in horizontal, activist, wider distributed and open-ended settings.[124] The Unfold case study, for instance, showed that a possible advantage of sharing is that other participants improve certain elements of the project that pose difficulties for the makers (in this case, air pressure or clay past). Another advantage is that sharing communicates the project in a broad way. Via sharing, however, makers and participants also risk comments on or unexpected uses of their projects.

122 Muller, 2002; Huybrechts et al, 2012.
123 E.g. Randell, 2004; Dourish & Button, 1996; Bardzell, 2010.
124 E.g. Hannemyr, 1999; Raymond, 2001.

In order to investigate what it means to make a product or process shareable, we mentioned that sharing is a common practice in open-source environments. However, within these contexts, sharing most often refers to making the functionality of a product 'accessible'.[125] This means that the ways in which a project functions and works, and how it is manufactured and how it can be used, are made transparent. However, as Dix states, if makers want others to participate in their work and even appropriate it for other ends, both the functionality and the intent of the product or work need to be visible.[126] This was also stated by Bardzell, who stressed the importance of an artefact to disclose the ways it interacts with a subject.[127] We therefore proposed to pay more attention to the sharing of meaning, besides to sharing the functionality of a project.

When we looked into how sharing was realised in the case study of l'Artisan Electronique, the importance of meaning became clear. This case explored the 'horizontal' practice of sharing a project, in which the maker/author is put in a position that is more or less equal to that of the participants. First, a considerable amount of functional documentation was shared, in the sense that the making process and its problems and opportunities were made transparent via Unfold's blog. Here, the design collective explained in detail how the RepRap printer functioned and was rebuilt to print clay, so others could repeat and change it. The makers socially rewarded interesting documentation that was shared by participants, including critiques of and improvements to the project, by blogging about them on their project weblog. Second, the makers' aim to share their vision and interpretation of the 3D process appeared to be of great importance to the project. The makers of the printer mainly aimed at stimulating reflection around today's approach to 3D printing in both commercial and open-source communities. Effectively, on Unfold's blog and other forums, a reflective process started about the future of 3D printing, design and pottery in which online participants discussed the project's opportunities. It was this more imaginative discourse around the meaning of the 3D printer that drove a large part of the international online discussion. It also stimulated many suggestions for improvements by online participants. This is similar to what Van Osch & Avital describe as a generative system being evocative and challenging participants to explore new perspectives, insights and actions via reflective dialogues.[128] The imaginative documentation of the meaning of projects is thus certainly something that both makers and participants can pay attention to when sharing their (contributions to) projects.

Modularity

The HCI, PD and CSCW literature also pointed out that sharing, or making a project accountable, is not the only factor that drives participation. Projects should

125 As mentioned by, for instance, Kanstrup, 2012.
126 Dix, 2007.
127 Bardzell, 2010.
128 Van Osch & Avital, 2009.

also allow some kind of affective modelling via offering participants opportunities, tools and social rewards.[129] As the case studies also showed, an open and flexible form may contribute to new creative applications of projects,[130] since people are able to experiment freely and might create projects that they would not have been able to produce from scratch.[131] In literature, this quality of participatory projects was referred to as modularity.[132] We discussed that this aspect of modularity should be understood broadly, as not only referring to making functions modular but also as a way to share meanings and open projects up to creative re-interpretation. The analyses of our case studies underlined this.

The case studies illustrated modularity as a second risky trade-off that makers and participants make in order to generate on-going participation. Important here was how the makers made their projects modular via their seamful character or by releasing them as unfinished, under-designed and interpretable. Zittrain referred to modularity as a project's capacity to be reprogrammed and repurposed via passing on means to make content, rather than passing on content.[133] The literature also underlined that creating patterns — as we mentioned earlier — is a way to make a design modular. Patterns provide a language to structure a design or parts of it. This makes design more flexible, modular and ultimately reusable.[134] Furthermore, the cultural field as well has inspired definitions of modularity. Manovich for instance, describes modularity as makers and participants making well-defined parts of functions and content related to the finished cultural object.[135] These can be used as building blocks for new objects. Manovich refers to two forms of modularity, being maker-driven and participant-driven modularity. The first type of modularity starts from a 20th-century notion, in which makers make finished projects, by using a small vocabulary of elemental shapes or modules. In this sense, modularity implies that the project, objects or software in the project are offered in pieces or patterns. They are small building blocks that can be reconfigured (like Lego bricks, wooden blocks, samples or electronic parts) by both makers and participants. This principle of modularity is illustrated by the Touchatag case. Manovich states that there is also a second type of modularity :

> ... that may appear like a contradiction in terms. It is modularity without a priori defined vocabulary. In this scenario, any well-defined part of any finished cultural object can automatically become a building block for new objects in the same medium. Parts can even "publish" themselves and other cultural objects

129 Fisher et al., 2004.
130 Huybrechts, 2011.
131 Open-source initiative, 2010.
132 See e.g. Zittrain, 2008.
133 Ibid.
134 Gamma et al., 1995.
135 Manovich, 2005.

> can "subscribe" to them the way you subscribe now to RSS feeds or podcast.[136]

This concept of modularity facilitates remixing, for instance. In remixing practices, modules from different sources (independent of their medium, while modularity is limited to a medium or source) are brought together. In their overview on media art, Tribe & Jana value remixability as a reflection of the changing status of artistic originality, in a context of mass-produced culture.[137] They point to the fact that, although the laws on intellectual property and access of material have become stricter, this remixing practice has kept on flourishing. This second approach to modularity can entail that makers and participants share or modify some parts of a project, allowing the project to be adapted or 'abnormally' transformed, such as a chair becoming a coat stand or magnets on the fridge turning into a message board.[138] This is the case in many projects that are created in the — already mentioned — context of Design for Hackability, DIY and DIWO. In the art world, examples are Duchamp's ready-mades, Höch's Dadaist photomontages and Pop Art's remixing of advertisements. Sampling and remixing practices also occur frequently in popular music: hip-hop or electronic dance music borrow and recombine musical fragments and create new versions of familiar songs.[139]

The Touchatag project was intended to be modular. Touchatag offered building blocks in the form of stickers and software to add digital information to these stickers. Next to these functional building blocks or 'patterns', they shared snippets of meaningful documentation of good practices around the project. These meaningful patterns appeared to be very important in order to motivate and inspire people to use the toolkit. As the Touchatag case study showed, the risk of using modularity was that it made it difficult to understand for non-technical experts. Using and matching the patterns in the Touchatag case requires — though sometimes little — insight in code and interaction. However, this risk also enabled participants to make their own version of the project and contribute to it as, for example, the collaborative architectural modelling-tool illustrated.

In the research phase of the Touchatag project, an early prototype of the toolkit was shared with many people in many forms to see what creative reuses would result from it. In this phase, there was no completely modular toolkit, but the maker team made 'on-the-spot', small adaptations to the toolkit in relation to the participant's needs of, for instance, playing a game. Modular elements thus resulted from the participatory sessions, inspired by both makers and participants, and illustrated its meaning as participant-driven. Once it was launched, the Touchatag venture offered a completely modular toolkit to participants.

136 Ibid., p.3.
137 Tribe & Jana, 2006.
138 Brandes & Erlhoff, 2009.
139 Tribe & Jana, op. cit.

Here, modularity was obviously defined in a maker-driven way. Although inspired by work with participants, it was mainly the Touchatag project team (i.e. the makers) that decided what was made modular and what 'seams' the design showed.[140] The project was careful, and tried to avoid too much uncertainty by not allowing participants to repurpose the tool in unexpected ways. However, when the Touchatag service ended its activities, it — as was the case in project-time — openly pointed to possible alternative software that people could use to continue using the hardware toolkit and thus appropriate it in a more participant-driven way.

In the project-phase and after the service was stopped, Touchatag used a very participant-driven concept of modularity. In the meantime, they held on to a more maker-driven, 'flexible', but not completely 'open' toolkit.[141] They limited the modularity to what people essentially needed to superficially tailor the toolkit: modular stickers that could be endlessly repositioned, a programming language that allowed to attach fragments of digital information to the stickers and snippets of documentation that could inspire the participants. On a functional level, they provided access to a DIY guide and to some applications that made it possible to reconfigure the toolkit. On a level of meaning, they shared documentation of good practices in repurposing the toolkit and comments by participants on the toolkit and the applications. Modularity is a way for makers and participants to give others the opportunity to flexibly further develop their projects — for instance, by remixing them — without the certainty that this will lead to results the maker intended or would approve of. The case study showed that although uncertainty can never be avoided when making projects modular, the degree of uncertainty that is allowed by the makers appears to be very diverse and can depend on, for instance, the phase the project is in.

Deviationism

To some extent, the Arduino too can be seen as an instance of a modular design. It is rather flexible and allows the participant to build all sorts of interactive products by taking advantage of a virtually endless array of sensors, actuators, Arduino shields, all sorts of hacked devices and so on. The Arduino case study is, however, even more illustrative of a third risky trade-off that resonates with the idea of generativity. We will call this particular risky trade-off 'deviationism'.

In his book on adversarial design, DiSalvo talks about the importance of making room for conflict and discussion in participatory projects, thereby shifting the traditional overemphasis on agreement and consensus.[142] We link deviationism to a process that creates divisions and separations within one 'thing' and generates new unexpected branches, adaptations or versions. Deviationism describes how participation in a participatory project can take the form of a deviation from the

140 E.g. Weiser, 1994.
141 Storni, 2009.
142 DiSalvo, 2012.

original intention and vision of the maker(s). This was very clear in the Arduino case study in which several deviant ideas and concepts were developed around what the Arduino was and how it should be developed further. These debates led to several alternative versions, such as the Freeduino. This specific risky trade-off entails that the engagement in participatory exchanges can lead to deviant results. Makers and participants can feel more or less comfortable with these deviant uses. The Arduino case study showed that deviant uses — such as the Freeduino — were mostly tolerated by the original makers, but led to some discussions.

From our literature review, we learned that — especially in the field of art — deviationism is part of a generative participatory project. Deviationism is a difficult factor to control, since makers cannot predict if the project is effectively changed or even contested and taken up by participants in new branches. This might explain why the literature we reviewed was more explicit about how to share a project or how to make a project modular, but contained no strong statements about deviationism. Looking at the case studies, minor deviant uses of the discussed platforms, such as the Lilypad Arduino, were explicitly supported, while more intense deviations, such as the Freeduino, were rather tolerated. When minor deviant uses were supported, the Arduino makers and participants invested time in following up how people used, reused, and reworked the project in their own organisation or work. This investment is risky and uncertain because original makers do not necessarily know beforehand what this investment will bring. For instance, we mentioned that, since the first development of the Arduino, the original developer invested time in managing continuous contact and collaboration with a growing global community of Arduino enthusiasts. Gradually, this community started to develop different versions fitting different purposes and design settings. Also, we saw that in order to support a project to branch into deviant forms over time, special attention to the possibility of distributed ownership is required.[143] The case study of Arduino underlined the importance of licenses to allow and facilitate this distributed ownership. The board schematics and design files of the Arduino are released under the 'Attribution share alike 3.0 Creative Commons' license, which allows producing copies of the board, redesigning it, or even selling boards that copy the design.

Especially this aspect of deviationism in generative projects — besides sharing and making projects modular — emphasises the uncertainties that makers and participants have to embrace in order to create ongoing, generative participation. Building towards ongoing participation asks for a lot of time and trade-offs and the results of building participation are never certain. Although specific actions may facilitate possible success in generating participation, they certainly never determine it.

143 See: Zittrain, 2008.

Conclusion

We want to end this chapter with a final reflection upon our literature review and empirical work. We approached all participatory projects that we studied as 'things', socio-technical assemblies that are continuously in movement. In the literature on participation, only a minor part of studies revolves around this continuous and on-going process of participation. In this chapter, we approached participation via the concept of generativity. Therefore, we presented an overview of this on-going practice and some in-depth case studies. Our analyses showed that — however advantageous — generative participatory projects involve risks and uncertainties. We approached generative projects as risky trade-offs between makers and participants, where choices are made in the hope that they will increase the generative participatory activity, but may lead to unexpected or unintended results. Specifically, we distinguished three risky trade-offs in relation to generativity, being shareability, modularity and deviationism (these three trade-offs are visualised in Image 32). The combination of risk-taking and uncertain outcomes may cause makers and participants to hesitate in trying to enable generativity. Still, we propose to stimulate makers and participants to engage in these trade-offs, since they can lead to interesting projects, as we believe that the Arduino, l'Artisan Electronique and Touchatag case studies showed. We distinguished the risky trade-offs in the case studies, but not as being determinant for participation. We also believe that more research is

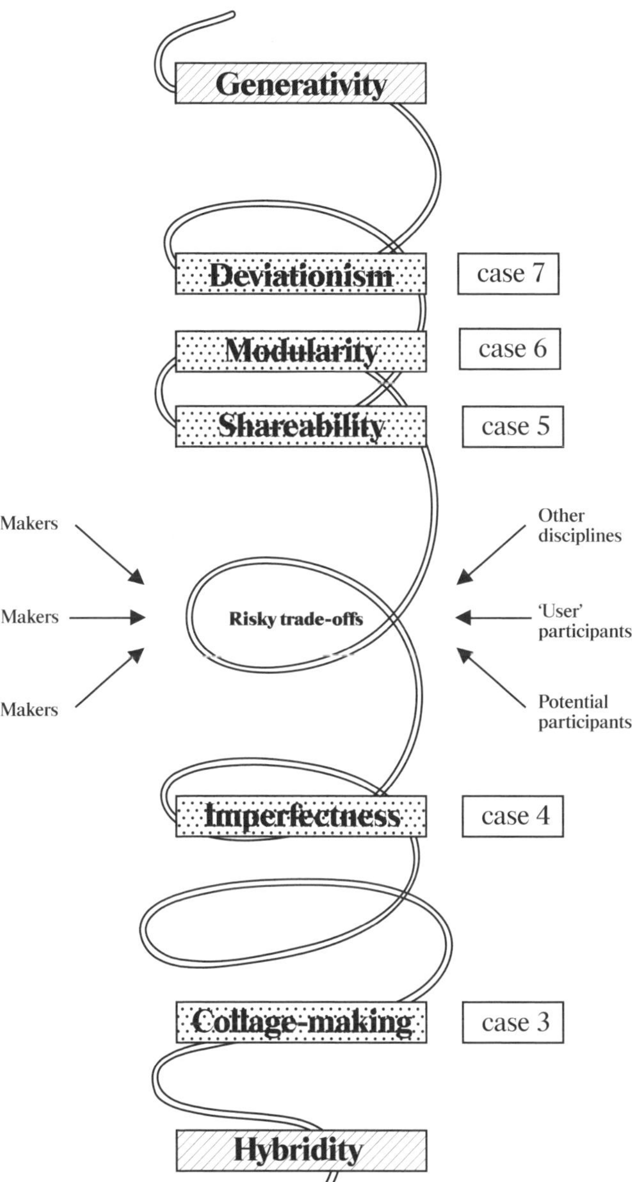

Image 32 **Visualisation of the three risky trade-offs related to generativity**

needed to uncover them in all their complexity.

Three aspects clearly deserve more attention for research into the generative potential of participatory projects. First of all, sharing in participatory projects still mostly points to how makers and participants exchange documentation of how a project 'works' or functions. However, the sharing of meaning and imagination appears to be very stimulating for the discussions among participants about the project. We see this as an interesting track for further study. Second, making a project modular does not mean it opens up itself completely for participation. We clearly distinguished multiple maker-driven and participant-driven forms of modularity. Makers still have the tendency — even when they make a project modular — to control what people can do with it. They are rather hesitant to tolerate, let alone support deviant uses. However, these deviant uses appear to be fruitful for the generative potential of the project. This brings us to our third point. As the Participatory Art literature shows, 'durational' participatory projects, extending beyond the initial participants and intentions, tolerate or support deviant uses.[144] Making a time investment in following up deviant developments of the project and providing feedback to participants contributed to this aspect. Also, allowing distributed ownership by setting up the appropriate project licenses can be helpful. It is especially this last aspect of deviationism in participatory projects that has been little explored, but appears to be a key trade-off that makers and participants involve in when engaging in participatory projects.

Mappings

Huybrechts, L. & Hendriks, N. .(2010). Antwerp: mapping Unfold. Available at: unfold.be and www.map-it.be/mapping-reports/mapping-unfold

Huybrechts, L. & Machils, P. (2009). Antwerp: mapping Alcatel-Lucent (Touchatag). Available at: www.alcatel-lucent.com and www.map-it.be/mapping-reports/mapping-smart-touch-browsing-through-smart-objects-around-you-touchatag

144 See our review of participatory art literature by e.g. O'Neill, 2011.

Conclusion
Participation Is a Risky Trade-off

When making art works, interfaces, products, services and toolkits (i.e. projects), artists and designers (i.e. makers) work in a great complexity and a variety of contexts (e.g. a museum context in contrast to a nursery home). Using a participatory approach can contribute to our understanding of these contexts, integrating the questions, needs and desires of the participants involved in the projects under development. In such an approach, participation means that makers engage with different, both professional and lay participants, contributing meaningfully to the creation process of a project. Participation can also be considered as a way to keep a project flexible and alive, even when the initial makers are less involved in it.

The participatory approaches and projects we looked at in this book are as diverse as the contexts they are situated in. Nonetheless, in their diversity we discovered some recurring aspects that may be informative for makers and participants, who (want to) engage in participatory projects. Although many definitions of participatory projects exist, we focused on the dynamics taking place between makers and participants. These dynamics are driven by the advantages that makers and participants want to gain from their involvement in a participatory process. At the same time, they also consist of the inevitable uncertainties that makers (have to) deal with when engaging in a participatory project. This is the reason why we characterised participatory projects by the on-going negotiations or 'risky trade-offs' that take place between makers and participants.

Participatory Projects are Risky Trade-offs

Participatory projects can be characterised by the *risky trade-offs* that continuously take place between makers and participants. Therefore, participatory projects are not defined by the objects they produce, such as a piece of technology with specific functions. Rather, we see them as socio-material assemblies where the partaking elements, being people and objects, mutually define and shape each other. We call these assemblies (of objects and people) '*things*', describing makers and participants who participate in collaborative — but also competing — activities around certain objects, topics, issues, contexts, et cetera, such as a specific technical issue.[1]

None of the elements involved in risky trade-offs (such as the makers, the participants or technical objects or issues) should be understood as determinants or prerequisites for (certain forms of) participation. Participation is not caused by putting certain specific 'recipes' in play. Rather, it is a process that is open-ended and difficult to control, in which makers, participants and their concerns and objects intersect. Both the process and the outcomes of the risky trade-offs (that makers and participants engage with) can therefore be satisfying, but they are always uncertain.[2]

We described how these trade-offs can take place in **two key moments** — project-time and use-time —

1 Latour, 2005.
2 Huybrechts et al., 2012.

and can demand, more or less strong or explicit participation from the people involved. In chapter 2, we focused on project-time. In project-time, the trade-offs are often strongly moderated by a (group of) maker(s) who organise people's participation with an eye on generating new ideas for future products or works. In use-time, however, trade-offs are mostly self-organised via a group of participants, often independently from the makers, with an infrastructure (such as a platform to exchange ideas around 3D printing) to organise their participatory exchanges. In chapter 3, we concentrated on these trade-offs that enable participation in use-time.[3]

To elaborate on risky trade-offs, we studied two levels on which participation takes place. First of all, we noticed that, in the exchanges between makers and participants, different types of participants are involved. Second, we zoomed in on the risky trade-offs themselves, which take place between makers and participants. Here, we focused on the — more complex — level of the 'thing', wherein people and objects interact. In this context, we discussed participatory projects via two concepts, being hybridity (specifically, in project-time) and generativity (specifically, in use-time).

Risky Trade-offs on the Level of Participants

In the first chapter, we observed that in participatory projects trade-offs take place between makers and different types of participants. During project-time, in the projects we discussed, makers engage with professionals from different disciplines. Also, all the projects we described involve — in more or less intense ways — 'user' participants or what are often called 'audiences' or 'users'. In use-time, the types of participants engaged in the project are diverse, being a mix between professionals and 'user' participants. Therefore, this type of participant is unpredictable. We called them potential participants, since they are participants who are not yet involved in the participatory projects but could become committed to the project in the future.

The types of participants (in relation to the makers) define the kinds of risky exchanges that take place in the projects we studied. To illustrate this, we will now give a short overview.

In a participatory project, working together with different disciplines can be very fruitful and sometimes even necessary.

This has an advantage.

— The uncertain differences between makers and participants from different professional disciplines can be a productive factor in the project, leading to new concepts or materials (e.g. the collaboration between the art collective Blast Theory and an engineering group led to the rethinking of current applications of mobile technology). However, there are also various uncertainties in-

3 Ehn, 2008; Huybrechts, 2011.

volved in working together with different disciplines.

— The participants need to get out of their comfort zones (in relation to the project) in order to participate in the project (in a constructive way). (Blast Theory, for instance, indicated how they stepped out of their own comfort zone and worked together with many different stakeholders (such as an engineering group with technological expertise, festival organisers, private partners and game players) throughout the whole process of *Uncle Roy All Around You*).

— The visions or viewpoints (of people from different disciplines) may be too different or too distinct from each other, which makes it difficult to work together constructively in a cross-disciplinary setup (e.g. the visions of the art collective Constant vzw and the technical partners on open technologies were quite different. Therefore, they limited their collaboration to a rather superficial exchange of material, instead of really co-creating technologies and concepts together).

Opening up a project to comments or contributions from 'user' participants can be an important goal of a participatory project.

This has several advantages.

— It can lead to outcomes that relate more to the daily experience of the participants (e.g. via an intense engagement with the local youth, the

Patching Zone (Go-for-IT!) made an innovative game concept, starting from a daily practice in the neighbourhood — dribbling).

— It can lead to creative outcomes that makers may not have foreseen (e.g. in the case of Go-for-IT!, the residents of the neighbourhood played one of the prototypes of a game — developed by the Patching Zone — in their own, personal and, for the Patching Zone unexpected ways).

— However, there are also various uncertainties involved in opening up a project to 'user' participants.

— Input by 'user' participants can lead to unexpected and uncertain outcomes, such as adapted versions of a product that do not entirely match with the makers' intentions (e.g. the art collective the Patching Zone created a game that used QR codes to involve participants in exploring a local neighbourhood. The game was, however, never really used by the participants because their mobile phones were not able to read the codes properly).

A participatory project can aim for handing over the project to a (large) group of potential participants that were not immediately involved in the project.

This has several advantages.

— Handing over the project to a (large) group of potential participants allows the project to transcend project-time, which means that participation does not stop when the project is finished (e.g. in the case of Arduino, the original collective created an environment which allowed the development of new alternative similar boards. By handing over the project to future participants, the Arduino gave way to, among other things, the Freeduino, Sanguino and Pinguino).

— It may affect the project unexpectedly in a positive sense, meaning that the projects evolve in a better, more beautiful, et cetera way than foreseen by the maker — participants — (e.g. the Lilypad Arduino is a platform for making interactive textiles via Arduino, which was not possible before. This makes the Lilypad Arduino very valuable to the makers of Arduino).
— Participants with unexpected areas of expertise can guide the project into new directions or markets. However, there are also various uncertainties involved in handing over a project to potential participants.
— It may lead the project in unexpected directions, that are even outside of the control of the initial makers (e.g. the Freeduino is a spin-off product from the Arduino, a platform for making interactive products and installations, starting from a different philosophy. Freeduino claims to be a free, unrestricted licence, in contrast to the Arduino's protected trademark).
— Makers can be confronted with unknown/

unfamiliar participants, whose backgrounds and interests are unclear.

Considering the engagements between the makers and the three types of participants, we can clearly distinguish the core meaning of a trade-off. While engaging in participatory exchanges involves many uncertainties, it can deliver new possibilities and outcomes for a project. These uncertainties and possibilities are slightly different in relation to the various participants. To understand these trade-offs in more depth and to discover how they differ in project- and use-time, we took into account the affordances of the objects for participation between makers and various participants. Based on this, we saw that interesting participatory projects can be characterised by two concepts, being (p. 104) 'hybridity' and (p. 190), 'generativity', associated with some specific trade-offs between makers and participants. Again, while we described these trade-offs, we did not propose them as prerequisites or 'recipes' that, undoubtedly, will lead to participation. These trade-offs will always induce uncertainty about their process and outcomes.

Risky Trade-offs on the Level of Things

Taking into account the objects that makers and various participants gather around, we distinguished two concepts that describe challenging participatory projects, being 'hybridity' (p. 104) and 'generativity' (p. 190).

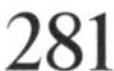

Hybridity

We used the concept of 'hybridity' to describe participatory projects that are situated on the border between participatory (participant-driven) and expert-based (maker-driven) approaches. Hybridity describes participatory projects that are constructed with in-between qualities.[4] This means that they are created by mixing elements (participants, objects, et cetera) from various domains, disciplines and contexts. These hybrid participatory projects form an in-between zone, a 'gluing element' or bonding agent that gathers disparate people, objects and contexts, stressing collectivism and shared ownership.[5] At the same time, it is a marginal space, carrying traits of previously disconnected or incompatible fields or discourses that do not belong to (one of) the participants, leading to uncertainty. Furthermore, hybridity refers to a situation of 'interpretative flexibility', in which projects generate different or alternative meanings for different social groups (makers of different disciplines, professionals and amateurs, journalists, et cetera). In these projects not only the ways in which people think about or interpret projects are flexible, but also the ways in which the projects are created.

We particularly focused on *project-time*, during which two main forms of risky trade-offs contribute to a hybrid character of participatory projects. These risky trade-offs include makers and participants exchanging via collage-making, on the one hand, and exchanging via (aspects of) projects with imperfect characteristics, on the other hand, as visualised in image 2.

We will now sum up these trade-offs that are characteristic for hybrid participatory projects.

Makers and participants in hybrid, participatory projects can engage in interesting exchanges via collage-making. Collages are made by recombining (characteristics of) people, objects and contexts.

This has several advantages.

— Teamwork between heterogeneous *participants* makes the project exciting and new for multiple parties involved.

— This teamwork can also contribute to the fact that the project meets the needs of many, diverse participants.

— Combining different aspects of various *objects* in a participatory project can lead to new product categories, services or concepts (e.g. the game that eventually was created by the Patching Zone elaborated on an existing practice in the neighbourhood, i.e. dribbling. This dribbling practice became the inspiration for a digital dribbling game that could be played in the streets, using the game rules of the old folk game 'Tic-Tac-Toe').

— By connecting different *contexts*, collage-making can lead to (long-term) intermingling of contextual knowledge, skills and expertise. However, there are also various uncertainties related to

4 Muller, 2002.
5 Bourriaud, 2002.

collage-making in hybrid, participatory projects.

- Teamwork between heterogeneous *participants* may lead to difficult collaborations, surprises and even conflicts in a project, which may hinder the project and therefore may not be desirable to the maker or the participants.
- By combining different aspects of various *objects* in a participatory project — by putting them in an unusual context or adding new functions to them — they become uncertain.
- By connecting different *contexts*, the project may not answer completely to the participants' expectations (e.g. as we mentioned above, the attempt of the Patching Zone to turn the city space into a game space by adding QR codes appeared to clash with the variety of mobile phones that were used in the particular neighbourhood).

Makers and participants may arrive at interesting hybrid, participatory projects via exchanging_(aspects of) projects with 'imperfect' characteristics.
This has several advantages.

- Insecure and imperfect roles of *participants* in the project can contribute to more empathy of the participants with other people's roles or to more self-reflection on their own roles. (e.g. by 'making themselves imperfect', by covering their ears and walking a distance, the design students of DESIGN.LIVES put themselves into B.'s shoes: a girl with a hearing impairment who was one of the active design partners in the DESIGN. LIVES design workshop).

— By creating imperfect *objects*, participants are engaged in an interpretative action resulting in stimulating their imagination and being encouraged to fill in gaps or gather clues about how the project works (e.g. because the design students and their participants staged a musical performance without sound — using coloured bottles — the participants could empathise more with the world of B.).
— By making some essential aspects of a *context* absent or extremely explicit, participants eventually gain more insight in the workings of a project for a specific context (e.g. in *Routes and Routines*, wearing shoes with various technological detectors slowed down walking in the city of Hasselt. This contributed to the fact that the participants experienced the use of technology in the city context more intensely).

However, there are also various uncertainties involved in playing with imperfection in hybrid, participatory projects.

— Imperfect roles of *participants* in projects can make participants feel alienated or not interested in the project. (e.g. Granny T., one of the active design partners in DESIGN.LIVES) took some of the design students to the nursing home, which radically changed the existing relationship between the design partner and the students and their respective roles. Eventually, this led to the students feeling alienated from the project).

- Imperfect *objects* may demand too much effort by or skills of participants, since they invite participants to compensate for the imperfections or guide them to a finished status (e.g. the Toucha-tag toolkit for attaching RFID stickers to daily life objects, is not an attractive tool for everybody, since it requires some knowledge and engagement to make the tool work).
- By playing with participants' imperfect knowledge of a *context*, participants may feel insecure (e.g. in 'DESIGN.LIVES', design students were introduced in a nursery home, the living environment of their active design partner. Their limited familiarity with this context lead to uncomfortable and inappropriate behaviour).

We gave an overview of several risky trade-offs that characterise hybrid participatory projects. The trade-offs taking place between people via collage-making and imperfect characteristics can clearly make both makers and participants feel insecure. This is related to their de-familiarising qualities. However, they do more than de-familiarise, by explicitly connecting makers and participants. In this way, they stimulate reflection on aspects of the project, leading the way to interesting processes and outcomes. We would like to stress that hybridity is just one of the concepts that describe the particularity of participatory projects. Many participatory projects can be explained via the concept of generativity. This concept is mostly associated with projects where makers set up an infrastructure to enable a group of participants to self-organise their participatory exchanges.

Generativity

With the term generativity we described projects wherein participants can continue to participate, even without a lot of support from the initial makers. The term 'generativity' is associated with the advantages of taking care of others and the production of something that contributes to the betterment of society, namely 'the interest in establishing and guiding the next generation.[6] It is also linked to an image of various distributed communities, on the internet, at home, in labs or in (small) organisations, that engage collectively in bottom-up and only little structured processes of unexpected creativity and change.[7]

While exploring the concept of generativity, we particularly focused on *use-time*. In use-time, things are mostly self-organised via a group of participants, often independently from the initial maker(s). Often, makers offer an infrastructure to the participants to organise their participatory exchanges themselves. Especially in use-time, we observed how participatory projects can gain a generative character via three

6 Erikson, 1950, p. 231.
7 E.g. Zittrain, 2008.

forms of specific risky trade-offs, being shareability, modularity and deviationism.

In the following part, we will discuss these three trade-offs.

Makers and participants can support the generativity of projects by making them shareable.

This has several advantages.

— Sharing makes it possible to engage new participants, who may improve certain elements of the project or can help to find solutions to particular problems (e.g. by sharing their project, the design collective Unfold received a lot of support from online participants to solve some concrete technical problems that they encountered during the making process of a 3D printing platform).

— By sharing, the project can be communicated to a wide audience and gain international attention. (e.g. by sharing their project worldwide over the Internet, Unfold's l'Artisan Electronique attracted the attention of an Israeli student who subsequently used some of the knowledge created during their project to build his own ceramic printer).

However, there are also various uncertainties involved in making a project shareable.

— Makers and participants are sometimes unsure about the amount or type of information they wish to share and which formats they can use to share in a qualitative and useful way. (e.g. Blast Theory felt uncertain about sharing the raw material of *Uncle Roy All Around You*, so they decided not to. The art collective explained that sharing is not their first interest and that it is a time-intensive process).

— In a sharing process, the documentation of functional and meaningful aspects of a project is important, but requires a lot of effort. Also, makers do not always know how to properly document these aspects.
— Via sharing, makers and participants can be confronted with unforeseen comments on or unexpected uses of their project, which can make them feel uncertain. (e.g. Touchatag was very careful about sharing certain aspects with participants, such as software, because they wanted to prevent the project from escaping the boundaries of control of the organisation).
— Via sharing, the ownership of ideas, designs and art works, etcetera can be at stake.

Makers and participants can support the generativity of projects by making participatory projects modular (meaning that makers and participants make well-defined parts of any finished cultural object into a building block for new objects.[8]

This has several advantages.

— Participants can make their own version of and contribution to the project. This may lead to an

8 Manovich, 2005.

enhanced feeling of ownership over the project (e.g. Alcatel-Lucent made the modular toolkit Touchatag that allows participants to make their own interactive objects and environments. This led to creative applications by participants, such as a toolkit for architects to collaboratively prototype buildings over the Internet).

— Elements or different modules of the project can be (re-)used by other new participants, extending the projects' lifetime (e.g. even though the Touchatag service has stopped working, online participants still use the toolkit for several ends. In this way, the project is still alive).

However, there are also various uncertainties involved in making a participatory project modular.

— Not all makers and participants are familiar with how to create for modularity (for instance, they may be uncertain about the amount of flexibility and challenges it should include), since this differs a lot from making finished objects.
— Using modularity can make the project difficult to understand for lay people or non-technical experts (e.g. the modular Touchatag stickers and software require more technical insight than a finished interactive application).
— Making a project modular makes it possible for other participants to take certain elements out of it, using them in contexts that the initial makers did not foresee or intend (e.g. Touchatag was adapted by hacker communities to hack the OV

chip card, which is used to pay for riding the Dutch public transport system).

Makers and participants can support the generativity of projects by embracing deviations (meaning that divisions and separations within one project can be created to generate new unexpected branches, adaptations or versions).
This has several advantages.

— Deviant uses show possibilities or pitfalls of the project that the initial makers and participants may not have foreseen or imagined (e.g. the 3D ceramics printing platform l'Artisan Electronique was improved by a suggestion of a designer, active on the 3D RepRap forum, to add a contemporary digital alternative of a pottery disk).
— Deviant uses generate wider attention for the project, often in unexpected contexts (e.g. the use of the Arduino in the fashion and textile industry was made possible via the Lilypad Arduino that can be integrated in textile to enable interactive applications).
— Deviant uses sometimes allow for continuation of the work that the initial makers did not have time for or interest in (e.g. initially, Touchatag sold the hardware with protected software. However, when the company ended their activities, it referred more freely to other possible software that could work on the hardware platform. This allowed others to continue a working process with Touchatag, although the makers are no longer involved in it).

However, there are also various uncertainties involved in embracing deviations.

— The project will have to tolerate or even support conflict and discussion, thus shifting the traditional overemphasis on agreement and consensus (e.g. while building the Arduino, i.e. the prototyping platform for interactive technologies and installations, there was discussion on the openness of the platform for participants' appropriations. This led to some deviating platforms, such as the Freeduino).
— Makers and participants will have to invest time in following up how people use, reuse and rework the project. This investment is uncertain because the original makers and participants do not necessarily know in advance what it will result in (e.g. Touchatag did a long-term investment in following up creative adaptations of their toolkit by participants. In the end, however, the tool and the surrounding service appeared not to match the long-term expectations of the organisation).
— Makers have the tendency to control what people can do with their projects and are therefore often hesitant towards deviant uses of the project.

We discussed three risky trade-offs that makers and participants engage in, when participating in a generative participatory project. These specific risky trade-offs contribute to a longer life span of the participatory project, by giving the participants means to continue them. This longer life span is, however, also associated with many uncertainties around, for instance, the ownership of the projects and possible misuses. Thus, in participatory projects there always has to be a balance between giving and taking. With this in mind, we end with a final reflection.

Afterword

Participatory projects are characterised by (risky) trade-offs between makers and diverse participants and can be described via the concepts of hybridity and generativity. We end with a reflection on some implications of these trade-offs for participatory projects and their makers and participants.

Many interesting participatory projects are hybrid in character. They involve makers and participants exchanging via collage-making (particularly in case study 3, Go-for-IT!) and via imperfect or unfinished aspects of projects that could be further elaborated on (particularly in case study 4, DESIGN.LIVES). Although these trade-offs appear to be fruitful for a lot of participatory projects, they can never function as 'recipes' (or determinants or prerequisites). Every participatory project demands a reflection on the extent to which a certain trade-off should be made in a certain context. For instance, one team of students that participated in the DESIGN.LIVES project became confused when some aspects of imperfection were introduced into the project, which was not conducive to participation. More specifically, the unfamiliarity with the contexts contributed to uncomfortable and even inappropriate behaviour. However, in another team — in which students were immersed in a role they were not perfectly familiar with (concerning not being able to hear) — this led to interesting exchanges between makers and participants. Therefore, it would be interesting to further study and compare experiences of makers and participants in participatory projects in which the trade-offs of collage-making and playing with imperfect characteristics are experimented with.

In some participatory projects makers try to engage participants not involved in the creation process, after the project is finished. We refer to this aspect as the generative potential of participatory projects. Next to the trade-offs that are typical for hybrid participatory projects, being collage-making and exchanging imperfect aspects of projects, three additional trade-offs between makers and participants appear to contribute to the generative potential of a participatory project: sharing, modularity and deviationism.

First of all, sharing documentation on the project between makers and participants appears to be successful in enabling participants to self-organise around (some aspects of) a project (as is the Case in Case study 5, l'Artisan Electronique). Therefore, makers and participants document (aspects of) the project and look for formats to share it with others. Here, it becomes clear that the exchange of both functional and meaningful documentation is important to engage participants to relate to and continue with the project. This aspect of integrating functional and meaningful documentation on projects is an interesting aspect for further study. Although the makers in the case studies we described (especially in Case study 1, *Uncle Roy All Around You*) were convinced about the potential of documenting, they felt uncertain about how to share this documentation. Ways of facilitating makers in dealing with this specific uncertainty concerning documentation, (e.g. by proposing them formats to share their projects with others and discussing the implications of each format), may be researched.

Second, by making a project modular, participants receive aspects of the project to handle, comment on or change. Modularity does not always have the same meaning in different participatory projects. We distinguish multiple maker-driven and participant-driven forms of modularity. In the maker-driven forms, makers still hold on to many aspects of the projects, even when they make a project modular. They are rather hesitant to completely open up the project to uses that differ from their initial expectations. This hesitation is also related to the fact that both makers and participants might have little experience in making projects modular. They are confronted with a lot of uncertainties about how to make the project flexible enough to stimulate easy changes. At the same time, they wonder how these easy interactions can provoke enough challenge for the participants (as became clear in Case study 2, *Routes and Routines* and 6, Touchatag). This aspect too deserves more research.

Finally, our cases have shown that generative

participatory projects can tolerate or support certain deviant uses (as was shown in case study 7, Arduino). Some projects even invest a lot of time in following up deviant developments of the projects by participants, by documenting them or by actively providing feedback. Also, they make deviant uses possible by allowing participants to really appropriate aspects of the project, via setting up the proper project licenses. We note that especially this last trade-off between makers and participants, in which the support for deviant uses plays a key role, deserves more attention from researchers in the future.

The title of this book suggests that participation is a risky trade-off. Indeed, this book provides some insights in the exchanges that take place in participatory projects between makers and participants. At the same time, it does not pretend that participatory projects are easy to engage in, since they confront all those involved with many uncertainties. However, we want to convince makers and participants to engage in participatory projects anyway, since there are so many reasons to do so, such as obtaining a longer life span for projects or creating more interesting concepts. Therefore, the book describes a variety of interesting practices, which inform makers and participants about the uncertainties as well as the advantages of choosing to engage in participatory projects.

Clay Analytics Workshop

Clay Analytics is a workshop format that tries to make the vocabulary that is touched upon in discourses around participation in art and design more tangible. The workshop was designed by Luna Maurer of Moniker in dialogue with Liesbeth Huybrechts (Social Spaces), author of this book. It uses clay and light play to make hands-on representations and even stories around words such as participation, user and maker, hybridity, autonomy, authorship, community and so on. Through making something (out of clay), the workshops initiate conversations and help generate ideas around participation.

www.socialspaces.be

http://conditionaldesign.org/workshops/clay-analytics

Contributors

Katrien Dreessen studied Communication Sciences at Vrije Universiteit Brussel (VUB), Belgium. After her studies, she started working in the field of user research at the research group SMIT-IBBT. Since 2008, she is part of the research group Social Spaces, participating in several research projects, including the set-up of FabLab Genk.

Denny K. L. Ho is Associate Professor in the Department of Applied Social Sciences, Hong Kong Polytechnic University, where his research has focused on social policy and action research methodology. Since 2008 he has collaborated with Dr Yanki C. Lee on design methodology for social participation. His major interest is in the relationship of solution-focus methods with the study and practice of design.

Liesbeth Huybrechts (1979) did her PhD about the relation between digital media, art, design and participation. She is head of research of the research unit Inter-actions, and researcher and lecturer in higher art education in the Media, Arts and Design Faculty in Genk, LUCA School of Arts/KU Leuven, Belgium. Within this context she is associated with the research group Social Spaces, exploring the social meanings, uses and applications of art and design (www.socialspaces.be). She also is involved in research and in mentoring students within the context of Cultural Studies KU Leuven and the Design Academy of Eindhoven, the Netherlands.

Yanki C. Lee is director of EXHIBIT CIC (www.exhibit-goldenlane.com), a social design agency in London. With an MA in Architecture from the Royal College of Art and a PhD in design participation from Hong Kong Polytechnic University, Dr Lee does research in the field of design methodology for participation and social innovation. From 2000 to 2011 she was a research fellow at the Royal College of Art Helen Hamlyn Centre for Design, London, and creator of www.designingwithpeople.org, the result of EPSRC funded i~design research project (2006-2010). As holder of the UK's BIS UK – China Fellowship of Excellence 2011, Dr Lee is currently director of the social design research lab at the Hong Kong Design Institute. www.yankilee.com

Selina Schepers (1986) graduated in 2009 as a Master of Philosophy (mPhil) in Cultures of Arts, Science and Technology at the University of Maastricht, the Netherlands. Currently, as a researcher at the research group Social Spaces I CUO, she is engaged in various research projects. As of 2012, she also became the research coordinator of Social Spaces I CUO. At the Media, Arts & Design-faculty (campus C-mine) in Genk, Belgium, she coordinates several design research-related courses.

Jessica Schoffelen (1981) lectures on research methods in (media) design at the Media, Arts & Design Faculty (LUCA School of Arts, Genk, Belgium). She was the coordinator of the bridging programme Communication & Media Design and of the postgraduate programme Social and Participatory Use of New Media. In her PhD research she explores how documentation of design projects can enable participation in the project (for which she is associated with the University of Hasselt). She is part of the research group Social Spaces and FabLab Genk.

Cristiano Storni is Lecturer in Interaction Design and Director of the MSc.\MA in Interactive Media at Computer Science and Information Systems department (Interaction Design Center, University of Limerick, Ireland). He holds a PhD in Information Systems and Organization from the Faculty of Sociology in the University of Trento, Italy. During his PhD, Cristiano has studied the impact of ICT on people, organizations and society. He particularly focused on Science and Technology Studies (STS), Actor Network Theory (ANT), Ethnography, Participatory and Interaction Design. His original background is in Communication Sciences with a focus on HCI and Cognitive Science (he is a graduate of the University of Siena, Italy). His research lies at the intersection of social science and design disciplines. His current research concerns design theory and practices, the social shaping of technology, especially ICT (with an interest on the notions of appropriation, participation, and empowerment) and in different application areas: Health Care, Web 2.0, open hardware and software, and social innovation. www.idc.ul.ie/people/cristiano-storni

Literature

Chapter 1

- Abbete, J. 1999. Inventing the Internet. Cambridge, MA: MIT Press.
- Adorno, T. & M. Horkheimer. 2002. Dialectic of Enlightenment, ed. by G. S. Noerr, trans. E. Jephcott, 94-137. Stanford, CA: Stanford University Press.
- Arnstein, S. R. 1969. A Ladder of Citizen Participation. JAIP 35 (4): 216-24.
- A.telier. 2011. Design Things. Cambridge, MA: MIT Press.
- Bauwens, M. 2007. Individual and Public. Amsterdam: The P2P Foundation. http://p2pfoundation.net/2.5_Individual_and_Public_(Nutshell).
- Beck, U. 1992. Risk Society: Towards a New Modernity. New Delhi: Sage.
- Benjamin, W. 1936. The Work of Art in the Age of Mechanical Reproduction. Los Angeles, CA: UCLA School of Theatre, Film and Television. www.marxists.org/reference/subject/philosophy/works/ge/benjamin.htm.
- Benkler, Y. 2006. The Wealth of Networks: How Social Production Transforms Markets and Freedom. New Haven and London: Yale University Press.
- Bishop, C. 2012. Artificial Hells: Participatory Art and the Politics of Spectatorship. London: Verso.
- Bowen, S. J. 2009. A Critical Artefact Methodology: Using Provocative Conceptual Designs to Foster Human-centred Innovation. Sheffield: Sheffield Hallam University, PhD diss.
- Bruns, A. 2005. Some Exploratory Notes on Produsers and Produsage. http://snurb.info/node/329.
- Callon, M., P. Lascoumes & Y. Barther. 2009. Acting in an Uncertain World: An Essay on Technical Democracy. Cambridge, MA: MIT Press.
- Daniels, D. 2004. Television-Art or Anti-Art? Conflict and Co-operation Between the Avant-Garde and the Mass Media in the 1960s and 1970s. www.mediaartnet.org/themes/overview_of_media_art/massmedia/.
- De Waal, M. & M. De Lange. 2008. The Mobile City: A Conference on Locative Media, Urban Culture and Identity. Rotterdam: The Mobile City. www.themobilecity.nl/background-information/lang_enconference-textlang_enlang_nlconferentie-tekstlang_nl/.
- Dekker, A., L. Huybrechts & P. Machils. 2010. Mapping (Version: 5.02.10). Brighton: offices Blast Theory.
- Devos, C. 2006. De kleermakers en de keizer. Ghent: Academia Press.
- Donath, J. 2004. Sociable Media. In The Encyclopedia of Human-Computer Interaction, ed. by W. Sims Bainbridge. Great Barrington, MA: Berkshire Publishing Group. smg.media.mit.edu/./Donath/SociableMedia.encyclopmedia.pdf.
- Dreessen, K., L. Huybrechts, T. Laureyssens, S. Schepers & S. Baciu. 2011. MAP-it: A Participatory Mapping Toolkit. Leuven: Acco.
- Eckberg, M. 2007. The Parameters of the Risk Society: A Review and Exploration. Current Sociology 55 (3): 343-66.
- Ehn, P. & R. Badham. 2002. Participatory Design and the Collective Designer. In PDC 02: Proceedings of the Participatory Design Conference, ed. T. Binder, J. Gregory & I. Wagner, 1-10. Malmö.
- Gauntlett, D. 2011. Making is Connecting: The Social Meaning of Creativity, From DIY and Knitting to YouTube and Web 2.0. Cambridge: Polity Press.
- Gaver, W., J. Beaver & S. Bendford. 2003. Ambiguity as a Resource for Design, 233-238. In CHI Letters. www.blasttheory.co.uk/bt/documents/ambiguity_CHI_2003.pdf.
- Giddens, A. 1999. Risk and Responsibility. Modern Law Review 62 (1): 1-10.
- Gold, R. 2007. The Plenitude: Creativity, Innovation, and Making Stuff (Simplicity: Design, Technology, Business, Life). Cambridge, MA: MIT Press.
- Hanseth, O. & C. Ciborra. 2007. Risk, Complexity and ICT. Cheltenham: Edward Elgar Publishing.
- Hawk, B., D. M. Rieder & O. Oviedo. 2008. Small Tech: The Culture of Digital Tools. Minneapolis: University of Minnesota Press.
- Hutter, B. M. & M. Power, eds. 2005. Organizational Encounters with Risk. Cambridge: Cambridge University Press.
- Huybrechts, L. & P. Machils. 2008. Place@Space. Hasselt: Z33. http://kunstencentrumz33wordpress.com

–. 2011. Participatory Creation is Risky: A Roadmap of Participatory Creation Processes and the Shifting Role of Creative 'Things'. Leuven: KULeuven, PhD diss.

–, K. Dreessen & S. Schepers. 2012. Mapping Design Practices: On Risk, Hybridity, and Participation. In PDC '12: Proceedings of the 12th Participatory Design Conference: Exploratory Papers, Workshop Descriptions, Industry Cases: Volume 2, 29-32. New York: ACM.

- Ito, M., D. Okabe & K. Anderson. 2007. Portable Objects in Three Global Cities: The Personalization of Urban Places. In: The Mobile Communication Research Annual Volume 1: The Reconstruction of Space and Time: Mobile Communication Practices, ed. by R. Ling & S. Campbell. New Brunswick, NJ: Transaction Book
- Jenkins, H. 2006. Convergence Culture: Where Old and New Media Collide. NY: NYU Press.

–, R. Puroshotma, K. Clinton, M. Weigel & A. J. Robison. 2005. Confronting the Challenges of Participatory Culture: Media Education for the 21st Century. www.newmedialiteracies.org/wp-content/uploads/pdfs/NMLWhitePaper.pdf.

- Jensen, C. S., C. R. Vicente & R. Wind. 2008. User-Generated Content: The Case for Mobile Services. IEEE Computer 41(12): 116-18.
- Laermans, R. 2002. Het cultureel regiem: Cultuur en beleid in Vlaanderen. Tielt: Lannoo.
- Lash, S. 2000. Risk Culture. In The Risk Society and Beyond: Critical Issues for Social Theory, ed. by B. Adam, 47-62. London: Sage Publications.
- Latour, B. 2005. Reassembling the Social: An Introduction to Actor-Network Theory. New York: Oxford University Press.

–. 2011. Networks, Societies, Spheres: Reflections of an Actor-Network Theorist. International Journal of Communication 5 (2011): 796–810.

- – & P. Weibel. 2005. Making Things Public: Atmospheres of Democracy. Cambridge, MA: MIT Press.
- Laurel, B. 1993. Computers as Theatre. Reading, MA: Addison-Wesley Professional – Leadbeater, C. 2008. We-Think: Mass Innovation, Not Mass Production: The Power of Mass Creativity. London: Profile Books.
- Leadbeater, C. 2008. We-think: Mass Innovation, Not Mass Production: The Power of Mass Creativity. London: Profile Books.
- Lupton, D. 2006. Sociology and Risk. In Beyond the Risk Society: Critical Reflections on Risk and Human Security, ed. by G. Mythen &
- S. Walklate, 11-24. Berkshire: Open University Press.
- Menger, P.-M. 2009. Le Travail Créateur: s'accomplir dans l'incertain. Paris: Gallimard-Seuil-Éditions de l'EHESS, coll. "Hautes Études".
- Milbrath, L. 1965. Political Participation: How and Why Do People Get Involved in Politics? Chicago: Rand McNally College Publishing Company.
- Murray, J. 1997. Hamlet on the Holodeck: The Future of Narrative in Cyberspace. Cambridge: Cambridge University Press.
- Nielsen, J. 2006. Participation Inequality: Encouraging More Users to Contribute. Warm Springs, CA: Nielsen Norman Group. www.useit.com/alertbox/participation_inequality.html.
- Norman, D. 2010. The Transmedia Design Challenge: Co-Creation. Jnd.org. www.jnd.org/dn.mss/the_transmedia_design_challenge_co-creation.html.
- Open Source Initiative. 2010. The Open Source Definition. www.opensource.org/ .
- O'Reilly, T. 2004. The Architecture of Participation. Cologne: O'Reilly Verlag GmbH & Co.KG. www.oreillynet.com/pub/a/oreilly/tim/articles/architecture_of_participation.html .

- Raessens, J. & J. Goldstein. 2005. Computer Games as Participatory Media Culture: Handbook of Computer Game Studies. Cambridge, MA: MIT Press.
- Rheingold, H., 2009. Course: Participatory Media Literacy. California: Social Text. www.socialtext.net/medialiteracy/index.cgi#.n.
- Sanders, E. B.-N. 2001. A New Design Space. In Proceedings of ICSID 2001 Seoul: Exploring Emerging Design Paradigm, 317-24. Oullim. Seoul: ICSID.
- Schäfer, M. T. 2008. Bastard Culture: User Participation and the Extension of Cultural Industries. Utrecht: University of Utrecht, PhD diss. www.scribd.com/doc/8594831/Bastard-Culture-User-participation-and-the-extension-of-cultural-industries.

  –. 2010. Bastard Culture: How User Participation Transforms Cultural Production. Amsterdam: Amsterdam University Press.
- Schäfer, M. T. 2011. How User Participation Transforms Cultural Production. Utrecht: University of Utrecht.
- Schepers, S., L. Huybrechts & K. Dreessen. 2011. MAP-it: On Risk, Friction and Releasing Control. Swedish Design Research Journal 2 (11): 32-38.
- Scott, A. 2000. Risk Society or Angst Society? Two Views of Risk, Consciousness and Community. In The Risk Society and Beyond: Critical Issues for Social Theory, ed. by B. Adam, U. Beck & J. van Loon, 34-47. London: Sage.
- Shanken, E. 2009. Art and Electronic Media, London: Phaidon Press.
- Shirky, C. 2009. Here Comes Everybody. London: Penguin Books.
- Simonsen, J. & T. Robinson. 2012. Routledge International Handbook of Participatory Design. Oxford: Routledge.
- Stengers, I. 2002. A 'Cosmo-Politics': Risk, Hope, Change. In Hope: New Philosophies for Change, ed. by M. Zournazi, 244-72. Annandale: Pluto Press Australia.
- Storni, C., 2011. Complexity in an Uncertain and Cosmopolitan World: Rethinking Personal Health Technology in Diabetes with the Tag-it-Yourself. PsychNology Journal 9 (2): 165-85.

  –. 2012. Artifacts Unpacking Design Practices: The Notion of Thing in the Making of Artifacts. Science Technology Human Values 37 (1): 88-123.
- Suchman, L. 1993. Foreword. In Participatory Design: Principles and Practices, ed. by D. Schuler & A. Namioka, vii-ix. Hillsdale, NJ: Lawrence Erlbaum Associates.

  –. 2006. Human-Machine Reconfigurations: Plans and Situated Actions. Cambridge, MA: Cambridge University Press.
- Tribe, M. & R. Jana. 2006. New Media Art. Cologne: Taschen.
- Twaalfhoven, A. 2010. Hand in hand. Boekman 22 (82): 62-63. Special issue Community Art.
- Van Erven, E. 2010. Op zoek naar de kern van de Nederlandse community art. Boekman 22 (82): 8-14. Special issue Community Art.
- Verba, S., K. L. Schlozman & H. E. Brady. 1995. Voice and Equality: Civic Voluntarism in American Politics. Harvard: Harvard University Press.
- Von Hippel, E. 2013. Open User Innovation. In The Encyclopedia of Human-Computer Interaction, ed. by M. Soegaard & R. F. Dam, 2nd ed. Aarhus: The Interaction Design Foundation. www.interaction-design.org/encyclopedia/open_user_innovation.html.
- Wagner, I., M. Basile, L. Ehrenstrasser, V. Maquil, J-J. Terrn & M. Wagner. 2009. Supporting Community Engagement in the City: Urban Planning in the MR-Tent. In Proceedings of C&T (Communities & Technologies), 185-94. University Park: Penn State University.
- Whittaker, S., L. Terveen, W. C. Hill. & L. Cherny. 1998. The Dynamics of Mass Interaction. In Proceedings of the 1998: ACM Conference on Computer-supported Cooperative Work, ed. by S. Poltrock & J. Grudin, 257-64. Seattle, WA: CSCW.
- Zielinski, S. 2006. Deep Time of the Media: Toward an Archaeology of Hearing and Seeing by Technical Means. Cambridge, MA: MIT Press.
- Zinn, J. 2004. Literature Review: Sociology and Risk: Social Context and Responses to Risk Network (SCARR). www.kent.ac.uk/scarr/publications/Sociology%20Literature%20Review%20WP1.04%20Zinn.pdf.

Chapter 2

– Adorno, T. & M. Horkheimer. 2002. Dialectic of Enlightenment, ed. by G. S. Noerr, trans. E. Jephcott, 94-137. Stanford, CA: Stanford University Press.
– Alexander, C., Ishikawa, S. & Silverstein, M. 1977. A Pattern Language: Towns, Building, Construction. New York: Oxford University Press.
– Almenberg, G. 2010. Notes on Participatory Art: Toward a Manifesto Differentiating it from Open Work, Interactive Art and Relational Art. Milton Keynes: AuthorHouse.
– Arns, I. 1997. Interaction, Participation, Networking Art and telecommunication. Karlsruhe: MediaArtNet. www.medienkunstnetz.de/themes/overview_of_media_art/communication/2/.
– Avital, M. 2011. The Generative Bedrock of Open Design. In Open Design Now! How Design Cannot Remain Exclusive, ed. by B. van Abel, L. Evers, R. Klaassen & P. Troxler, 48-58. Amsterdam: Bis Publishers.
– Barok, D. 2009. On Participatory Art: Interview with Claire Bishop. Prague: Workshop Monument to Transformation. www.academia.edu/771895/On_participatory_art_Interview_with_Claire_Bishop.
– Baudrillard. 1994. Simulacra and Simulation, trans. S.F. Glaser. Michigan: University of Michigan Press. Originally published as Simulacres et simulation (Paris: Galilée, 1981).
– Bauman, Z. 1993. Postmodern Ethics. Oxford: Blackwell Publishers.
– Bell G., M. Blythe & P. Sengers. 2005. Making by Making Strange: Defamiliarization and the Design of Domestic Technologies. ACM Transactions on Computer-Human Interaction 12 (2): 149-73.
– Bermel, A. 2001. Artaud's Theatre Of Cruelty (Plays and Playwrights). London: Methuen Drama.
– Bhabha, H. K. 1994. The Location of Culture. London: Routledge.
– Bijker, W. E., T. E. Hughes & T. Pinch, eds. 1987. The Social Construction of Technological Systems: New Directions in the Sociology and History of Technology. Cambridge, MA: MIT Press.
– Bishop, C. 2006. Participation. London: Whitechapel.
–. 2012. Artificial Hells: Participatory Art and the Politics of Spectatorship. London: Verso Books.
– Bourriaud, N. 2002. Relational Aesthetics. Paris: Les Presses du réel. Originally published as Esthétique relationelle (Paris: Les Presses du réel, 1998).
– Braden, S. 1978. Artists and People. London: Routledge and Kegan Paul Ltd.
– Bucciarelli, L. L. 2002. Between Thought and Object in Engineering Design. Design Studies 23 (3): 219-31.
– Chen, S. 2005. Task Partitioning in New Product Development Teams: a Knowledge and Learning Perspective. Journal of Engineering and Technology Management 22 (4): 291-314.
– Clifford, J. 1997. Routes: Travel and Translation in the Late Twentieth Century. Cambridge, MA: Harvard University Press.
– Cross, N. & A. Clayburn Cross. 1995. Observations of Teamwork and Social Processes in Design. Design Studies 16 (2): 143-70.
– Dalsgaard, P. 2008. Experiential Design: Findings from Designing Engaging Interactive Environments. In Advances in Human-Computer Interaction, ed. by S. Pinder, 85-106. Rijek: InTech.
– Davis, L. J., ed. 1997. The Disability Studies Reader. New York: Routledge.
– Devlieger, P., F. Renders, H. Froyen & K. Wildiers. 2006. Blindness and the Multi-Sensorial City. Antwerpen and Apeldoorn: Garant.
– Dorst, K. & N. Cross. 2001. Creativity in the Design Process: Co-evolution of Problem-Solution. Design Studies, 22 (5): 425-37.
– Dunne, A., 1999. Hertzian Tales: Electronic Products, Aesthetic Experience and Critical Design. London: RCA CRD Research Publications.
– & F. Raby. 2001. Design Noir: The Secret Life of Electronic Objects. Basel (etc.): Birkhäuser.
– & F. Raby. 2001. Placebo Project: London: Studio Dunne and Raby. www.dunneandraby.co.uk/content/projects/70/0.

- Ehn, P., 1988. Work-Oriented Design of Computer Artifacts. Hillsdale, NJ: Lawrence Erlbaum Associates.
  –. 2008. Participation in Design Things. In Proceedings of the Tenth Anniversary Conference on Participatory design 2008, 92-101. New York: ACM.
  – & R. Badham. 2002. Participatory Design and the Collective Designer. In: PDC 02: Proceedings of the Participatory Design Conference, 1-10. Malmö, Sweden: PDC02.
  – & M. Kyng. 1987. The Collective Resource Approach to Systems Design. In Computers and Democracy: A Scandinavian Challenge, ed. by G. Bjerknes, P. Ehn & M. Kyng, 17-57. Brookfield, VT: Avebury.
- Finlay, L. 2005. Reflexive Embodied Empathy: A Phenomenology of Participant-Researcher Intersubjectivity. The Humanistic Psychologist 33 (4): 271-92.
- Flusser, V. 1999. About the Word Design. In Vilém Flusser on Design (Version: 13.01.09), D. Barrington. London: Everyone Forever. www.everyoneforever.com/content/2008-01-13/vilem_flusser_on_design/.
- Friedman, J. 1998. Review: Routing Roots and Rooting Routes: A Cosmopolitan Paradox. Current Anthropology 39 (5): 733-34.
- Gaver, W., J. Beaver & S. Bendford. 2003. Ambiguity as a Resource for Design. In Proceedings of the SIGCHI Conference on Human Factors in Computing Systems, 233-40. New York: ACM. www.blasttheory.co.uk/bt/documents/ambiguity_CHI_2003.pdf.
  – & H. Martin. 2000. Alternatives: Exploring Information Appliances through Conceptual Design Proposals. In Proceedings of the SIGCHI Conference on Human Factors in Computing Systems, 209–16. New York: ACM.
- Gold, R. 2007. The Plenitude: Creativity, Innovation, and Making Stuff (Simplicity: Design, Technology, Business, Life). Cambridge, MA: MIT Press.
- Greenbaum, J. & M. Kyng. 1991. Design at Work: Cooperative design of Computer Systems. Hillsdale: NJ: Lawrence Erlbaum Associates.
- Helen Hamlyn Centre. 2007. About Inclusive Design. London: RCA. www.hhc.rca.ac.uk/research/id/index.html.
- Huybrechts, L. 2011. Participatory Creation is Risky: A Roadmap of Participatory Creation Processes and the Shifting Role of Creative 'Things'. Leuven: LKULeuven, PhD diss.
  –, T. Coenen, T. Laureyssens & P. Machils. 2009. Living Spaces: A Participatory Design Process Model Drawing on the Use of Boundary Objects. International Reports on Socio-Informatics 6 (2). www.iisi.de/fileadmin/IISI/upload/IRSI/IRSIV6I2.pdf
  –, K. Dreessen & S. Schepers. 2012. Mapping Design Practices: On Risk, Hybridity, and Participation. In PDC '12: Proceedings of the 12th Participatory Design Conference: Exploratory Papers, Workshop Descriptions, Industry Cases: Vol. 2, 29-32. New York: ACM.
  – & A. Wilkinson. 2010. For Them: Designing for or With, Some or One. Brussels: Design Vlaanderen.
- Joselit, D. 2007. Feedback: Television Against Democracy. Cambridge and London: MIT Press.
- Karasti, H. & K. Baker. 2008. Community Design: Growing One's Own Information Infrastructure. In Proceedings of the Tenth Conference on Participatory Design. Bloomington, IN: CPSR; New York: ACM Press.
- Kelly, O. 1984. Community, Art, and the State: Storming the Citadels. Stroud: Comedia.
- Kester, G. 2011. The One and the Many: Contemporary Collaborative Art in a Global Context. Durham: Duke University Press.
- Kim, A. J. 2000. Community Building on the Web: Secret Strategies for Successful Online Communities. Berkeley, CA: Peachpit Press.
- Kluitenberg, E. 2008. Delusive Spaces: Essays on Culture, Media and Technology. Rotterdam: Institute of Network Cultures and NAi Publishers.
- Latour, B. 2005. Reassembling the Social: An Introduction to Actor-Network-Theory. Oxford: Oxford University Press.
  – & P. Weibel. 2005. Making Things Public: Atmospheres of Democracy.

Cambridge, MA: MIT Press.
- Lee, Y. & J. Bichard. 2006. From Inclusive User Research Processes to Universal Design Outputs: The Cases of an Inclusive Design Education Programme. In Proceedings in the IAUD, 2nd International Conference on Universal Design, Kyoto: IAUD.
  –. 2008. Design Participation Tactics: The Challenges and New Roles for Designers in the Co-Design Process. CoDesign 4 (1): 31-50.
- Lefebvre, H. 1992. The Production of Space. Oxford: Basil Blackwell.
- Ljungblad, S. & L. Holmquist. 2007. Transfer Scenarios: Grounding Innovation with Marginal Practices. In CHI '07: Proceedings of the SIGCHI Conference on Human Factors in Computing Systems, 737-46. New York: ACM. www.sics.se/fal/publications/2007/transfer-scenarios-CHI.pdf.
- Lynch, K. 1960. The Image of the City. Cambridge, MA: MIT Press.
- Meikle, J. 2001. Twentieth Century Limited: Industrial Design In America 1925–1939. Philadelphia: Temple University Press.
- Merkel, C. B., L. Xiao, U. Farooq, C. H. Ganoe, R. Lee, J. M. Carroll & M. B. Rosson. 2004. Participatory Design in Community Computing Contexts: Tales from the Field. In PDC '04: Proceedings of the Eight Conference of Participatory Design: Artful Integration: Interwaving Media, Materials and Practices Vol. 1, 1-10. New York: ACM.
- Muller, M. J. 2002. Participatory Design: The Third Space in HCI. In The Human-Computer Interaction Handbook: Fundamentals, Evolving Technologies and Emerging Applications, ed. by J. A. Jacko & A. Sears. Hillsdale: NJ: Lawrence Erlbaum Associates, 2003.
- Nigten, A. 2006. Processpatching: Defining New Methods in aRt&D. London: SMARTlab Programme in Performative New Media Arts, Central Saint Martins College of Art & Design, University of the Arts, PhD diss. processpatching.net/Publishing.
- O'Neill, P. 2009. Three Stages in the Art of Public Participation: The Relational, Social and Durational. €urozine 39. www.eurozine.com/articles/2010-08-12-oneillen.html.
- Papanek, V. 1985. Design for the Real World: Human Ecology and Social Change. London: Thames & Hudson.
- Preece, J. 2000. Online Communities: Designing Usability, Supporting Sociability. Hoboken, NJ: Wiley.
- Raley, R. 2009. Tactical Media (Electronic Mediations). Minneapolis: University of Minnesota Press.
- Rancière, J. 2002. The Aesthetic Revolution and Its Outcomes. New Left Review 14: 133-51.
  –. 2010. Dissensus: On Politics and Aesthetics. London: Continuum International Publishing Group.
- Ross, K. 1983. Henri Lefebvre on the Situationist International. October 79 (Winter 1997). www.notbored.org/lefebvre-interview.html.
- Sanders, E. B.-N. 2008. On Modeling: An Evolving Map of Design Practice and Design Research. Interactions XV (6): 13-17.
- Schäfer, M. T. 2010. Bastard Culture: How User Participation Transforms Cultural Production. Amsterdam: Amsterdam University Press.
- Schuller, D. & A. Namioka. 1993. Participatory Design: Principles and Practices. Hillsdale, NJ: Lawrence Erlbaum Associates.
- Sengers, P., K. Boehner, S. David & J. Kaye. 2005. Reflective Design. In Proceedings of the 4th Decennial Conference on Critical Computing 2005, 49-58. New York: ACM. http://cemcom.infosci.cornell. edu/mainsite/uploads/pubs/Reflective%20 Design.pdf.
- Shklovsky, V. 1917. Art as Technique. In Contemporary Literary Criticism: Modernism Through Poststructuralism, ed. by R. Con Davis. New York and London: Longman Press.
- Stallman, R. 1999. The GNU Operating System and the Free Software Movement. Open Sources: Voices from the Open Source Revolution. www.gnu.org/gnu/thegnuproject.html.

- Storni, C. 2012. Artifacts. Unpacking Design Practices: The Notion of Thing in the Making of Artifacts. Science Technology Human Values 37 (1): 88-123.
- The Patching Zone (2010). Go for IT! (Version: December 2009). Rotterdam: Patching Zone. http://go-for-it-rotterdam.nl/ and www.patchingzone.net.
- Tomico, O., J. W. Frens & K. Overbeeke. 2009. Co-Reflection: User Involvement for Highly Dynamic Design Processes. In Proceedings of ACM: CHI 2009 Conference in Human Factors in Computing Systems, 2695-98. New York: ACM.
- Trienekens, S. & D. W. Postma. 2010. Verbinden door te ontwrichten. Special issue Community Art. Boekman 22 (82): 22-29.
- Turner, J. F. C. 1977. Housing by People: Towards Autonomy in Building Environments. New York: Pantheon Books.
- Twaalfhoven, A. 2010. Hand in hand. Special issue Community Art. Boekman 22 (82): 62-63.
- Vague, T. 2000. The Boy Scout's Guide to the Situationist International: The Effect the S.I. Had on Paris '68 and All That: Through the Angry Brigade and King Mob to The Sex Pistols (Version: 05.07.08). Baltimore: nothingness.org. http://library.nothingness.org/articles/SI/en/display/240.
- Vallance, R., S. Kiani & S. Nayfeh. 2001. Open Design of Manufacturing Equipment. In CIRP: 1st International Conference on Agile, Reconfigurable Manufacturing. Ann Arbor: Regents of the University of Michigan.
- Van Erven, E. 2010. Op zoek naar de kern van de Nederlandse community art. Special issue Community Art. Boekman 22 (82): 8-14.
- Van Oenen, G. 2008. Babylonische maakbaarheid: Lessen van New Babylon voor de hedendaagse publieke ruimte. Open 15: 36-59.
- Wenger, E. 1998. Communities of Practice: Learning, Meaning, and Identity. Cambridge, MA: Cambridge University Press.
- Winschiers-Theophilus, H., S. Chivuno-Kuria, G. Kapuire, N. Bidwell & E. Blake. 2010. Being Participated: A Community Approach. In PDC '10: Proceedings of the 11th Biennial Participatory Design Conference, 1-10. New York: ACM.
- Zielinski, S. 2006. Deep Time of the Media: Toward an Archaeology of Hearing and Seeing by Technical Means. Cambridge, MA: MIT Press.

Literature Chapter 3

- Arnstein, S. R. 1969. A Ladder of Citizen Participation. JAIP 35 (4): 216-24.
- Avital, M. 2011. The Generative Bedrock of Open Design. In Open Design Now!: How Design Cannot Remain Exclusive, ed. by B. van Abel, L. Evers, R. Klaassen & P. Troxler, 48-58. Amsterdam: Bis Publishers.
  – & Te'eni, D. 2006. From Generative Fit to Generative Capacity: Exploring an Emerging Dimension of Information Systems Fit and Task Performance. In Proceedings of the 14th European Conference on Information Systems (ECIS 2006), 138. Göteborg.
- Bardzell, J. 2010. Feminist HCI: Taking Stock and Outlining an Agenda for Design. In CHI '10: Proceedings of the SIGCHI Conference on Human Factors in Computing Systems, 1301-10. New York: ACM.
- Bauwens, M. 2007. Individual and Public. Amsterdam: The P2P Foundation. http://p2pfoundation.net/2.5_Individual_and_Public_(Nutshell).
- Bhabha, H.K. 1994. The Location of Culture. London: Routledge.
- Björgvinsson, E., P. Ehn & P. A. Hillgren. 2010. Participatory Design and 'Democratizing Innovation'. In PDC '10: Proceedings of the 11th Biennial Participatory Design Conference, 41-50. New York: ACM.
- Bödker, S. 1999. Computer Applications as Mediators of Design and Use: A Developmental Perspective. Aarhus: University of Aarhus, PhD diss.
- Brandes, U. & M. Erlhoff. 2009. NID – Day – to – Day REDESIGNING THE DESIGNED (Version: 14.09.09). www.be-design.info/24d10/Writings.htm.
- Bruns, A. 2008. Blogs, Wikipedia, Second Life and Beyond: From Production to Produsage. New York: Peter Lang.
- Buechley, L., E. Paulos, D. Rosner & A. Williams. 2009. DIY for CHI: Methods, Communities, and Values of Reuse and Customization. In Proceedings CHI

EA '09: Extended Abstracts on Human Factors in Computing Systems, 4823-26. New York: ACM.

- Carroll, J. 2002. A Field Study of Perceptions and Use of Mobile Telephones by 16 to 11 Years Old: A Field Study. Journal of Information Technology Theory and Application 4 (2): 49-62.
  –, S. Howard, J. Peck & J. Murphy. 2003. From Adoption to Use: The Process of Appropriating a Mobile Phone. Australian Journal of Information Systems 10 (2): 38-48.
- Chalmers, M. 2003. Seamful Design and Ubicomp Infrastructure. In Proceedings of Ubicomp 2003 Workshop on Location-Aware Computing.
  – & A. Galani. 2004. Seamful Interweaving: Heterogeneity in the Theory and Design of Interactive Systems. In DIS '04: Proceedings of the 5th Conference on Designing Interactive Systems: Processes, Practices, Methods, and Techniques, 243-252. New York: ACM Press.
- Chomsky, N. 1972. Language and Mind. New York: Harcourt Brace Jovanovich.
- Ciborra, C. 1992. From Thinking to Tinkering: The Grassroots of Strategic Information Systems. The Information Society 8 (4): 297-309.
  – & O. Hanseth. 2000. Introduction: From Control to Drift. In From Control to Drift: The Dynamics of Corporate Information Infrastructures, ed. by C. Ciborra et al., 1-11. Oxford: Oxford University Press.
- Clifford, J. 1997. Routes: Travel and Translation in the Late Twentieth Century. Cambridge, MA: Harvard University Press.
- DelFanti, A. & J. Söderberg. 2012. Bio/Hardware Hacking. Journal of Peer Production 2. http://peerproduction.net/.
- DiSalvo, C. 2009. Design and the Construction of Publics. Design Issues 25 (1): 48-63.
  –. 2012. Adversarial Design. Cambridge, MA: MIT Press.
  –, K. Boehner, N.A. Knouf & P. Sengers. 2009. Nourishing the Ground for Sustainable HCI: Considerations from Ecologically Engaged Art. In CHI '09: Proceedings of the SIGCHI Conference on Human Factors in Computing Systems, 385-94. New York: ACM.
  –, A. Light, T. Hirsch, C. A. Le Dantec, E. Goodman & K. Hill. 2010. HCI, Communities and Politics. In CHI EA '10: Exteded Abstracts on Human Factors in Computing Systems, 3151-54. New York: ACM.
  –, I. Nourbakhsh, D. Holstius, A. Akin & M. Louw. 2009. The Neighborhood Networks Project: A Case Study of Critical Engagement and Creative Expression Through Participatory Design. In Proceedings of the Tenth Anniversary Conference on Participatory Design 2009, 41-50. Indianapolis: Indiana University.
  – & Dourish, P. 2003. The Appropriation of Interactive Technologies: Some Lesson from Placeless Documents. Computer Supported Cooperative Work 12 (4): 465-90.
  – & G. Button. 1996. On "Technomethodology": Foundational Relationships between Ethnomethodology and System Design. In Proceedings of the SIGCHI Conference on Human Factors in Computing Systems, 19-26. New York: ACM.
- Dix, A., 2007. Designing for Appropriation. In Proceedings of the 21st British HCI Group Annual Conference on People and Computers: HCI...But Not as We Know It: Volume 2, 27-30. Swinton: British Computer Society.
- Dreessen, K., L. Huybrechts, T. Laureyssens, S. Schepers & S. Baciu. 2011. MAP-it: A Participatory Mapping Toolkit. Leuven: Acco.
- Eglash, R., J. Croissant, G. Di Chiro & R. Fouché, eds. 2004. Appropriating Technology: Vernacular Science and Social Power. Minneapolis and London: University of Minnesota Press.
- Ehn, P. 2008. Participation in Design Things. In Proceedings of the Tenth Anniversary Conference on Participatory Design 2008, 92-101. Indianapolis: Indiana University.
- Erikson, E.H. 1950. Childhood and Society. New York: W. W. Norton & Company.
- Fisher, G., E. Giaccardi, Y. Ye, A. G. Sutcliffe & N. Mehandjiev. 2004. Meta-design: A Manifesto for End-User Development. Communications of the ACM 47 (9): 33-37.

- Galloway, A., J. Brucker-Cohen, L. Gaye, E. Goodman & D. Hill. 2004. Design for Hackability. In *DIS '04: Proceedings of the 5th Conference on Designing Interactive Systems: Processes, Practices, Methods, and Techniques*, 363-66. New York: ACM.
- Gamma, E., R. Helm, R. Johnson & J. Vlissides. 1995. *Design Patterns CD: Elements of Reusable Object-Oriented Software*. Indianapolis, IN: Addison-Wesley Publishing Co.
- Gaver, W., J. Beaver & S. Bendford. 2003. Ambiguity as a Resource for Design. In *CHI '03: Proceedings of the SIGCHI Conference on Human Factors in Computing Systems*, 233-40. New York: ACM.
- Gergen, K.J. 1994. *Toward Transformation in Social Knowledge*, 2nd ed. Sage: London.
- Gershenfeld, N. 2005. *FAB: The Coming Revolution on Your Desktop: From Personal Computer to Personal Fabrication*. New York: Basic Book.
- GNU. 2013. *GNU General Public License, version 1*. Boston: Free Software Foundation. www.gnu.org/licenses/old-licenses/gpl-1.0.html.
- Haddon, L., E. Mante, B. Sapio, K.-H. Kommonen, L. Fortunati & A. Kant, eds. 2005. *Everyday Innovators: Researching the Role of Users in Shaping ICTs*. Dordrecht: Springer.
- Hannemyr, G. 1999. Technology and Pleasure: Hacking Considered Constructive. *First Monday* 4 (2). www.firstmonday.org/issues/issue4_2/gisle/" www.firstmonday.org/issues/issue4_2/gisle/.
- Hardware Slashdot. 2013. *Don't Forget the Arduino*. New York: Slashdot. http://hardware.slashdot.org/story/08/10/24/0343244/open-source-hardware-for-fun-and-for-profit.
- Harris, J. & A. Henderson. 1999. Better Mythology for System Design. 1999. In *CHI '99: Conference on Human Factors in Computing Systems*. New York: ACM.
- Hartmann, B., S. Doorley & S. R. Klemmer. 2006. *Hacking, Mashing, Gluing: A Study of Opportunistic Design and Development: Technical Report*. Stanford University Computer Science Department.
- Henderson, A. & M. Kyng. 1992. There's No Place Like Home: Continuing Design in Use. In *Design at Work: Cooperative Design of Computer Systems*, ed. by J. Greenbaum & M. Kyng, 219-40. Hillsdale, NJ: Lawrence Erlbaum Associates.
- Himanen, P. 2001. *The Hacker Ethic and the Spirit of Information Age*. New York: Random House.
- Huybrechts, L. 2011. *Participatory Creation is Risky: A Roadmap of Participatory Creation Processes and the Shifting Role of Creative 'Things'*. Leuven: KULeuven, PhD diss.
- –, K. Dreessen & S. Schepers. 2012. Mapping Design Practices: On Risk, Hybridity, and Participation. In *PDC '12: Proceedings of the 12th Participatory Design Conference: Exploratory Papers, Workshop Descriptions, Industry Cases: Vol. 2*, 29-32. New York: ACM.
- Kanstrup, A.M. 2012. A Small Matter of Design: An Analysis of End Users as Designers. In *PDC '12: Proceedings of the 12th Participatory Design Conference: Research Papaers: Vol. 1*, 109-18. New York: ACM.
- Kornberger, M. & S.R. Clegg. 2004. Bringing Space Back in: Organizing the Generative Building. *Organization Studies* 25 (7): 1095-1114.
- Kuznetsov, S. & E. Paulos. 2010. Rise of the Expert Amateur: DIY Projects, Communities, and Culture. In *NordiCHI '10: Proceedings of the 6th Nordic Conference on Human-Computer Interaction: Extending Boundaries*, 295-304. New York: ACM Press.
- Kwon, M. 2002. *One Place After Another: Site-Specific Art and Locational Identity*. Cambridge, MA: MIT Press.
- Latour, B. & P. Weibel. 2005. *Making Things Public: Atmospheres of Democracy*. Cambridge, MA: MIT Press.
- Le Dantec, C. 2012. Participation and Publics: Supporting Community Engagement. In *CHI '12: Proceedings of SIGCHI Conference on Human Factors in Computing Systems*, 1351-60. New York: ACM.

- Leadbeater, C. & P. Miller. 2004. The Pro-Am Revolution: How Enthusiasts Are Changing Our Economy and Society. London: Demos.
- Lemhachheche, R. 2005. Design for Appropriation of Ubiquity in Information Systems. International Reports on Socio-Informatics 2 (2): 60-63.
- Levy, S. 2010. Hackers: Heroes of the Computer Revolution. Sebastopol, CA: O'Reilly Media.
- Lievrouw, L. 2006. Oppositional and Activist New Media: Remediation, Reconfiguration, Participation. In Proceedings of the Ninth Conference on Participatory Design: Expanding Boundaries in Design, Vol. 1, 115-124. New York: ACM Press.
- Lovink, G. 2008. Zittrain's Foundational Myth of the Open Internet. Amsterdam: Institute of Network Cultures. http://networkcultures.org/wpmu/geert/2008/10/12/zittrains-foundational-myth-of-the-open-internet/.
- Lynch, K. 1972. What Time Is This Place? Cambridge, MA: MIT Press.
- MacKay, H. & G. Gillespie. 1992. Extending the Social Shaping of Technology Approach: Ideology and Appropriation. Social Studies of Science 22 (4): 685-716.
- MacKenzie, D. & J. Wajcman, eds. 1999. (org. 1985). The Social Shaping of Technology. Buckingham and Philadelphia: Open University Press.
- MacLean, A., K. Carter, L. Lestrand & T. Moran. 1990. User-Tailorable Systems: Pressing the Issues with Buttons. In CHI '90: SIGCHI Conference on Human Factors in Computing Systems, 175-82. New York: ACM Press.
- Manovich, L. 2005. Remixing and Remixability. http://imlportfolio.usc.edu/ctcs505/ManovichRemixModular.pdf.
- Milbrath, L. 1965. Political Participation: How and Why Do People Get Involved in Politics? Chicago: Rand McNally College Publishing Company.
- Moran, T. P. 2002. Everyday Adaptive Design. In DIS '02: Proceedings of the 4th Conference on Designing Interactive Systems, 13-14. New York: ACM Press.
- Muller, M. J. 2002. Participatory Design: The Third Space in HCI. In The Human-Computer Interaction Handbook: Fundamentals, Evolving Technologies and Emerging Applications, ed. by J. A. Jacko & A. Sears. Hillsdale, NJ: Lawrence Erlbaum Associates.
- Nissenbaum, H. 2004. Hackers and the Contested Ontology of Cyberspace. New Media and Society 8 (2): 195-217.
- Norman, D. 1998. The Invisible Computer. Cambridge, MA: MIT Press.
- O'Neill, P. 2009. Three Stages in the Art of Public Participation: The Relational, Social and Durational. dérive 39. www.eurozine.com/articles/2010-08-12-oneill-en.html.
- O'Neill, P., & C. Doherty, eds. 2011. Locating the Producers: Durational Approaches to Public Art. Antennae Series 4. Amsterdam: Valiz.
- Open Source Initiative. 2010. The Open Source Definition. www.opensource.org/.
- O'Reilly, T. 2005. What Is Web 2.0? Design Patterns and Business Models for the Next Generation of Software (version 09/30/2005). Cologne: O'Reilly Verlag GmbH & Co.KG. www.oreilly.de/artikel/web20.html.
- Phillips, P. C. 1992. Temporality and Public Art. In Critical Issues in Public Art: Content, Context and Controversy, ed. by H. F. Senie & S. Webster. Washington and London: Smithsonian Institution Press.
- Pierson, J., E. Mante-Meijer & E. Loos, eds. 2011. New Media Technologies and User Empowerment. New York: Peter Lang Publishers.
- Ramocki, M. 2007. DIY: The Militant Embrace of Technology. ramocki.net. http://ramocki.net/ramocki-diy.pdf.
- Randell, R. 2004. Accountable Technology Appropriation and Use. In Proceedings of the 2004 ACM NordiCHI Conference on Human-computer Interaction, 161-70, New York: ACM Press.
- Raymond, E. 2001. The Cathedral & the Bazaar: Musings on Linux and Open Source by an Accidental Revolutionary. Sebastopol, CA: O'Reilly Media.
- RepRapWiki. 2013. Community Portal. www.reprap.org/wiki/RepRapWiki:Community_portal.

- Rheingold, H. 2000. The Virtual Community: Homesteading on the Electronic Frontier. Cambridge, MA: MIT Press.
- Robinson, M. 1993. Design for Unanticipated Use. In ECSCW '93: Proceedings of the Third European Conference on Computer-Supported Cooperative Work, 187-199. Norwell, MA: Kluwer.
- Schäfer, M.T. 2008. Bastard Culture: User Participation and the Extension of Cultural Industries. Utrecht: University of Utrecht, PhD diss. www.scribd.com/doc/8594831/Bastard-Culture-User-participation-and-the-extension-of-cultural-industries.
- Schön, D.A. 1979. Generative Metaphor: A Perspective on Problem-Setting in Social Policy. In Metaphor and Thought, ed. by A. Ortony. Cambridge: Cambridge University Press.
- Sengers, P., K. Boehner, S. David & J. Kaye. 2005. Reflective Design. In Proceedings of the 4th Decennial Conference on Critical Computing: Between Sense and Sensibility, 49-58. New York: ACM.
- Silverstone, R. & E. Hirsch, eds. 1992. Consuming Technologies: Media and Information in Domestic Spaces. New York: Routledge.
- Spiekermann, S. & F. Pallas. 2006. Technology Paternalism: Wider Implications of Ubiquitous Computing. Poiesis & Praxis: International Journal of Technology Assessment and Ethics of Science 4 (1): 6-18.
- Stallman, R. 1999. The GNU Operating System and the Free Software Movement. In Open Sources: Voices from the Open Source Revolution. Sebastopol, CA: O'Reilly Media. www.gnu.org/gnu/thegnuproject.html
  –. 2008. Free Software Free Society: Selected Essays of Richard M. Stallman. Boston: Free SoftwareSociety. http://shop.fsf.org/product/free-software-free-society/.
- Storni. 2008. Interview with Massimo Banzi. Conducted via Skype.
  –. 2009. The Ambivalence of Engaging Technology: Artifacts as Products and Processes. In Proceedings of NORDIC Design Research Conference 2009.
  –. 2012. Artifacts Unpacking Design Practices: The Notion of Thing in the Making of Artifacts. Science, Technology and Human Values 37 (1): 88-123.
- Suchman, L. 2007. Human-Machine Reconfiguration: Plans and Situated Actions 2nd ed. Cambridge (etc.): Cambridge University Press.
- Tapscott, D. & A. Williams. 2006. Wikonomics. London: Atlantic Books.
- Thompson, C. 2008. Build It: Share It: Profit: Can Open Source Hardware Work? Wired Magazine 16 (11) www.wired.com/techbiz/startups/magazine/16-11/ff_openmanufacturing?currentPage=all.
- Touchatag (n.d). What is Touchatag. Antwerp: Touchatag. www.touchatag.com/.
- Tribe, M. & R. Jana. 2006. New Media Art. Cologne: Taschen.
- Toffler, A. 1984. The Third Wave. New York: Bantam.
- Unfold (n.d). Congratulations. Antwerp: Unfold. http://unfoldfab.blogspot.be/2012/08/congratulations.html.
- Vallance, R., S. Kiani & S. Nayfeh. 2001. Open Design of Manufacturing Equipment. In CIRP 1st International Conference on Agile: Reconfigurable Manufacturing.
- Van Osch, W. & M. Avital. 2009. Collective Generativity: The Emergence of IT-Induced Mass Innovation. Proceedings of JAIS Theory Development Workshop. Sprouts: Working Papers on Information Systems 9 (54): 9-54.
- Von Hippel, E. 2005. Democratising Innovation. Cambridge, MA: MIT Press.
- Wagner, I. & E. Balka. 2005. Supporting Configuring as Appropriation Work. International Reports on Socio-informatics 2 (2): 85-92.
- Wakkary, R. & K. Tanenbaum. 2009. A Sustainable Identity: The Creativity of an Everyday Designer. In Proceeding of the 27th Annual SIGCHI Conference on Human Factors in Computing Systems (Boston, USA), 365-374. New York: ACM Press.
- Wark, M. 2004. A Hacker Manifesto. Cambridge, MA: Harvard University Press.
- Weiser, M. 1991. The Computer for the 21st Century. Special issue, Scientific American 265 (3): 94-104.
- Weiser, M. 1994. Creating the Invisible Interface (Invited Talk). In UIST '94:

Proceedings of the 7th ACM Symposium on User Interface Software and Technology, 1. New York: ACM.
- – & J. S. Brown. 1996. The Coming Age of Calm Technology, Xerox PARC.
- Winograd T. & F. Flores. 1986. Understanding Computer and Cognition. Norwood, NJ: Ablex Publishing Corp.
- Zandee, D.P. 2004. A Study in Generative Processes: The Art of Theorizing. Cleveland, OH: Case Western Reserve University, PhD diss.
- Zielinski, S. 2006. Deep Time of the Media: Toward an Archaeology of Hearing and Seeing by Technical Means. Cambridge, MA: MIT Press.
- Zittrain, J. 2008. The Future of the Internet and How to Stop It. New Haven, CT: Yale University Press.

Literature Conclusion

- Bourriaud, N. 2002. Relational Aesthetics. Paris: Les Presses du réel. Originally published as Esthétique relationelle (Paris: Les Presses du réel, 1998). http://wiki.mediamind.org/images/3/38/Bourriaud.pdf.
- Ehn, P. 2008. Participation in Design Things. In Proceedings of the Tenth Anniversary Conference on Participatory design 2008, 92-101. New York: ACM, 2008.
- Erikson, E. H. 1950. Childhood and Society. New York: W. W. Norton & Company.
- Huybrechts, L. 2011. Participatory Creation is Risky: A Roadmap of Participatory Creation Processes and the Shifting Role of Creative 'Things'. Leuven: KULeuven, PhD diss.
- Latour, B. & P. Weibel. 2005. Making Things Public: Atmospheres of Democracy. Cambridge, MA: MIT Press.
- Muller, M. J. 2002. Participatory Design: The Third Space in HCI. In The Human-Computer Interaction Handbook: Fundamentals, Evolving Technologies and Emerging Applications, ed. by J. A. Jacko & A. Sears. Hillsdale: NJ: Lawrence Erlbaum Associates.
- Zittrain, J. 2008. The Future of the Internet and How to Stop It. New Haven, CT: Yale University Press.

Index

Colophon

Participation Is Risky: Approaches to Joint Creative Processes
Editor Liesbeth Huybrechts
Antennae Series n° 10 by Valiz, Amsterdam

Contributors Katrien Dreessen, Denny K.L. Ho, Liesbeth Huybrechts, Yanki Lee, Selina Schepers, Jessica Schoffelen, Cristiano Storni
Translation Dutch-English Leo Reijnen
Copy editing Leo Reijnen, Elke Stevens
Production Pia Pol
Design Metahaven
Paper inside Munken Print 100 gr 1.5, hv satinated mc 115 gr
Paper cover Bioset 240 gr
Printing and binding Ten Brink, Meppel
Publisher Valiz, Amsterdam, 2014 www.valiz.nl

ISBN 978-90-78088-77-6

This book is initiated by **Social Spaces (www.socialspaces.be)** and **KULeuven Cultural Studies (Jan Baetens and Fred Truyen)**, in collaboration with **BAM (Flemish Institute for Visual, Audio-visual and Media Art)**, **Valiz Publishers**, supported by the **Flemish Art Fund 'Kunstendecreet'** and the **Dutch Mondriaan Fund**, to gain more insight into the characteristics of participatory projects in art and design.

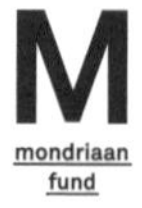

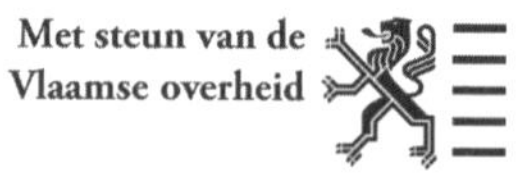

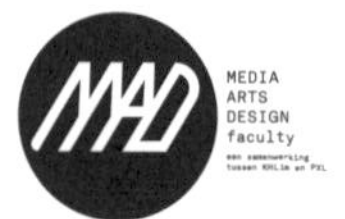

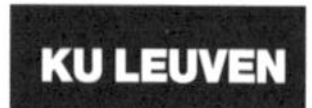

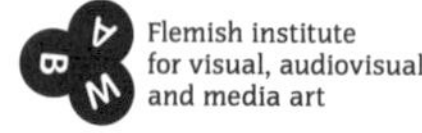

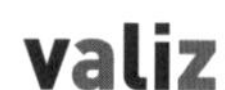

Distribution:
USA: D.A.P., www.artbook.com
GB/IE: Anagram Books, www.anagrambooks.com
NL/BE/LU: Coen Sligting, www.coensligtingbookimport.nl
Europe/Asia/Australia: Idea Books, www.ideabooks.nl

ISBN 978-90-78088-77-6
NUR 656, 651
Printed and bound in the Netherlands

Antennae Series:

The Fall of the Studio: Artists at Work
edited by Wouter Davidts & Kim Paice
Amsterdam: Valiz, 2009 (2nd ed.: 2010),
ISBN 978-90-78088-29-5

Take Place: Photography and Place from Multiple Perspectives
edited by Helen Westgeest
Amsterdam: Valiz, 2009, ISBN 978-90-78088-35-6

The Murmuring of the Artistic Multitude: Global Art, Memory and Post-Fordism
Pascal Gielen (author)
Arts *in* Society
Amsterdam: Valiz, 2009 (2nd ed.: 2011),
ISBN 978-90-78088-34-9

Locating the Producers: Durational Approaches to Public Art
edited by Paul O'Neill & Claire Doherty
Amsterdam: Valiz, 2011, ISBN 978-90-78088-51-6

Community Art: The Politics of Trespassing
edited by Paul De Bruyne, Pascal Gielen
Arts *in* Society
Amsterdam: Valiz, 2011 (2nd ed.: 2013),
ISBN 978-90-78088-50-9

See it Again, Say it Again: The Artist as Researcher
edited by Janneke Wesseling
Amsterdam: Valiz, 2011, ISBN 978-90-78088-53-0

Teaching Art in the Neoliberal Realm: Realism versus Cynicism
edited by Pascal Gielen, Paul De Bruyne
Arts *in* Society
Amsterdam: Valiz, 2012 (2nd ed.: 2013),
ISBN 978-90-78088-57-8

Institutional Attitudes: Instituting Art in a Flat World
edited by Pascal Gielen
Arts *in* Society
Amsterdam: Valiz, 2013, ISBN 978-90-78088-68-4

Dread: The Dizziness of Freedom
edited by Juha van 't Zelfde
Amsterdam: Valiz, 2013, ISBN 978-90-78088-81-3